ADV

"Written with concision, elegance, and anecdotal verve, this book combines cutting-edge science and the experience-based insights of a master clinician. Lou Cozolino's guide to applied neuroscience will be a treasured resource for therapists, physicians, and counselors for a long time to come."

—**Gabor Maté, M.D.**, author,
*In The Realm of Hungry Ghosts:
Close Encounters With Addiction*

"Few people have Cozolino's clear understanding of the indivisible nature of mind, brain, and body. Fewer still can make these concepts so accessible, accurately describing the brain as a social organ and humans as complex beings that have been shaped by evolution. Exploring the interface of science and psychotherapy, this book encourages us to know relationship as our natural habitat and to appreciate the conscious and unconscious layers of communication that influence us."

—**Mary L. Meador, M.D.**, Board Certified Family Physician
in private practice, Education Chair for Global Association
of Interpersonal Neurobiology, Teacher of Science
of Interpersonal Neurobiology, Portland Community
College, Lecturer and author on integrating Interpersonal
Neurobiology into healthcare, education, and families

"Lou Cozolino's new book is a must-have for all therapists and practitioners who support and care for individuals who carry with them pain and hurt. It is a way of looking through the lens of knowledge about the brain, mind, and body to understand deeply the ways in which relationships offer the resources for healing and transformation. Lou is a thoughtful and kind guide to the neuroscience of clinical work. (You will want to read the book again and again. Each time, you will discover something new.)"

—**Joe Tucci, Ph.D.**, CEO of the Australian Childhood Foundation

THE NORTON SERIES ON INTERPERSONAL NEUROBIOLOGY

Louis Cozolino, PhD, Series Editor
Allan N. Schore, PhD, Series Editor, 2007–2014
Daniel J. Siegel, MD, Founding Editor

The field of mental health is in a tremendously exciting period of growth and conceptual reorganization. Independent findings from a variety of scientific endeavors are converging in an interdisciplinary view of the mind and mental well-being. An interpersonal neurobiology of human development enables us to understand that the structure and function of the mind and brain are shaped by experiences, especially those involving emotional relationships.

The Norton Series on Interpersonal Neurobiology provides cutting-edge, multidisciplinary views that further our understanding of the complex neurobiology of the human mind. By drawing on a wide range of traditionally independent fields of research—such as neurobiology, genetics, memory, attachment, complex systems, anthropology, and evolutionary psychology—these texts offer mental health professionals a review and synthesis of scientific findings often inaccessible to clinicians. The books advance our understanding of human experience by finding the unity of knowledge, or consilience, that emerges with the translation of findings from numerous domains of study into a common language and conceptual framework. The series integrates the best of modern science with the healing art of psychotherapy.

A NORTON PROFESSIONAL BOOK

LOUIS COZOLINO

THE POCKET GUIDE TO NEUROSCIENCE FOR CLINICIANS

W. W. NORTON & COMPANY

Independent Publishers Since 1923

New York • London

Copyright © 2020 by Louis Cozolino

All rights reserved
Printed in the United States of America
First Edition

For information about permission to reproduce selections from this book, write to
Permissions, W. W. Norton & Company, Inc., 500 Fifth Avenue, New York, NY 10110

For information about special discounts for bulk purchases, please contact
W. W. Norton Special Sales at specialsales@wwnorton.com or 800-233-4830

Manufacturing by LSC Harrisonburg
Production manager: Katelyn MacKenzie

Library of Congress Cataloging-in-Publication Data

Names: Cozolino, Louis J., author.
Title: The pocket guide to neuroscience for clinicians / Louis Cozolino.
Description: First edition. | New York : W.W. Norton & Company, [2020] |
"A Norton professional book." | Includes bibliographical references and index.
Identifiers: LCCN 2019044448| ISBN 9780393713374 (paperback) |
ISBN 9780393713381 (epub)
Subjects: | MESH: Cognitive Neuroscience—methods | Brain—physiology |
Mental Processes—physiology | Psychotherapy—methods |
Psychophysiology—methods | Handbook
Classification: LCC QP360.5 | NLM WL 39 | DDC 612.8/233—dc23
LC record available at https://lccn.loc.gov/2019044448

W. W. Norton & Company, Inc.,
500 Fifth Avenue, New York, N.Y. 10110
www.wwnorton.com

W. W. Norton & Company Ltd.,
15 Carlisle Street, London W1D 3BS

1 2 3 4 5 6 7 8 9 0

TO MY DEDICATED STUDENTS,
EAGER NEOPHYTES TO LIFETIME LEARNERS,
WHO INSPIRE ME TO KEEP ON EXPLORING,
WRITING, AND TEACHING.
THIS ONE'S FOR YOU!

CONTENTS

INTRODUCTION

Learning is the only thing the mind never exhausts, never fears,
and never regrets.

—LEONARDO DA VINCI

About the time as I began my training as a therapist during the
1970s, I happened to read an article about the brain for a class in biological psychology. At the time, the brain and the mind were considered to be completely separate entities, studied in different academic
departments, with no thought of connecting the two. Because I was
impressed by how various forms of brain damage cause difficulties similar to those seen in mental illness, I began reading everything I could find in the very limited neuroscience literature of the
time. For some reason, I have continued to explore brain-behavior
relationships ever since. When I began, no two academic subjects
seemed more distinct than psychotherapy and neuroscience—but a
lot has changed.

There is an inherent challenge in understanding the role of the
brain in human experience. The English language leads us to think
of the brain, mind, body, relationships, and culture as distinct and
discrete concepts, which has spawned many dissociated fields of
study. This suggests that each can be studied independently and
understood without reference to the others. As you will learn in
the following pages, understanding the human brain requires a syn-

thesis of all of these disciplines. For biopsychosocial organisms like ourselves, to discuss one is, by necessity, to invoke the others.

The purpose of this book is to broaden and deepen your clinical thinking through an understanding of neuroscience, brain development, epigenetics, and the role of attachment in brain development. While no book can prepare you for all eventualities, I will provide you with examples of how I apply many findings from scientific studies. As you might imagine, this is an ongoing learning process which, after decades, I still find both challenging and exciting.

A fundamental assumption of my work is that each client's presenting problems, cognitive and emotional styles, and defenses have been shaped through an interaction of genetics, temperament, and prior experiences. The way I conceptualize clients is also informed by developmental, systems, and attachment theory, with some Buddhist philosophy mixed in. I sometimes use techniques from cognitive-behavioral therapy (CBT), Gestalt, eye movement desensitization and reprocessing (EMDR), mindfulness, or play therapy in the context of a general psychodynamic conceptualization and a Rogerian approach. Based on this eclectic foundation, I use what I know about the brain and the mind as conceptual glue to organize these various perspectives and techniques into a coherent and focused whole.

Many things contribute to positive change in psychotherapy. At its core, psychotherapy is a joining of hearts and minds in an effort to alleviate suffering. It combines a healing relationship and new ways of thinking and feeling. Most human suffering results from inadequate availability, empathy, and compassion. Healing comes from offering these human qualities in combination with the knowledge and techniques that support psychological, emotional, and behavioral growth.

As Salvador Minuchin famously said, "Human beings are snails. We carry our shells of memory with us, and we are them" (Minuchin & Nichols, 1993). The vast majority of the problems we treat as psychotherapists result from this shell of memory. If we think beyond the everyday idea of memory, like recalling where we left the car keys, we will come to learn that the shells of memory contain the unconscious memories of our attachment histories, how our bodies learned to experience and express emotions early in life, and what we absorbed from our parents' childhoods. We also have memories carried by genetic programming formed by the experiences of our grandparents, great-grandparents—all the way back to our primate ancestors.

An appreciation of our snail-like qualities requires an understanding of how memory, consciousness, and all human experience have emerged from the deep history of our species. It includes knowledge of evolution, neuroanatomy, and how the systems of our brains work together to give rise to who we are, how we thrive, and why we suffer. This knowledge can be extremely useful for our clients. It can help them to understand why they do what they do, experience their lives in certain ways, or experience symptoms that leave them feeling crazy and out of control.

Despite the widely accepted notion that advances in science are the result of monumental paradigmatic shifts, in reality, most scientific progress occurs through incremental steps. These small steps are driven largely by new inventions and measurement tools combined with meticulous observation and newer, more inclusive theories. As my biology professor E. A. Carlson has written, "Scientists are not solving a jigsaw puzzle. Most of the time they have no idea where innovation will lead, and the paradigm, if it exists, is a constantly changing one." If you are seeing clients, thinking about what is happening, learning new information, and combining it with what you already know, you are a part of the incremental advancement of the field. I offer this book as an invitation to the exploration of the sciences and psychotherapy. I further encourage you to question my ideas, draw new conclusions, and create theories of your own.

THE POCKET GUIDE TO
NEUROSCIENCE FOR CLINICIANS

PART I

Brain, Mind, and Self

THE EMERGENCE OF
THE SOCIAL BRAIN

Kindness is the language that the deaf can hear and the blind can see.

—MARK TWAIN

The brain has long been the subject of human fascination—this has never been as true as it is today. For most of recorded history, the brain was thought to be just another organ, like the liver or the kidneys, while our sense of self was thought to reside in the heart. With the emergence of phrenology and neurology, the idea that the brain somehow organized personality and behavior gradually gained prominence. As religious and mythological beliefs began to diverge from scientific investigation, the concept of the brain as the organizer of experience took hold. The newer notion of the brain as a social organ emerged only in the last few decades, and with it, the field of social neuroscience.

The more we've come to understand how our brains work, the more we've realized that significant portions are dedicated to connecting us with others. These findings have made it possible to forge fields like affective neuroscience and psychoneuroimmunology. We've learned from these interdisciplinary studies that models of psychotherapy focused exclusively on individuals and their internal experiences reveal but a small portion of the information relevant to healing. Further, focusing on thinking, feeling, behavior, somatic experience, relationships, or culture alone limits our ability to comprehend our clients and leverage psychotherapy as an agent of change. The consistent message of recent research is that minds are always embodied, encultured, and embedded within the context of relationships. When we forget their ultimate interdependence, we come to objectified and superficial understandings of the people we treat. As Wilhelm Reich once said, "We arrive at a catastrophic comprehension of the psychic surface." For this reason, I begin with a discussion of the social brain, and how it is built, regulated, and modified. These are all central topics for psychotherapists, parents, and teachers and the most important reasons to become *neurofluent*.

THE SOCIAL BRAIN

Out of yourself and into the team.
        —UNIVERSITY OF ALABAMA LOCKER ROOM SIGN

The social brain refers to two primary concepts. The first is that the brains of social animals (like ourselves) contain multiple neural systems that are partly or wholly dedicated to receiving, processing, and transmitting information to others. For example, we have a neural system (called the fusiform face area) dedicated to the recognition of right-side-up faces that switches off when faces are turned upside down. Upside-down faces get transferred to our object recognition systems, which is why we find it much harder to recognize inverted faces. Damage to the primitive core of the prefrontal cortex can result in a loss of empathy, sympathy, and compassion. The same circuits are also involved in the organization of our attachment schema and our ability to regulate our emotions. Humans have also evolved to automatically communicate their states of body, emotion, and mind to one another. Research in physiology has shown that our internal organs are automatically linked to our facial expressions to give others a real-time readout of our internal biological state. We also have things called mirror neurons designed to create an internal representation of the actions, expressions, and emotions of others within our own bodies. This allows us to be able to feel our own version of what others are feeling, especially strong emotions like pain, fear, disgust, love, and joy. This is especially important for the parents of young children, who need to read the primitive expressions of comfort and distress acted out by their children. These and a host of other findings serve as the foundation of our understanding of the social brain.

The notion that "genetics is destiny," assumes that the genes we inherit from our parents shape our bodies, brains, and minds, while experience has little influence on development. The opposite notion of a tabula rasa (blank slate) suggests that everything we are is the result of how we have been conditioned by experience. We now know that we are born with both genetic input that guides the basic organization of our brains and also that many brain systems are highly dependent on postnatal experience, especially those involved in social relating. These systems, specifically those related to attachment and affect regulation, are of particular importance to the field of psychotherapy and are said to develop in an experience-dependent manner.

Most neural systems dedicated to social connectedness are shaped by an interaction between our genetic inheritance and our lived experience. The complex wiring of our brain is shaped to adapt to the particular relationships in which we grow up. As social animals, this adaptation strategy most likely maximizes the survival of both the individual and the tribe. Of course, this is not without its problems. The brains of many children are shaped to people and situations that are not good models for survival outside the family and thus, are poorly suited to long-term adaptation. This certainly describes many of the clients who come to us seeking help. Our challenge is to make their unconscious adaptational patterns conscious, and then modify them in ways more in line with their present situation and long-term goals.

Human infants are born into the most abject dependency, connection equals survival. So we all enter the world with a basic rule: The first order of business is to attach to our parents and trigger their bonding instincts to take care of us. We stare into their eyes, grab their fingers, smile and coo, and cry when they leave us alone, making it clear that we want and need them. For at least the first decade of life, our caretakers and immediate family are our entire world. The input we receive from these interactions teaches us how to get what we want, regulate our fears, teach us if we are lovable, and what we can expect from others in the future.

Think about the game of peekaboo we play with our children. We hide our face with our hands, then expose our face, and say "Peekaboo!" with wide eyes, an exaggerated smile, and a high-pitched voice. The baby's eyes and mouth open wide, and then the baby gives us a big smile and maybe even an open-mouthed laugh. What just happened in our brains? First, the surprise and big smile stimulated metabolic activity in both the baby's and the parent's brain, delivering extra glucose and oxygen to support learning. We both experience surges of oxytocin, dopamine, and serotonin triggered by our mutual enjoyment, making us feel good and making us want to do it again. (Again! Again!) Epigenetic processes within the baby's brain trigger neuroanatomical growth that supports a sense of joy and creates the building blocks of long-term well-being. Changes in the parents' brains support deepening attachment, physical health, and emotional well-being. Parenting, grandparenting, and caring for any child, turn out to be good medicine for all of us at any age.

A good example of this is the epigenetic translation of these pleasurable experiences into the building of endorphin receptors on the baby's amygdala. The more of these receptors we build, the more the endorphins in our nervous system keep the amygdala downregulated, decreasing our vulnerability to stress, anxiety, and fear. This is one of the many physiological variables related to qualities like ego strength, grit, or resilience.

In stark contrast to this situation are the many children who lack quality caretakers, attentive others, or positive stimulation. Within the brains of these children, opposite biochemical and neuroanatomical processes occur that lead them to be more vulnerable to stress. This is why children with a greater number of adverse social experiences during childhood (e.g., parental psychopathology, exposure to domestic violence) are far more likely to experience psychological, physical, and adaptational difficulties later in life. Our social experiences are translated, for better and worse, into the neurobiological structure of our brains and tend to stabilize over time. Early trauma is truly a gift that keeps on giving, and a suffering child often grows into a suffering adult.

SOCIOSTASIS

> *We know from daily life that we exist for other people first of all, for whose smiles and well-being our own happiness depends.*
>
> —ALBERT EINSTEIN

Brains connect to one another, regulate one another, and attune to one another in ways that enhance emotional resonance and support coordinated group behavior. They also allow for some negative phenomena like groupthink, mob mentality, and group hysteria. As opposed to our other organs, which focus exclusively on homeostatic balance within the body, our brains are in a constant regulatory dance with those around us. Our brains are also filled with images, emotions, and incessant internal dialogues that guide our moment-to-moment experience. We are clearly wired to function as individuals embedded within multiple groups, balancing our own needs with the needs of those around us. A good proportion of the inner voices we experience is the internalization of the rules of the group that helped us function in tribes back into prehistory. The judge and jury we carry around in our heads keep us in line via social referencing and shame, constantly reminding us to stay in line and go along with the herd.

The fact that the brain is a social organ is also reflected in the many insights afforded us by systemic family therapy. The notion that the family is a complex biological organism (as proposed by Murray Bowen decades ago) is supported by the discovery that we regulate each other's arousal, mood, and immunological functioning. This process of sociostasis is the mechanism by which a family's behavior becomes organized around the regulation of anxiety. The role of the identified patient, the breakdown of open communication, and the formation of dysfunctional alliances are all driven by sociostatic processes and the attempt to regulate both the conscious and unconscious anxiety of many powerful family memories. The common adult experience of going back home and regressing to old patterns of thoughts, behaviors, and feelings clearly reflects this natural tendency. This is also why being in either good or bad relationships has many health benefits and risks.

Relationships have a powerful influence on both psychological and physical well-being. We now have a better understanding of why patients with schizophrenia who return home after hospitalization to hostile and critical relatives have much higher rates of relapse. It makes sense that the presence of supporting others and the kindness of a doctor or nurse decreases healing time, medication use, and days of hospitalization. We now know the epigenetic mechanisms of action that cause a mother's postpartum depression to affect the structure of her infant's brain in ways that make him or her more vulnerable to problems with bodily regulation, weight gain, and emotional well-being.

By utilizing the basic Rogerian principles of warmth, congruence, and positive regard, therapists leverage their connection with their clients' social brain networks in support of neuroplasticity and positive change. Via sociostasis, a positive therapeutic relationship can modulate arousal, activate the biochemistry of bonding, enhance neuroplastic processes, and support neural network integration. By treating clients as worthy of our attention and care, we activate mirror neuron systems that allow for learning through imitation, support plasticity, and boost the courage to try new ways of being. Roger's emotional stance toward his clients parallels parenting attitudes supportive of secure attachment. Nurturing connections have been shaped by evolution to create a state of brain and mind that opens us to learning, self-reflection, experimentation, and exploration. Many therapists who see therapy as a technical intervention they perform on a client, as opposed to a human journey they take with a client, can easily miss the power of sociostasis to drive positive therapeutic change.

THE SOCIAL SYNAPSE

> *We share with insects the mysterious instinct to build complex societies.*
>
> —E. O. WILSON

There is no such thing as an individual neuron. N
unable to connect with and develop a functional r
other neurons die. The surviving neurons work to

the functional neural networks upon which we depend for everything from breathing to consciousness. As you probably already
know, individual neurons are separated by small gaps called synapses. Although the word "gap" implies emptiness, these gaps are
actually filled to capacity with a wide array of chemical substances
that carry out highly sophisticated communication. Commonly
called neural transmission, this relentless chemical gossip allows
each neuron to live, grow, and build functional relationships with
one another. Over vast expanses of evolutionary time, synaptic
transmission has grown increasingly intricate to meet the needs of
ever more complex brains.

Synaptic transmission is the first stage of a three-step messenger
system that shapes individual neurons into fully integrated neural
systems. The second step consists of changes in the internal environment of the cell that result from the types of stimulation it receives.
The particular combination of chemical stimulation, as well as its
intensity and duration, regulates the internal chemical environment
of the neuron. In the third step, the chemical environment triggers
our DNA (contained in the nucleus) to become available for expression. This third messenger system, also called transcription genetics
or epigenetics, is the mechanism for the conversion of our experiences into the wetware of our brains. Just as bees combine to create
a hive and humans combine to create a tribe, neurons combine to
create the nervous system. While neurons got here first, the drive
toward interconnection is conserved across the levels of evolutionary complexity.

The social synapse is the space between us, the medium through
which we communicate with and link to one another. When we
smile, wave, and say hello, our behaviors are transferred across the
social synapse to the sense organs of others—their cell surface, if
you will. Receptors in the sense organs of the other convert these
electrical and mechanical messages into electrochemical impulses
hin their brains. These signals stimulate internal biochemical

changes, new behaviors, and the sending of messages back across the social synapse. From the moment we are born, our survival depends upon connecting to those around us through touch, smell, sights, and sounds. If we are able to connect with available and nurturing others, we will bond, attach, and survive.

The relationships we are embedded in directly impact the second and third messenger systems in our brains. A basic assumption is that loving connections and secure attachments build healthy and resilient brains, while neglectful and insecure attachments can result in brains vulnerable to stress, dysregulation, and illness. How we are treated by others impacts synaptic transmission and influences the internal environment of neurons and the epigenetic processes that build our brains. This mechanism of action explains why early attachment has such a powerful influence on who we become. During early periods of exuberant neural growth, our experiences are converted into neural infrastructures that make us either more resilient or more vulnerable to the mental and physical illnesses we suffer later in life.

The social synapse has an exceedingly broad bandwidth ranging from the conscious communication of words, sustained facial expressions, and touch to unconscious messages via pupil dilation, scent, and fleeting facial microexpressions. Dilated pupils signal others that we see them as trustworthy and that it is safe to approach, while blushing lets others know we are aware that we have committed a social faux pas and feel embarrassed by our transgression. Both of these reactions are not under conscious control but evolved as automatic and unconscious forms of social communication. Scientists continue to uncover new ways in which we are linked, imitate each other, coordinate our behaviors, and build each other's brains.

THE BIOCHEMISTRY OF ATTACHMENT

*The deepest principle in human nature is the craving to be
appreciated.*

—WILLIAM JAMES

Evolutionary processes of natural selection have shaped our drives
to bond and attach. Neurochemicals such as oxytocin, vasopressin, and endorphins, initially emerging to shape reward and physical pain, were later leveraged to make us feel better when with our
loved ones and anxious when we are apart. The central brain structures of the social motivation system include the amygdala, anterior
cingulate, and orbital medial prefrontal cortex. These neural circuits and neurochemicals are involved with everything from parental instincts, attachment, and pair bonding to empathy, compassion,
and altruistic behavior.

Oxytocin and vasopressin in mammals evolved from the molecules that control sexual behavior and egg laying in reptiles, reflecting that reproduction is the deep history of all attachment. Referred
to as "the peptides that bind," oxytocin and vasopressin modulate
bonding, social behavior, and anxiety in a wide range of species.
They are primarily produced in the hypothalamus and sent down
into the pituitary gland and up into the limbic system and cortex.
Oxytocin has also been found to be generated and released in the
amygdala and the heart, reflecting their central role in both anxiety
and attachment. At its core, attachment is the regulation of anxiety via proximity to others. The effects of oxytocin are to direct a
child's attention toward its mother while driving maternal behavior and inhibiting her irritability and aggressiveness. For example,
when an infant suckles at its mother's breast, the nipple triggers the
hypothalamus to release oxytocin into the bloodstream, triggering
a sense of well-being in the mother as well as contractions of the
muscles of her breasts to force milk to the nipples.

Oxytocin, and it male equivalent Vasopressin, facilitating pair bonding, attachment, and the maintenance of monogamy in a number of mammalian species. Its antagonistic relationship with testosterone leads to a decrease in aggression and sexual behavior in males in caretaking relationships. The amount and quality of maternal behavior toward pups correlates with the amount mothers received during infancy, and with the number of oxytocin receptors in regions of their social brains that modulate maternal behavior and anxiety. The growth of oxytocin receptors is stimulated through epigenetic processes triggered by maternal attention during infancy.

The touch, pressure, and warmth of another increase oxytocin and decrease blood pressure, which may explain why intimate relationships and massage improve physical and emotional well-being. Oxytocin and vasopressin also support the protein synthesis necessary for neuroplastic processes involved in learning, which is why positive emotional connections with teachers result in better educational outcomes. It is also important to know that oxytocin blocks dopamine receptors, which helps to prevent habituation to those we love—in contrast to all of those things we buy only to find they lose their appeal after we get them home. Thus, evolution has used multiple reward systems to keep us focused on staying close and taking care of one another.

The primitive attachment circuits have come to serve as the infrastructure of how we think and feel about other individuals, and humanity in general. With higher levels of oxytocin, we pay more attention to faces, movements, and social cues from others. Increasing oxytocin levels have been shown to promote trust and empathy, increase the consideration of the perspective of others, and enhance communication during conflict. This is probably why a little oxytocin will generally increase generosity and charitable contributions, and also enhance prosocial behavior in people with autism.

In the context of psychotherapy, these systems can all be tapped into via a warm and supportive therapeutic relationship. The good news for all of us is that attachment circuits remain plastic through-out life, as evidenced by the intense love that grandparents often experience for their grandchildren. These neural hubs and the biochemistry that drives them are key levers of psychotherapeu-tic change. Techniques, clinical knowledge, and experience are all important, but it is the relationship that creates the state of mind and brain that allows a client to benefit from them.

LEVERAGING SOCIOSTASIS

The meeting of two personalities is like the contact of two chemical substances: if there is any reaction, both are transformed.

—C. J. JUNG

The term "placebo effect" is generally thought of as a person's ability to feel better after taking a sugar pill, without receiving any actual medication. It is so pervasive that any good research study must include a placebo to be considered solid research. Those who do feel better when taking the placebo are generally regarded as weak, eas-ily influenced, and perhaps not really ill in the first place. However, before the rise of biological interventions to cure disease, belief, motivation, and inspiration were seen as central components of heal-ing. Through countless millennia of pre-technological healing, the power of the mind to influence the body was both recognized and leveraged by shamans, faith healers, and old country doctors.

The word "placebo," Latin for "I shall please," reflects the idea that responding to an inactive treatment results from the patient's desire to live up to the doctor's expectations. This desire to please can be amplified by the doctor's status, bearing, and reputation. These factors, combined with a positive reaction to someone mak-ing an effort to help us, are sociostatic mechanisms that impact our biochemistry, neuroanatomy, and conscious experience. It has been mat.

suggested that a better term for this sociostatic process is a "meaning response" that can be applied to the power of the effect of social beliefs on an individual. For example, Chinese Americans born during those years considered inauspicious have been found to have significantly shorter life spans, an effect that is proportional to how strongly they hold to traditional cultural beliefs. In another important example, drugs usually have the strongest results just after they are released, become less effective over time as negative reports, side effects, and doubts about them become public.

Parallel research in education has shown that when teachers are given false IQ results and told which children in their classroom were about to bloom over the next academic year, the randomly chosen bloomers showed greater gains in total IQ and reasoning compared to the control group. These students were also rated by their teachers as more intellectually curious, better adjusted, happier, and less needy of approval than the students in the control group. The power of the meaning response and the mechanisms that transmit them across the social synapse are undeniable.

How do the meanings we hold translate into the biochemistry of the brain? The impact of the meaning effect is an example of top-down (cortical to subcortical) modulation of neurochemistry and immunological activity. The general impact of the meaning effect is improved cognitive and immunological functioning via increased levels of dopamine and serotonin, more protein synthesis, and decreased levels of cortisol. These changes increase positive feelings and optimism about the future, whether it is healing or succeeding in the classroom and at work. More specific effects are tied to the symptoms for which people are seeking treatment. For example, positive meaning effects in the treatment of pain are mediated via beta-endorphins (internally generated opioids), the chemicals that result in "runner's high" and provide us with a buffer against pain when we experience physical injury. Brain regions involved are the anterior cingulate, insular cortex, and thalamus, all rich in opioid receptors.

Individuals suffering with Parkinson's disease who benefit from the meaning effect show changes in the subthalamic nuclei and the nigrostriatal dopamine system, the regions of the brain known to be involved with their symptoms. Those with depression show increased activation in serotonergic networks, decreases in amygdala activity, and an overall shift from subcortical to cortical activation. Thus, both general and specific effects suggest that the mind is capable of converting the meanings contained within successful social interactions into specific neurochemical substances that mimic the pharmacological effects of targeted medication. While there exists a wide spectrum of miraculous technological medical interventions, we may be throwing the baby out with the bathwater when healers become strictly medical technicians. There is little doubt that the combination of technology and leveraging millions of years of human evolution via sociostatic processes and the placebo effect is a most powerful combination.

THERAPY AND REPARENTING

Love cannot live where there is no trust.

—EDITH HAMILTON

There are many ways in which psychotherapy parallels good-enough parenting. Through the therapeutic relationship, we are attempting to modify the same circuits of attachment, emotional regulation, and autobiographical memory that were shaped during childhood. We also use the same attentive and nurturing sociostatic processes to help our clients regulate their anxiety, provide them with challenges at the edge of their capabilities, and help them to articulate their thoughts, feelings, and experiences. All of these aspects of psychotherapy are central to positive parenting, secure attachment, and building resilience.

We leverage the transference relationship to bring past struggles with parents into the present moment to make them available for conscious consideration and modification. Transference and attachment are always activated during a therapy relationship. Both are implicit memory systems based on early relationships triggered in the context of current relationships. Both attachment schema and transference reactions come in multiple forms. So always keep in mind that what we are seeing with each client is a particular reaction in a specific situation that may not reflect how they respond in other situations. We have to gather much information before we can have confidence in our interpretation of attachment or transference.

One way to think about the beginnings of therapy is a combination of two things: (1) an attempt to establish some kind of working relationship in the face of whatever resistances clients bring with them, and (2) discovering the deeper narrative below the surface story they disclose. A major challenge for the newer therapist is not getting stuck in the content of the surface narrative. It is easy in the early years of our careers to mistake building a relationship with allowing the client to lead the sessions and taking everything they say as truth. The fact that we have two levels of narrative is embedded in the evolution of our social selves, the complexity of our brains, and the fact that our two brain hemispheres are capable of different ways of perceiving and navigating experiences.

From the perspective of neuroscience, what we see as resistance is the reflection of a complex network of implicit emotional, somatic, motor, and sensory memories. It is the brain-mind's best guess about what is necessary to survive today based on what happened long ago. Our primitive brain works on a strict assumption that past experience is the best predictor of how to survive in the present.

The more stressed or frightened we become, the more likely we will regress to familiar patterns of interacting with the world. We see this all the time in children who develop new skills, only to see them disappear in the face of anxiety and trauma. Therefore, resistance isn't something that we have to wait out in order to start the real therapy. Coming to understand and work with a client's resistance is a central component of therapy. From the perspective of neuroscience, these patterns of implicit memory that create closed logic, emotional frailty, and repetitive behaviors all maintain suffering. A core aspect of successful therapy is embracing resistance as an accomplishment that allowed the client to survive stressful circumstances. By embracing resistance, you take away the need to employ resistance, which allows the client to be less anxious, less defensive, and more open to change. This is the highest and best use of sociostasis in both parenting and psychotherapy.

FANCY FARMS

> *I like it when my mother smiles. I especially like it when I make her smile.*
>
> —ADRIANA TRIGIANI

About a month ago I had some time free time between meetings and decided to find somewhere to eat. As I walked along an unfamiliar street, I noticed a boutique supermarket up ahead and decided to have a look. A few minutes later, sandwich in hand, I headed to a counter with stools facing out the front window. After I sat down, I noticed, just outside the store, tables and chairs that looked much more comfortable. As I was gathering up my things to relocate, I noticed something that made me slowly sink back onto my stool. At an outside table, directly across from me, was a mother sitting across from her one-year-old in a stroller. What stopped me was the look on the child's face as her mother picked up her phone.

I flashed to memories of the films I had seen of infants' reactions to their mothers holding a still face, and I was curious to see how this child would react to having her mother's face replaced with the back of a phone. The heavily tinted glass separating us guaranteed I could observe them without being detected. The mother played her role perfectly, holding up the phone in front of her in a way that replaced her face with the smooth metal surface of her smartphone. At first, the baby looked interested in the phone and watchfully tracked her mother's hand movements as she swiped left and right, up and down. I set the stopwatch on my phone and set it in front of me so I could make notes about the timing of their interactions. At 15 seconds, the baby began to protest, rhythmically kicking her feet and letting out an occasional yell. It seemed clear that she was trying to capture her mother's attention. The mother played her role perfectly as she proceeded to swipe, take a few selfies, add captions, and post them to social media.

This continued until the 50-second mark, when the little one seemed to deflate. She suddenly became lethargic, looked about, and then hung her head limply down and to the left. After a while, she began to look up and around again: At 74 seconds, she seemed to notice a bird hopping by, people passing, the wind moving the colorful umbrellas overhead. One after another, they captured and then lost her attention. Her face became strained, as if she was angry or had a stomachache, and she began to shake her legs, occasionally let out a yell, and looked up from time to time to see the back of the phone. At 103 seconds, she became less active and soon looked deflated once again. At this point I became aware of how deflated I began to feel. I also felt the physical urge to reach and pick her up. My mind flashed on how many ti done the same thing to my own son.

At 157 seconds, the mother put down her phon her coffee. When she looked down at the baby, I in my own body, and the words "Thank God" mind. If this were my research project, I would have called it off as too inhumane. Now, at 176 seconds, the mother was trying to get the little one's attention, but she no longer seemed interested. There were no visible responses to the mother's words or gestures, just the baby's limp head hanging to the left and her blank stare. Was this intentional avoidance, a state of hopelessness, or emotional exhaustion? Her mother seemed to shrug it off and stopped trying to get her child's attention. She took another sip of her coffee and returned to her phone, her child now seemingly indifferent to her actions. A few seconds later the mother stood up and pushed the stroller away as she looked at her phone.

As I finished my sandwich and headed off to my next meeting, my informal naturalistic, single-subject study rolled around in my mind. Early observational attachment research noted that parents who were dismissive or intermittently available tended to have children who developed insecure patterns of attachment. It was those mothers who were good at being available and responsive to their children's requests for engagement that had children who were secure in their attachments and developed adaptive affect regulation and good attentional abilities. The social synapse now has a new and ever-present competitor that leads us to bypass those in front of us for those who are at a distance. I wonder how our devices will impact the development of our children's brains. For the first time, I began to wonder if the constant availability of devices and the intentionally addictive nature of the tech industry will prove to have a deleterious impact on the emotional security of future generations.

2

THE DEVELOPING BRAIN

Anyone who does anything to help a child is a hero to me.

—FRED ROGERS

An understanding the developing brain begins with questioning the very definition of the brain. It is made up of millions of neurons connected in billions of ways that transmit energy and information in what the neuroscientist Antonio Damasio aptly describes as a "government of systems." Instead of the departments and agencies of the Washington bureaucracy, our brains contain countless neurons organized into neural systems that are dedicated to the entire range of adaptive functions—from seeing and walking to thinking and feeling. Thinking of the brain as a complex set of interacting neural systems provides us with the broad context for neurofluency. It is the proper development and integration of these systems that leads to both optimal functioning and mental health.

Neurofluency Principle 1: The brain consists of a government of systems.

The fact that the brain consists of a government of neural systems is highlighted by the patterns of skills and deficits of individuals on the autistic spectrum. Genetically triggered neurodevelopmental abnormalities undermine the growth and integration of different neural networks, resulting in patterns of both over- and underdevelopment. This is why it is not uncommon for individuals on the spectrum to have deficits in language and social communication while possessing extraordinary strengths in visual and numeric memory. In contrast, individuals with Williams syndrome are deeply empathic and attuned to others, yet incapable of basic self-care and independent living. Autism and Williams syndrome clearly point out that abilities like emotional attunement and arithmetic computation are organized in separate and dissociable neural networks subject to independent genetic, gestational, and developmental disruptions.

Each of our neural systems has a deep history that reflects its survival value either now or at some point in our evolutionary past. Our brains contain the evolutionary history of our species and of the other animals, plants, and single-celled organisms that came before. The same is true of our bodies; the bones of our inner ears that allow us to hear were once part of the jaws of our reptilian ancestors; the bones at the base of our spine are the remnants of the tails that helped our monkey predecessors to live safely high in the trees. Another way in which we embody our evolutionary past is how our brains change during the life cycle. The neural system in each of us has its own developmental course as we develop, mature, and grow old, which reflects the changing demands placed on members of troops and tribes at each stage of life. Our brains embody our survival both as individuals and as members of social units.

Neurofluency Principle 2: Each neural system has its own adaptational and evolutionary history.

As we age, each neural system has its own developmental course; some stay the same, some improve, while others decline.

For example, the memory system for faces stays relatively strong throughout life, while the system dedicated to our memory for words peaks around age 25 and slowly declines thereafter. As we age, we get better at expert skills we already possess but find it more difficult to learn new information. Attachment systems stay strong throughout life while emotional arousal and reactivity downshift. This is why grandparents can love their grandchildren as much as their own children and get less upset at things that once bothered them. In essence, the pattern of aging across neural systems has been shaped to serve the historic needs of our tribes during our life cycle.

Neurofluency Principle 3: The brain is both an individual and social organ.

It is in the context of our social evolutionary history that the difficult-to-explain peculiarities of development begin to make sense. My favorite example is the seemingly inexplicable desire of young children to hear the same story or watch the same movie again and again. When he was 3 years old, my son would beg me to read him the same story every night. Although he already knew it by heart, he would insist on the same reading in the same way. If I made a mistake or substituted a word to make it more interesting to me, he would correct me and insist I go back and do it correctly. Another experience we likely share is the tendency for our elders to repeat the same stories again and again, usually beginning with the line, "Have I ever told you about . . ."

This tendency to repeat stories, called "off-task verbosity" by 20-something cognitive researchers, is no more a coincidence than my son's desire to hear the same stories again and again. This lock-and-key mechanism of storytelling and listening served as the transmitter of history and culture over eons of preliterate evolutionary history. The stories needed to be passed on, and the brain was programmed and timed for grandparents and grandchildren to link up across the generations. Once again, thinking of the brain in the context of our Paleolithic past helps us to make sense of apparently illogical behavior in the present.

NEURODIVERSITY

Talent perceives differences; genius unites.

—WILLIAM BUTLER YEATS

One of evolution's key strategies is the maximization of diversity through sexual reproduction, where the genetic diversity of two unrelated individuals maximizes the probability of healthy offspring (thus the incest taboo). Through the interaction of genetics and experience, each of us ends up with a unique combination of neural networks and patterns of activity reflected in our abilities, disabilities, personalities, and behaviors. Some are born with a more active amygdala that leads them to be anxious and vigilant while others are more exploratory, love to take risks, and are excited to find out what's around the next curve. Still others may have a higher number of neurons and glia cells in their parietal lobes that provide them with greater visual-spatial abilities. The variations are nearly endless, making each brain a unique experiment of nature.

> *Neurofluency Principle 4*: Each brain is an expression of biodiversity and a unique experiment of nature.

The natural diversity we see among individuals likely reflects historical differences that supported the survival of the tribe during countless generations of the evolution of our species. As social animals, we have been shaped to survive as both individuals and members of our tribe, for if the tribe doesn't survive, neither do the individuals of which it is composed. The two simultaneous evolutionary mandates, taking care of ourselves and taking care of others, are likely the biological origins of our morals, ethics, and laws. The dynamic tension between individual and group survival drives conflict both within and between tribes, countries, ethnicities, and religions. The Darwinian struggle for survival can be witnessed at every level, from the smallest neurons to the mightiest nations.

NEURODYNAMICS

Just like the brain consists of billions of highly connected neurons,
a basic operating unit in a neural network is a neuron-like node. It
takes input from other nodes and sends output to others.

—FEI FEI LI

What we think of as a normally functioning brain is the result of many systems developing, integrating, and communicating with one another. When any of these three processes are disrupted, we may observe psychological symptoms. If systems do not develop that process the internal emotional states of another, we are vulnerable to experiencing others as objects and failing to anticipate their reactions to our behaviors (sociopathy). If messages from our bodies aren't communicated from our insular to cingulate cortex, we may find it impossible to be consciously aware of our bodily states and even our emotions (alexithymia). In high states of arousal, our cortical executive systems may become inhibited, resulting in an ongoing dissociation among networks of thinking, feeling, sensing, and behaving. This neural dissociation results in vulnerability to unregulated arousal, nightmares, flashbacks, and disconnection from others (post-traumatic stress disorder, PTSD).

Neurofluency Principle 5: Communication and integration are key components of optimal brain health.

A central factor in understanding the brain is the importance of the integration of neural systems. Although we tend to think in terms of certain regions of the brain being responsible for specific functions, it is just as true that proper brain functioning relies on the communication, coordination, and integration of the functioning of multiple regions and networks. Neural networks involve patterns of excitation and inhibition between different brain regions that regulate and modify their activity. An important aspect of neurofluency is an appreciation for both the hubs of activity and the networks in which they operate.

A good example of neurodynamics central to psychotherapy is the relationship between the amygdala and the region of the prefrontal cortex just above the eyes called the orbital-medial prefrontal cortex (OMPFC). The amygdala, the primitive executive and the center of our fear circuitry, is fully mature at birth while the systems in the OMPFC that regulate it are not developed. Early relationships with caretakers shape the circuits between the amygdala and OMPFC, which stores the memories of how well others are able to regulate our anxiety. The implicit memories stored in this network manifest as what are called secure and insecure patterns of attachment. Although there is more to the neuroscience of attachment than this one circuit, the neurodynamics within this particular system have a powerful and lasting impact on how we relate to others.

THE DEVELOPING BRAIN

The only source of knowledge is experience.

—ALBERT EINSTEIN

The cultural biases baked into our view of aging have led the study of brain development to be primarily focused on children and adolescents. This dogmatic blindness has led us to think of the brain as having a few years of exuberant early development, followed by a plateau in young adulthood, followed by a long decline thereafter. Despite all the evidence to the contrary, prejudices about aging in popular culture and in the scientific community have led us to miss the biological truth that brain development is a dynamic and complex process that continues from birth until death. Further, it has been shaped over unmeasurable time to be in sync with the needs of those around us.

Neurofluency Principle 6: Our brains continue to develop and adapt throughout life.

The brain is a social organ of adaptation that is reshaped successively throughout life to meet the ever-changing survival demands of the individual and the tribe. The flow of these developmental changes has been woven into genetic codes that guide brain development in fairly consistent ways. Our brains (like our gut) remain essentially Paleolithic in nature and are more in sync with the life course of our hunter-gatherer ancestors than our current technological society. What this means is that much of how our brain develops only makes sense in light of our evolutionary and social histories. Put in a slightly different way, brain development is linked to the traditional demands of tribal life of thousands of years ago.

Our attachment circuitry starts off highly active and remains robust due to its survival value to both the individual and the tribe. On the other hand, the memory circuitry of the hippocampus and frontal regions develops slowly during childhood, making it difficult to impossible for most of us to access conscious autobiographical memory from the early years of our lives. Attachment circuitry reaches a sensitive period during adolescence and young adulthood, when we traditionally had to transition out of childhood, mate, have children, and assume the roles and responsibilities of adulthood. These changes required forming new attachments outside of our immediate families. By contrast, the hippocampal-cortical systems involved in new learning begin an early decline during adulthood. This is most likely due to the fact that, for most of our evolutionary history, there wasn't that much new to learn after age 25, and adulthood only consisted of a few decades at best. Remembering new names and faces, computer passwords, and where we put the car keys did not burden our tribal ancestors.

Neurofluency Principle 7: Every neural system has its own developmental timetable.

The first thing most people think of when they consider the developing brain is that it grows larger. Along with a larger brain come more sophisticated thoughts, behaviors, and skills. These are the two obvious changes we witness in our children as birthdays pass. At least early in life, bigger brains and more sophisticated abilities do go hand in hand. However, the ways the brain develops also change over time. While early in development the brain is growing in size and computing power, midlife presents a brain diminishing in size while expanding in both sophistication and problem-solving capacity. These improvements are due to the increasing connectivity of neural systems and their participation in solving complex problems.

Brain development is full of strategies that seem to contradict everyday common sense. One was to vastly overproduce neurons during gestation and have them compete for survival after birth. Neurons compete to connect with other neurons to become part of a functional system sustained and expanded through continued stimulation. The lack of stimulation to the shunned neurons causes them to die—a process called apoptosis—while the surviving neurons expand in size and connectivity. The brain grows larger during childhood because of the growth of new dendrites of the surviving neurons as the overall number of neurons decreases. During the first years of life, quantity is systematically replaced by patterns of connectivity and complexity. Like us, neurons survive because they connect with others and exchange energy and information.

Another aspect of brain development is the myelination of the neural axons. In this process, Schwann cells throughout the brain cover the axons in a fatty substance that looks like the snack called a pig in a blanket found at sports bars. This layer of white fat serves as an electrical insulator for the current that flows through the neuron on its way to firing and stimulating its neighbors. The bundles that connect different regions of the brain are primarily made of myelinated axons and are called white matter because of the color of the myelin. At a systemic level, brain development can be measured by the degree of connectivity among regions that need to share information and work together to perform specific tasks. Sensory and motor networks connect to allow us to do things like grasp objects and navigate the environment while those dedicated to memory and appraisal integrate so we can distinguish between familiar and unfamiliar others.

Neurofluency Principle 8: The cortex is shaped in an experience-dependent manner.

Because the brain doesn't develop in a linear fashion, we use our caretakers' brains as scaffolding early in life. Compare, for example, the fear circuits of the amygdala that are fully mature by birth with the cortical systems dedicated to regulating fear that take years to develop. During infancy and childhood, we rely on our caretakers to serve this yet-to-develop regulatory function. The way in which our caretakers help us to deal with fear and anxiety shapes our own developing circuitry between our amygdala and prefrontal cortex. How this circuit becomes organized is reflected in how we relate to others and our ability to regulate our emotions. As our brains develop, our experiences shape the architecture of our neural circuitry, making our brains a living expression of our learning histories.

There are also genetically timed bursts of neural growth called critical and sensitive periods that propel certain abilities to come online at specific times during development. Good examples are the emergence of stranger anxiety around 8 months and the burst of language development at around 18 months. The challenges of childhood at home, at school, and in the community are mostly tailored to the adaptive skills of the age group they serve. Research has shown that these periods of enhanced growth must interact with exposure to specific challenges and stimuli in order to be fully taken advantage of. Children who are neglected or abused during early critical periods of attachment often have great difficulties in making up for the negative experiences during important developmental windows.

The development of the teenage brain is characterized by the reorganization of networks involved in abstract thinking, emotional regulation, attachment, and reward. This sensitive period is driven by the social expectations that traditionally came along with adolescence to reorganize attachments in line with peer groups and mating, and take on the responsibilities of adulthood. Because modern Western society has postponed the timing of these challenges, many adolescents are a poor fit for the ongoing dependency they must adapt to. They may gravitate to violent video games, challenging sports activities, and promiscuous sexual behavior in an attempt to fulfill their genetic mandates. If this could be fully recognized by society, perhaps the timing of education could be modified and supplemented with activities and adventures more in line with the developing brain.

As we mature into adulthood, the connectivity among neural regions increases as the white matter communication bundles continue to mature. The ability to regulate our emotions also increases because of the maturation of cortical-amygdala connections. These and many other changes parallel the demands placed on adults to do the consistent heavy lifting of the family and tribe and to employ sound judgment in the best interest of those who depend on them. This process continues into the later years of life as we shift to the roles and responsibilities of elders: nurturing children and grandchildren, transmitting the stories, values, and cultures of the tribe, and dealing with spiritual and complex social problems of the family and tribe.

Some abilities, like remembering new information, peak around age 25 and begin to slowly decline thereafter. Others, like attachment, stay strong throughout life because of the necessity to nurture children, grandchildren, and new friends as old ones pass away. The primary developmental process during the last third of life is the increased participation of more areas of the brain in the service of complex problem solving, especially in the areas of interpersonal dispute resolution and the appropriate allocation of resources. These were the high-level abstract skills necessary for the maintenance and survival of the tribe through many millions of years of primate/human evolution.

THE BRAIN IN THE CONSULTING ROOM

Healing is a matter of time, but it is sometimes also a matter of opportunity.

—HIPPOCRATES

As a social organ of adaptation, our brains' first job is to join the web of relationships into which we are born. The newborn brain lacks perspective and experience, so it accepts the demands of its environment as a given, and invests in figuring out what is needed to survive. When we sit across from a client, years or decades later, we are relating to the totality of their developmental history. An appreciation of this deep complexity helps us to avoid accepting simplistic and prepackaged solutions for the human dilemma. A one-size-fits-all approach will never have a high frequency of success with such a diverse and complex species as our own.

Take, for example, my client Rochelle; a married, 50-year-old African American mother of four. She came to therapy complaining of anxiety, depression, and a concern about her increasing dependence on marijuana. Associated with these complaints were escalating levels of tension and fighting with her husband. Relevant life changes over the previous year included her husband's retirement and her youngest (and last) child leaving home. These changes resulted in a loss of identity and meaning for both of them. As I learned more about the history of their relationship, it became clear that the seeds of their marital conflicts were in place during their courtship. The fulfillments and challenges of family, career, and raising their children had allowed both of them to avoid these issues as well as the unresolved trauma from both their childhoods. As an old wise woman once told me, "What you resist, persists!"

Trauma is a word we use to describe our reaction to stressful and threatening experiences. If a child is brought up in a safe environment, with plenty of resources and attentive caretakers, her brain is shaped (in an experience-dependent manner) to navigate and succeed in the world in which she finds herself. If another child, similar in most respects, finds himself in a dangerous, deprived, and isolated life, his brain goes about the business of adapting to these conditions. The adaptations these two children make will consist not only of observable behaviors but also of their neuroanatomy, psychology, biology, epigenetics, mind, and spirit. In essence, early experiences shape the wetware of our brains and program the algorithms organizing our minds.

Rochelle's father was a popular musician, and her mother, an intelligent and competent homemaker, allowed her a comfortable and predictable life, one that looked "very good on paper." The fact that her family was intact, that they lived in a fine home and took nice vacations, led others to see her as a lucky and even spoiled child. All of her "luck" confused Rochelle about the legitimacy of her sad thoughts and painful emotions. "If I'm upset or unhappy, it must be my fault." But what was on paper was far different from her own experience. Her famous father, whose many fans loved and respected him, was also an unpredictable and violent alcoholic. Sometimes he would come home irritable and impatient, so that, instead of running to greet him, Rochelle would be sure to hide, stay quiet, and be careful not to draw attention to herself. Those were the good times. In bad times, he came home drunk, angry, and out of control, taking his rage out on his wife and children, especially Rochelle's older brother, who bore his name. In addition to navigating this home life, Rochelle's mother was careful to caution all of her children to always put on a good front and never to tell anyone what happened at home out of fear of damaging her father's reputation and their privileged lifestyle.

Rochelle's story is not an unusual one—it has been told innumerable times by the countless victims of violence and addiction. What might be new for you is looking at this scenario from the perspective of Rochelle's developing brain. Two overarching questions are (1) how did her brain adapt to her childhood environment, and (2) how have these adaptations impacted her relationship with her husband so many decades later?

Growing up in an environment characterized by uncertainty and danger, Rochelle's fear circuitry was shaped to be on constant alert and go to code red when her father was around. The likely biological outcomes are higher resting levels of adrenaline, cortisol, and dopamine, and lower levels of serotonin, all of which combine to enhance startle response, scan the environment for danger, and look for evidence of threat where none may exist. Research has shown that observing physical violence or being the victim of verbal abuse may even have a negative impact on a victim's ability to see and hear things clearly and accurately later in life. Sensory circuits appear to slow in their development, perhaps as a way to adapt better by not listening or seeing the details of painful input. Such a child's attachment circuitry will be shaped in a way that will make her experience of others feel more tenuous, uncertain, and less safe. In addition, the functioning of her immunological system will be impaired and make her more vulnerable to both physical and mental illness later in life if not during childhood.

Although Rochelle's family had considerable financial resources, they lacked emotional stability and security. And even though her parents could have afforded to send her to therapy, this never would have even been considered. For one, Rochelle wasn't consciously aware of her anxiety and depression. Also, the introduction of a therapist into the family system would have been too big a threat to her father's authoritarian control. What little emotional resources the family had were invested in day-to-day survival. As Rochelle told me, "We never knew whether Dr. Huxtable or Ike Turner was coming home, so we were always on alert and figuring out ways to keep things calm and safe." Rochelle's brain was shaped similarly to those of prey animals, such as mice and deer, trying to stay out of sight while ever vigilant for predators. I could tell by Rochelle's interactions with her husband that her brain was distorting her experience of him in line with her early experiences with her father.

From what I could tell, Rochelle's husband, Winston, was struggling with his own issues of anxieties and self-esteem. Rochelle experienced Winston's emotional struggles as dangerous, making her frightened and overreactive during their interactions. She was unable to relax when he was at home, which now was most of the time. His presence felt to her either like an attack or a precursor to one. As a child, she was never able to establish appropriate boundaries between herself and others because no one in her family had boundaries. So now with Winston, she was defenseless against any of his negative emotions; his emotions automatically triggered her own.

We generally focus on the emotional aspects of trauma and forget that they can result in disorders of attention and cognition. The primary reason for this is because our brains are incapable of separating thoughts from feelings. Thinking serves at the pleasure of emotion, so the biology and emotions of anticipatory anxiety and fear will lead the cortex to create explanations for these feelings. Rochelle's brain and mind led her to interpret many of Wilson's neutral statements as either threats or attacks. And this worked both ways; one of Rochelle's "jokes" about Winston was, "I see him in the morning and say, 'Good morning,' and he says, 'And just what do you mean by that?'" Many couples get trapped in patterns of interactions like this, reverberations of childhood trauma or past betrayals in their current interactions. Trauma changes the brain and mind and alters not only the way we feel but also the way we process information.

Although some may believe that everyone has a sense of self, an internal world, and the experience of personal boundaries, many don't possess them. Rochelle did develop an extraordinary sensitivity to the facial expressions, postures, and movements of others, as any successful prey animal would. She was known to her siblings, friends, and her husband as exquisitely aware of their needs and emotions, and had developed the reputation of being an exceptionally attentive parent and caretaker. Because Rochelle hadn't developed a sense of her own self, she was unable to leverage any of these finely honed abilities to her own benefit.

The self is a product of the imagination that ties together emotional, somatic, and visceral experience with autobiographical and working memory. It is not an evolutionary instilled process triggered by a gene into a critical period, but rather an outgrowth of social relating whereby others see you as a separate and integrated being. They assume you have your own experience and ask you to articulate and share it. All of the energy and attention in Rochelle's family was focused on day-to-day survival, and there was no time to worry about Rochelle or her siblings as the entire family had to live in the head of their frightening father.

Winston's parents were both high-powered businesspeople and socialites who had little time for him. In many ways, his brain had been shaped very differently than Rochelle's, but they shared the desperate insecurity of not having attentive parents and growing up lacking a safe haven within which to establish an ability to self-soothe and regulate their emotions. Each was at a point in their lives when they needed to gain a sense of security and reassurance from the other. Each disappointed the other on a daily basis—there just wasn't enough emotional security in their relationship to go around.

In Winston's brain, security was tied to his proximity to Rochelle, similar to the way a young child with insecure attachment clings to the mother for comfort and safety. This led him to experience fear whenever Rochelle was away and any expression of independence by Rochelle as abandonment and rejection. This reaction triggered Rochelle's fear of being trapped, and a battle would ensue. While they had functioned as highly successful adults for decades, the stressors activated their early experiences. The result was that their relationship quickly shifted from an adult partnership to two desperate children trying to get each other to be the adult they needed to take care of them and make them feel safe.

"Realizing at fifty-five that you don't know who you are is a shock," Rochelle told me near the beginning of one of our sessions. "What if I figure out who I am, and I don't want to be married anymore? Then what do I do?" She's so right! It's difficult at any stage of life to discover that you have outgrown an old way of being and need to build a new sense of self. In your teens, it's age appropriate, and you have plenty of company. If this developmental process is put off for decades, you not only go it alone, but you risk hurting the people who have assumed that the act you've been putting on was really you. For Rochelle, realizing she was devoid of boundaries and lacking a solid sense of self was an important first step in facing the challenge ahead of her.

Rochelle discovered that if I asked her how she was, her mind would immediately think of all the people in her life, and if none of them were having difficulties, she would respond, "I'm fine." Not only did she not think of herself when asked how she was doing, but that it had never occurred to her that anyone would be interested. Rather, she saw herself as a conduit to connect others without leaving an impression or, as she put it, "leaving a mark." So our work began here—interrupting these automatic and unconscious assumptions organized in childhood and beginning to focus on herself. She needed to be aware of what was going on in her body, how she was feeling, and what was important to her in the moment. As this work progressed, I pushed her to think about what she would like to do for herself, what made her feel special, or to pick things to do that she never would have thought she had the right to pursue.

As small pieces of her sense of a separate self began to coalesce, we had something to build a boundary around. We then used some meditation and guided imagery techniques to help her build an imaginary inner space for her to retreat to. We then used the resulting state of mind to practice being with Winston without monitoring his feelings, worrying about his needs, or obsessing about how she was failing him. She gradually worked her way out of living in his head and inhabiting her own. It takes time to build a self, just as it does during the long turbulent years of the transition from childhood to adulthood. It's always important to remind our clients that this is a slow process; otherwise they start to attack themselves for being behind schedule and can be hit with the same shame they felt as a child for not being worthy of the attention they needed in the first place. All things in due time.

3

PRIOR TO CONSCIOUSNESS

The mind is like an iceberg; it floats with one-seventh of its bulk above water.

—SIGMUND FREUD

The interaction of our brains, bodies, and relationships, give rise to the human mind. Information and energy are sent, received, and responded to while, through a narrow window of consciousness, we attempt to make sense of it all.

What is referred to as the unconscious by psychoanalysts, and implicit processing by neuroscientists, is mediated via a set of early evolving and early developing "fast" neural systems. These fast systems are driven via our senses, motor experiences, and bodily processes, all of which are nonverbal and inaccessible to conscious reflection. Evidence of the activity of these fast systems is all around us every day. If we touch a hot stove, get cut off while driving, or are able to return a fast tennis serve, our bodies react faster than our conscious awareness. These fast systems are likely all that our ancestors had for millions of years until the recent emergence of what we call conscious awareness.

The later-evolving systems involved in conscious awareness emerge from a complex interaction of sociality, culture, and the larger brains they require. Along the way, narratives, imagination, abstract thought, and self-awareness also emerged. These more complex processes involve multiple neural systems, many more synapses, and take considerably longer to process than reflexes, impulses, and somatic reactions. In this chapter, I will attempt to create a broad map of what happens in the brain during the half second it takes the brain to construct the components of our conscious experience. Because our memories (and books like this) are organized into narratives with beginnings, middles, and ends, we try and understand consciousness in the same way. However, the feedback systems in our brains work forward and backward in time, making neural processing more similar to the complex interactive systems like those which create oceans currents, tornadoes, and shape those interesting patterns in your cup as cold milk mixes with hot coffee. Simple linear models of cause and effect just don't suffice.

THE CONSTRUCTION OF CONSCIOUSNESS

What lies behind us and what lies ahead of us are tiny matters compared to what lives within us.

—HENRY DAVID THOREAU

We don't know how our brains construct consciousness, but neuroscientists generally believe that it arises from the convergence of multiple neurobiological processes. Our best guess is that conscious experience emerges through a combination of functions like working memory, learned behaviors, social interactions, language, and culture. The time between the triggering of electrochemical activation in our brains and when this firing arises into conscious awareness is thought to be approximately one half second. This half second is enough time for the neural activation of 100 billion neurons and 100 trillion synaptic connections to construct conscious experience.

Neurofluency Principle 9: Fast systems of implicit memory influence our experience of the world prior to conscious awareness.

Despite the fact that we experience the world around us and within us as if we are in the present moment, we are actually about a half second behind the present moment. When gurus tell us to "Be Here Now," the best we can do is to be here almost now. Just as our bodies, behaviors, and attachment to others have been shaped by natural selection to enhance survival, so has the nature and quality of our conscious awareness. But being aware of this half-second delay would be very disruptive to our ability to navigate the world. It might be like watching a movie when the film and soundtrack are out of sync.

While the illusion of living in the moment makes sense from a survival standpoint, it leads to a number of profound misunderstandings about ourselves. The first is that we are not influenced by implicit and unconscious processes—how could we be if we are living in the moment? It also leads to the illusion that we are in possession of all the information relevant to understanding our situation and making good decisions. Because we are unconscious of the half-second gap between brain activation and conscious awareness, we assume it doesn't exist. This leads to genuinely honest confusion in our clients when they ask, "How could things that happened decades ago still affect me?" It also leads to social challenges where people don't believe in implicit biases and prejudices because they don't consciously experience themselves as prejudice. They are unaware of their unseen biases embedded in the half second between sensation and perception that shapes their experience.

Neurofluency Principle 10: Conscious awareness depends upon slow systems of explicit memory to organize experience.

Another illusion shaped by survival is that our eyes are the center of our awareness which makes us feel like we control our actions from a space behind our eyes. This illusion has probably been shaped by a number of factors, including the increasing dominance of visual perception over the course of human evolution, the importance of hand-eye coordination in negotiating the physical world, and our cultural emphasis on thinking over feeling and doing. The downside of this illusion is that we underestimate the contribution of our other senses and the importance of somatic, visceral, and motor processing in shaping our experience. It also leads us to emphasize brain-based interventions for healing and underemphasize the importance of bodily and sensorimotor activities.

THE ARCHITECTURE OF IMPLICIT PROCESSING

Life is all memory, except for the one present moment that goes by so quickly you hardly catch it.

—TENNESSEE WILLIAMS

The Flash, a popular member of the Justice League, possesses the power of "the speed force," which allows him to accelerate to velocities that render him invisible to others. As he speeds through space, he is able to do good deeds like change the course of a speeding bullet or pull the rug out from under an enemy. Although those around him don't even notice his momentary absence, they observe that the bullets fired in their direction miss them and that their foes fall to the ground without apparent cause. Flash is a good metaphor for the speed at which our neural systems are able to construct consciousness. Just like the other members of the Justice League stuck in the standard flow of time, we only witness the results of our fast systems. Bullets don't go off course, but emotions are triggered, information distorted, and perceptions reshaped within the fast layers of implicit processing. We just experience the results of all this activity, which we interpret as our objective perception of the world.

Neurofluency Principle 11: We experience the events in the world around up approximately one half second after they occur.

In the normal flow of time, a half second goes by so quickly that we can hardly sense it. But like the Flash, the electrochemical messages transmitted throughout our nervous systems can do a great deal in almost no time at all. With the goal of adaptation through the prediction and control of our environments, our speed force allows us to make rapid decisions based on the smallest amount of information. Our brains use memory as their main predictive tool, especially for threatening situations. Although it seems to us that we are responding to the outside world, 90% of the brain's activity is in response to other activity within the brain. This is where our brains are comparing our sensations to past experiences in an attempt to perform a preemptive action in the service of survival. This is as true for withdrawing our hand from a hot stove as for reacting with avoidance to the offer of attention from others if this has been a source of pain in the past. This is likely why past behavior is the best predictor of future behavior.

A brain's job is to support the survival of the creature in which it resides. Long before animals developed anything as sophisticated as a brain, we possessed receptors that would detect nutrients and toxic substances in the environment to trigger life-sustaining approach-avoidance reactions. These receptors evolved into our immunological system, which detects bodily invasion by unfamiliar and potentially toxic substances. Others were dedicated to maintaining our internal homeostatic balance, monitoring things like temperature levels, oxygen supply, and blood pressure to trigger action when we needed to cool down, breathe more, or relax in order to maintain homeostasis. The nervous system evolved to monitor, assess, and trigger appropriate adaptive responses.

Neurofluency Principle 12: During the half second between sensation and perception, implicit memory systems shape our cognition and behavior.

The two most basic divisions of the nervous system are the central nervous system (CNS) and the peripheral nervous system (PNS). The CNS includes the brain and spinal cord, whereas the PNS is composed of the autonomic nervous system (ANS) and the somatic nervous system. The autonomic and somatic nervous systems are involved in the communication between the CNS and the sense organs, glands, and the body (including the heart, intestines, and lungs). The ANS has two branches, called the sympathetic and parasympathetic nervous systems. The sympathetic system controls the activation of the nervous system in response to a threat or other basic drives. The parasympathetic system balances the sympathetic system by fostering conservation of bodily energy, digestion, immunological functions, and repair of damaged systems. A third system, referred to as the smart vagus, operates in parallel to the parasympathetic branch of the ANS and is dedicated to fine-tuning bodily reactions in the service of social engagement.

The hypothalamic-pituitary-adrenal (HPA) axis regulates the secretion of hormones involved with the body's response to stress, the regulation of digestion, the immune system, and energy storage and expenditure. The immediate reaction to stress is vital for short-term survival, while the rapid return to normalization after the threat has passed is essential for long-term survival. Prolonged stress results in systemic damage and eventual breakdown. The long-term effects of negative parenting experiences, failures of attachment, and early trauma are mediated via the HPA system.

AT THE CENTER OF IT ALL: THE AMYG.

*Bad news sells because the amygdala is always looking for
something to fear.*

—PETER DIAMANDIS

The contemporary human amygdala has been highly conserved
during evolution and descends directly from our reptilian and
mammalian ancestors. Its main role is as an organ of appraisal of
positive and negative stimuli designed to trigger approach, avoidance, and freeze reactions. It is activated by both external stimuli
and internal input from the body and different systems of memory.
As the human brain has become increasingly complex, the amygdala has remained at the core of input and output circuits to appraise
moment-to-moment experience. When we are faced with danger,
the amygdala exerts its veto power over the other two cortical executive systems and takes control of our actions and reactions. It sits
at the nexus between descending information from the cortex and
information sent up from the viscera and bodily senses. It is also
at the apex of descending circuits to the brain stem and body in
response to threat and attraction. All of these reasons explain why
the amygdala appears to serve as a fulcrum of neural processing.

Neurofluency Principle 13: The amygdala is the center of our
first and most primitive executive system.

The amygdala is best known for its role in assessing for danger and
triggering the fight-flight-freeze response but also becomes active in
response to positive stimuli. In the complex and delicate dance of relationships, it plays a central role (in collaboration with the OMPFC) in
the evaluation of the dos and don'ts of day-to-day social interactions.
In fact, while the size of the hippocampus correlates with the complexity of the demands of navigating physical space, the amygdala's

size of our social networks. Making all of
ıires constant feedback from memory net-
rning experiences, making the amygdala
ɔth implicit and explicit memory.
..ygdala causes deficits in many human functions,
ʽ appraisal of social information, visual memory, and the
.ʊry recognition of fear and anger. It becomes more active in
social interactions when someone looks directly at us or when we
perceive a lack of fairness either to ourselves or to others. Amygdala activation varies with degrees of attachment security and the
availability of oxytocin, and individuals with antisocial personality
disorders tend to have a smaller amygdala. A central physiological
manifestation of secure attachment is a higher threshold of amygdala
activation for anxiety than those with an insecure attachment schema.

Humans and other primates evolved from small mammals similar to moles and hedgehogs, whose social interactions are guided
primarily by olfaction. In these animals, the amygdala evaluates
smells for clues of safety, danger, and mating. As visual information became increasingly important during primate evolution, the
amygdala came to also appraise facial expressions, eye gaze direction, gestures, and posture for social information. Faces judged to
be untrustworthy, verbal and written threats from others, and seeing fearful faces all activate different areas of the amygdala. Damage
results in a loss of socially appropriate behavior, decreased eye contact during interactions, and the loss of social status.

NEUROCEPTION AND SOCIAL ENGAGEMENT

There is more wisdom in your body than in your deepest philosophy.
—FRIEDRICH NIETZSCHE

The ubiquity and automatic nature of human relationships, from the
first moments of life, leads us to take them very much for granted.

They are, however, an incredible evolutionary accomplishment that has required our brains to greatly evolve in both size and complexity. Just as our immunological systems have to differentiate between familiar and foreign substances that enter our bodies, our social brains have to be able to identify how to safely navigate the social environment. In addition to distinguishing friend from foe, and kin from stranger, evolution also faced the challenge of better regulating emotions in close, sustained contact. As bigger brains led to children being born earlier in development to enhance survival of the mother, mothers needed to be able to read the increasingly primitive communication from their babies in order to care for them.

While basic approach-avoidance defensive strategies suffice for nonsocial animals, caretaking, cooperation, and group coherence require subtle and continuous emotional self-regulation. Mammals have to know not only whom to approach, but when, how, and for what purpose. We also sometimes have to stay in proximity to those we don't fully trust or toward whom we need to be deferential. We need to have different reactions to the same information based on whether it is coming from a friend or foe, superior or subordinate, adult or child, relative or stranger. The infinite subtleties of social interactions require a system of bodily and emotional regulation that is finely calibrated to a range of social situations. This is where the all-or-nothing nature of the sympathetic fight-flight-freeze mechanisms of the ANS and HPA are just not up to the task. An important contribution to our understanding of implicit processing has come from the neurophysiologist Steven Porges. His notions of polyvagal theory, the social engagement system, and neuroception add to our understanding of how brains connect, communicate, and regulate one another.

At the core of Porges's theories is a recognition of the sequential evolution of three separate autonomic subsystems in social mammals. The first two are the parasympathetic and sympathetic branches of the ANS, which we have already discussed. The more primitive parasympathetic system relies on the unmyelinated networks of the 10th cranial nerve system (the vagus nerve), which controls bodily shutdown, immobilization, and freeze reactions in response to stress and danger. The second is the mobilization or fight-flight system, which depends on the sympathetic branch of the ANS. The third system, which is the focus of Porges's social engagement system, relies on the later-evolving myelinated branch of the vagal system, which modulates sympathetic arousal.

Neurofluency Principle 14: The social engagement system provides a more refined method of affect regulation than the ANS.

According to Porges, it is the evolution and development of this "smart" vagal system that allows us to modulate autonomic arousal and emotional expression to promote social contact, emotional attunement, and more sophisticated caretaking. The same system also innervates the muscles of our eyes, faces, mouths, and ears to enhance social-emotional communication. He suggests that the vagal system evolved as a refinement of the ANS to provide more subtle regulation of visceral and autonomic activity and enhance our abilities to engage with others without activating fight-flight responses. Where the main ANS works like an on/off switch, the smart vagus provides us with a volume control on our arousal and social interactions.

Although the vagus is called the 10th cranial nerve, it is better described as a complex bidirectional feedback system that functions outside of the spinal cord. Because it has both sensory and motor fibers, it is an information-processing system that provides us with another conduit of processing bodily and social information below the level of conscious awareness. Information from the social engagement system, which Porges refers to as neuroception, is fed to the amygdala and cortex to provide input for social engagement, such as recognizing and reading facial expressions and other forms of social input.

Motor fibers of the vagus originate in the nucleus ambiguus and the dorsal motor nucleus. The dorsal motor nucleus is the source of the "vegetative vagus" and helps to regulate respiration and digestion with projections to the trachea, lungs, and gastrointestinal tract. The nucleus ambiguus drives the smart vagus, which processes emotion, motion, and interpersonal communication, with projections to the heart, palate, larynx, and bronchi. The addition of the smart vagus allows us to become excited and stay engaged with others by regulating sympathetic arousal, negative amygdala involvement, or adrenal activation. This makes arousing engagements, such as sustained caretaking, affiliation, and cooperation, possible positive experiences devoid of defensiveness or attack.

The tone of the vagus refers to the system's ability to regulate the heart and other target organs. Children with poor vagal tone have difficulty suppressing emotions in situations demanding their attention, making it difficult for them to engage with their parents, sustain a shared focus with playmates, and maintain attention on important material in the classroom. The development of vagal tone appears to be experience dependent and impacted by the quality of attachment relationships during childhood. For example, infants with greater vagal tone elicit more attuned behavior from their parents, which, in turn, helps them to develop greater vagal regulation. Vagal tone translates our experience with caretakers into the more stable bodily and emotional reactions we bring into subsequent relationships.

Good-enough parenting not only teaches appropriate responses in challenging interpersonal situations, it also builds the neural circuitry required to successfully carry them out. As adults, good vagal regulation allows us to become upset, anxious, or angry with a loved one without withdrawing, rejecting, or becoming physically aggressive. It allows us to engage in relationships, use them to regulate affect, and internalize them to aid in self-regulation. The role of the smart vagus in linking the primary muscles of the face, mouth, and throat to our bodily states allows both us and those we are engaged with to have a real-time readout of our gut reactions during interpersonal interactions. The smart vagus brings visceral-emotional background (tone) to all of our experiences and provides a broad soundtrack to our lives. All of the particular situations that we experience in consciousness are colored by this background biology, which perhaps results in different temperaments that make some people see the glass as half full or half empty, tend to be social or unsocial, or approach others in a friendly or unfriendly way.

INTUITION, DECISION MAKING, AND SOMATIC MARKERS

We do not live to think. . . . We think in order that we may succeed in surviving.

—JOSÉ ORTEGA Y GASSET

Theories of decision making, especially in the field of economics, have traditionally been based on a rational application of cost-benefit analyses. Yet most of us have the sense that there is more to making good decisions than drawing up a list of pros and cons. While we are thinking things through, it seems that other processes are going on inside us that influence our choices, sometimes overriding what we think is most logical. A highly successful gambler, business strategist, or athlete always seems to have a sixth sense about what to do, an intuition they may not even be able to articulate, which helps them to beat the odds.

What we call intuition is likely based in implicit information processing taking place within the fast system of neural processing.

It is likely that intuition consists of a combination of multiple data streams appraised by the amygdala to have an overall positive or negative valence. The neuroscientist Antonio Damasio found that individuals with damage to the OMPFC, amygdala, or somato-sensory cortex had difficulty making good choices in complex situations. He believed that this was because subliminal bodily and emotional input to the amygdala had been cut off. The core of the theory is that we evolved to use information from our bodies, such as muscle tone, heart rate, endocrine activity, and so on, to make rapid decisions about how to navigate the physical and social worlds. Through these somatic markers, we unwittingly rely on primitive appraisal networks to guide our conscious decision-making process.

Neurofluency Principle 15: Somatic markers provide input into our decision making via implicit memory systems embedded in neural networks that organize bodily and sensory experience.

Somatic markers, like the unconscious appraisal described in the polyvagal social engagement system, influence the construction of conscious experience. "Decision making" is another way of saying "appraisal"—whether to make a big bet or trust someone in a business deal is a more abstract expression of the basic question of what we approach and avoid. Somatic markers are an excellent example of conservation in evolution, where older systems are retained and interwoven with later-evolving ones to enhance survival. It would make evolutionary sense for us to use more primitive systems to both support and reinforce later-evolving systems in complex decision making. Economists who once performed their analyses based on models of rational capitalism have come to learn that their models do not account for the emotion-based decision making of individuals and groups.

LESSONS FROM BUDDHISM

To live is to suffer, to survive is to find some meaning in the suffering.

—FRIEDRICH NIETZSCHE

Some readers may find it curious that a book about neuroscience in clinical practice would include a section about Buddhist philosophy. This initial confusion might be caused by the idea that Buddhism is a religion like Islam, Judaism, or Christianity. In fact, the teachings of Buddhism center around an understanding of the workings of the brain and mind based on 2,000 years of meditative self-observation. I believe that Buddhists are the experts on human consciousness and how the body, brain, and social relationships lead to the emergence of the mind and the construction of conscious experience.

Most forms of psychotherapy rely upon the expansion of self-awareness in the service of being freed from self-destructive patterns of thought, emotion, and behavior. The core beliefs of CBT, the unconscious determinants from early childhood experience used in psychoanalysis, and the existential dilemmas of the humanistic therapies are all present in the teachings of Buddhism. Western psychotherapists tend to focus on the differences among the conceptual schools rather than appreciating their similarities. This is likely because we are so desperate to feel like we have an understanding of the mind instead of being in awe of its complexity.

The Buddhist's goal, like the goal of any therapist, is to bring liberation from suffering. In the last century, these teachings have spread around the world and are most evident today in the various schools of meditation and the mindfulness movement in the Western hemisphere. We don't have to leave our own beliefs behind or become Buddhists to benefit from Buddha's teachings. In fact, I don't even consider him to be the founder of a religion, but rather, one of the world's first psychologists.

Although neuroscientists have yet to figure out the origin of consciousness, they are beginning to develop a model of its various contributing factors. The thinking of Western scientists is in the process of slowly evolving beyond a view of consciousness as a rational process generated by the executive functions of the mind. They are discovering, as Antonio Damasio and Steve Porges described, that many implicit and unconscious processes have come to shape it. In Buddhism, the five aggregates are seen as combining to give rise to consciousness:

1. The physical world, body, and sense organs (visceral and somatic experience)
2. Experiencing an object as pleasant, unpleasant, or neutral (appraisal)
3. Perception and cognition registering an object's familiarity (memory)
4. Mental formations, impulses, and volition habits (thought patterns and habitual behaviors)
5. Consciousness—that which discerns (the observing self and metacognition)

Together, the five aggregates give rise to our experience of consciousness. The ability to appraise the value of the people and things around us (amygdala and OMPFC) leads us to be dissatisfied with what we have and to want something else. The existence of memory creates the ability to obsess about the negative aspects of the past and be anxious about what will arise in the future (amygdala, hippocampus, and temporal cortex). Negative and self-destructive patterns of thoughts, feelings, and behaviors lead us to engage in repetitive experiences, while our attachment to our ideas of self-identity leads us to be burdened with guilt, shame, regret, and low self-esteem.

The core principle of Buddhism—the one that is most central

to Western psychotherapy—is that life's suffering is related to how we think about ourselves, others, and the future. Notice the similarity to CBT's cognitive triad; perhaps Aaron Beck was a Buddhist in a former life. All forms of therapy, including Buddhism, accept that pain is a natural part of life. We inevitably have illnesses, lose loved ones, grow old, and die. Pain is inevitable, but because suffering is a product of the mind, it is optional, if we can learn to control our thoughts. To express it in a slightly different way, pain is woven into nature while suffering is the result of how the mind constructs our experience of pain. Suffering is the anguish we experience from worry about not getting the things we need or losing the things that we have. It is the anticipatory anxiety and catastrophic thinking we can connect to not getting an A, being overweight, or not getting married and having a baby according to schedule. Suffering is a result of the dissatisfaction created by our minds, no matter how much we have or how well we are doing.

Buddhist psychotherapy is not so different from many of the types of therapy practiced in the West. The goal is to decrease suffering by distinguishing between external reality and the creations of our minds that lead to suffering. What is called enlightenment is the realization that our minds create the world, and we have the power to change our experience for the better, which includes living with less suffering, by remaining mindful of the illusions created by the mind and its attachment to these creations that are not real. Most clients don't come to therapy to become enlightened, but they do wish to become less symptomatic, engage in less self-destructive behaviors, and have a more positive engagement with life. As Freud wrote, the goal of therapy is not perfection, but to lessen pathological patterns of thoughts, feelings, and behaviors. Therapy should go on long enough to allow the client to be free to love and work.

FREE WILL AND FREE WON'T

Between stimulus and response there is a space.
In that space is our power to choose our response.
In our response lies our growth and our freedom.

—VIKTOR FRANKL

The illusion of free will has obvious survival advantages, the foremost of which is the ability to be confident, assertive, and action oriented in challenging and dangerous situations. The downside is that when we have time to think things through, we are limited by our belief that our conscious awareness is all there is, and that we have access to all relevant and necessary information. This is akin to thinking that global warming is no longer a problem on a snowy day. Psychotherapy, in all of its forms, attempts to address and sometimes unpack the architecture of the fast system to discern how our experience is biased prior to conscious awareness.

Self-reflective capacity and an openness to questioning one's assumptions is a key predictor of positive outcome in psychotherapy. These are the main ingredients for exploring aspects of consciousness that usually go unseen. One of our main roles as therapists is to give our clients a glimpse of the fact that what they assume to be objective reality is actually a product of their own mind. At the point of this realization some flee, some argue, and others become fascinated. If they stay with it, they come to learn that their histories, encoded in things like attachment schemata, transference, and shame programming, contribute to and even shape their day-to-day experience. This awakening can lead to making new decisions about their behaviors, emotions, and relationships. Once they realize they are living according to an unconscious script, they have the possibility for edits and even rewrites.

The core of many anxiety treatments is a combination of exposure to the feared stimulus, staying in its presence instead of fleeing (response prevention), and learning how to be calm in situations that have caused arousal in the past. Changing behavior that's based in the programming of the half second between sensation and perception has a similar biology and a parallel process of change. The first step is awareness—transition from unconscious acting-out to learning to observe what is happening. Don't expect not to do it; just add conscious awareness to the mix. Say you want to drink less alcohol yet find yourself regularly drinking to excess. Instead of just drinking as a reflex, be aware that you have the impulse to have a drink, find out what feelings are driving the behavior, and pay attention to the consequences.

> *Neurofluency Principle 16*: It is not clear how much free will
> we have when it comes to our automatic thoughts, but it is
> clear that we are capable of exercising free won't in acting
> with accordance with them.

Adding awareness to previously reflexive behavior adds cortical activation and the possibility of regulation and inhibition of impulses buried within the implicit half second. We need cortical activation to gain control of unconscious reflexes and habits. Once you are more present and aware while doing the behavior you wish to change, add some conscious thinking to the reflex. In the example of excessive drinking, ask yourself what you are feeling when the impulse to drink takes hold. You might find you are vaguely aware of being a bit anxious or lonely when the reflex is activated. The reflex and the effects of drinking may have served to keep you from being consciously aware of being anxious or lonely.

Many of us may not be able to be aware of our feelings during an event, and only become aware of them hours or days later. That's just another thing to become aware of. When I use this strategy with clients, I find that the time between the behavior and the awareness slowly decreases until they are able to recognize the feeling an hour later, then right after the first drink, and eventually, before they even reach for a drink. When the reflex is closely followed by the awareness, then you have the option to engage in free won't. The awareness creates the possibility of free will, while without it we are robots that are controlled by the programming contained within the half second. We still might not decide to change our behaviors, but at least we are closer to being in control than a puppet on a neural string.

DIGGING MY OWN GRAVE

The major task of the 20th century will be to investigate the subsoil of the mind.

—HENRI BERGSON

I received a call from a woman who asked if I could help her 33-year-old daughter Dora. Lupa told me that Dora had been a successful model in her late teens and early 20s and seemed happy until five years ago. "She went from being a happy, social person," Lupa said, "to avoiding people and staying home almost all of the time." She suspected that whatever was wrong was somehow related to the end of Dora's marriage to a "bad guy" who was no longer in the picture. Dora refused to talk to her mother about what happened or discuss why she had changed. Lupa had been trying to get her to see someone for the past couple of years, and she finally agreed as long as her mother would come with her, so we set up an appointment for later that week.

As I opened the door to my waiting room, I was struck by the contrast between the two women. Lupa was smallish and round, with a beaming smile in a beautiful face. Dora, tall and thin, sat with a twisted posture and expressionless face. I could see the resemblance between the two, but only in the geometry of their faces; one full of life, the other barely alive. My first impression was how much worse Dora looked than Lupa's description led me to envision. Mom jumped up and led the way, while Dora rose slowly and hesitantly entered my office. Lupa was excited to have finally gotten her daughter to a therapist and launched into her description of Dora, past and present. Dora resumed her twisted posture, stared off into space, and seemed many miles away.

After 10 minutes, I asked Dora if it was all right if her mom went to the waiting room, and she agreed. We sat in silence for a while before I said, "Your mom has a lot to say," which made Dora roll her eyes and crack a small smile. I could see that she wasn't going to speak on her own, so I started asking questions about her concerns, general health, and any symptoms she might be experiencing. She attributed most of her problems to fatigue, listed a number of illnesses she thought she might have, and lamented at how incompetent doctors are. I listened carefully, jotted some notes, and realized that creating a trusting connection with Dora would most likely take a while.

As she described her last few years in a slow monotone, I began to wonder if she would qualify for a diagnosis of major depression and thought of whom I might refer her to for a medication consultation. As all this was taking place, I noticed that whenever there was a noise from either the interior hall or an outside window, she would wince slightly and lean her body to the right. It looked as if either something had approached her from the left or she was having a small muscle cramp. I noted that her physical reaction was the same regardless of where the sound came from, which I found unusual. I made a note of this but didn't ask her about it given the early stage of our relationship. Over the first few sessions, we continued to get to know one another, found a few points of connection, and even shared an occasional light moment. She came to accept that she was depressed, and we went about scheduling consultations with a pharmacologist and physician for a general physical.

Dora denied physical or sexual abuse during childhood, although she did confide experiences of domestic violence before her mother left her father and came to the United States. She reported ending her marriage because her husband had difficulties with anger, and she remembered him hitting her on two occasions. She describes leaving him because, she said, "I didn't want my mother's life." As sessions passed, I continued to notice her wincing reaction in response to sounds, and a couple of times when I shifted in my seat or got up to retrieve a pen or a tissue. About two months into therapy, during a quiet moment, I said, "Dora, I've noticed a few times now that when you hear a sound or if I move, you seem to wince a bit on your left side." She seemed confused by my words, so I demonstrated with my own body what I saw. "Like this," I said. She continued to look at me with a perplexed expression, so I asked her to imitate and even exaggerate what I was doing and asked her to tell me if any thoughts or feelings came to her. She tried it once or twice without a reaction, but the third time her body froze. She looked startled and then began to tremble. A few seconds later, she ran out of my office, leaving her purse and sweater behind.

After she left, I sat musing about what had happened and thought about clues to this kind of response I might have missed. At the end of the hour when I called her house, Lupa answered and told me that Dora had just arrived and gone directly into her room. I asked her to have Dora call me when she felt up to it. Although I didn't hear from her, I held her next appointment and she showed up. This was a different Dora; no longer distant and lethargic, instead agitated and frightened. "I'm guessing that what I said about your body movements at our last session triggered something powerful inside of you. Any idea what it might be?" She was silent for a while and slowly began to quietly sob. "It just broke me apart, after holding myself together for all these years, just that one thing you said broke me apart." "Can you tell me what my words broke apart?" She sat quietly for about a minute and then told me this story.

"When I was 25, I met this guy who said he was crazy about

me and couldn't wait to marry me. Working as a model, most of the guys I met were either gay or real creeps, but this guy seemed real. We got married pretty quickly, maybe 3 months. My mother was so mad at me. Anyway, things were good for a while but then he began to change. Staying out all night, upset and angry all the time—he went from treating me good to treating me really bad. The first time he hit me I couldn't believe it. All I could think about was watching my mother getting hit by my father when I was little. The next time it happened, around midnight after he had a few drinks, I told him I was going to leave him. He stood frozen for a long while, got this strange look in his eyes, and then went into the garage. He was making a lot of noise and I could hear him throwing stuff all over. I was wondering if he was packing his things to leave me. When he came back in, I could hardly recognize him. He looked like an angry demon. He grabbed me, dragged me into the garage, and stuffed me into the trunk of the car. I was screaming and kicking, but he was too strong. He ripped off my shoes and glasses, threw them on the floor, and slammed the lid shut.

"It seemed we drove forever, probably on highways because we hardly stopped. I could tell it had become daytime because the trunk got really hot and it was hard to breathe. Then it got really bumpy for a while until we came to a stop. I could hear him walking around outside and unloading stuff from the backseat. I yelled at him but he wouldn't talk to me. I was so hot, so thirsty—I started to get scared when I realized I wasn't sweating anymore. I thought I was gonna die. I was getting weaker and weaker. I was crying, but no tears were coming out. I must have fallen asleep or passed out and when I woke up the trunk was cooler, so I thought it must be nighttime. All of a sudden I heard the key in the lock, and the lid popped open. It was dark. There was nothing but sand all around, and Leo was standing there, staring at me and holding a shovel." Dora stopped here and started to shake, so I brought her some water and reminded her that she was safe now and these were memories from the past. I reassured her again and again that she was safe.

After a while she began again. " 'Get out and dig!' he yelled at me and pointed a gun at my head. I was shocked to see him with a gun and at first couldn't understand why he wanted me to dig. As I climbed out of the trunk and he shoved the shovel into my chest, I realized that he was making me dig my own grave. I must have gone into shock, because I only have small pieces of memory. I probably dug for quite a while, because when I came to, I was lying in a big hole. Maybe he dug some of it. I just don't know. My head and ribs were throbbing. It was totally dark, and I was alone in the middle of nowhere. I walked for a long time until I got to a road and eventually someone drove by and took me to a police station. I made a police report, borrowed enough money to get home, and slept for two days. I never told my mother, and when I woke up I decided to make believe that it never happened. I tried so hard to forget it that I think I actually did. When you made me do those movements, the wincing movements, I had a flash of pain in my left rib, and the pain made me remember him hitting me with the shovel and breaking them. Then it all started coming back as if it happened yesterday. It's like I forgot about it and didn't forget at the same time. Very strange shit."

In early childhood (and afterward during states of high arousal), our amygdala functions as the executive brain. Experiences associated with threat are stored in primitive unconscious systems of sensory, motor, visceral, and emotional memory. Afterward, these nonconscious memories can be triggered by anything that the amygdala associates with them, from a smell, to the touch of a hand, to the sight of some long-forgotten image. The fact that most of our neural processing functions below the level of awareness allows us to perform many different functions and tasks simultaneously. However, it creates problems for us when these primitive memories organized by the amygdala break into consciousness and negatively interfere with adaptive, healthy functioning. Although Dora actively repressed these memories from consciousness for many years, they still guided her emotions and behaviors, rendering her a prisoner in her own home. Pointing out her wincing and her dramatic reaction made her hidden memories public and subject to reflection and sharing. It's at this point where the process of integrating these memories into conscious awareness and healing from her trauma can begin. The "de-repression" of memories is often the first step toward coming to grips with overwhelming traumatic experiences and beginning the process of healing.

4

ATTACHMENT,
BRAIN, AND MIND

There is no abstract "human nature," fixed and immutable. . . .
Human nature is the totality of historically determined social
relations, hence an historical fact.

—ANTONIO GRAMSCI

In the Western world, we have been taught to separate the heart
from the mind, the hard from the soft sciences, and the healing
sciences from the arts. We also romanticize intimate relationships
and resist illuminating them with the cold light of science. When
my son was born, a few people asked me if my interest in brain
development interfered with my paternal instincts. Did I experience him in a more distant and analytical way than I might have if I
were ignorant of what was going on inside his skull? All I can say is
that I don't think so. In addition to all the normal feelings of bonding, warmth, and love, I marveled to see the concepts I had studied
over the years unfolding before my eyes. My study of neuroscience
turned out to be no match for the biochemistry driving my paternal
responses.

When I took my initial steps into the study of neuroscience in the 1970s, attachment and brain research lived in separate universes. During graduate school, I had a morning child development class in a large sun-filled hall at the western border of campus. After lunch, I walked 30 minutes east to a basement lab to study the hippocampi of rats and the visual cortex of chimpanzees. It was truly a double life. Neither world had any interest in the other, and no one could fathom my interest in both. The truth is that I wasn't certain myself—I was following a deep intuition that was hard to articulate and difficult to defend.

As the decades have passed, the two fields have slowly discovered one another in powerful ways. It is now impossible for neuroscientists to ignore the importance of early nurturance whenever they study a social species. Some have even started breeding their own experimental animals to control for the influences of early experience on the brain. On the other side, those who study child development are coming to appreciate how early experience is translated into the very substance of the brain. Developmental psychologists, educators, and therapists now understand that the underlying biological processes of infancy and childhood are the mechanisms through which early interactions are translated into adult experience and behavior. In answer to the question, What do early nurturance, maternal care, and attachment schema have to do with neuroscience and the human brain? The answer turned out to be just about everything.

THE ENCULTURED BRAIN

Freedom is the consciousness of necessity.

—KARL MARX

As humans became increasingly social, the period of childhood dependency expanded well beyond those of most other species. Our brains develop slowly as they adapt to the behaviors, beliefs, and rituals of those around us. Through countless interactions, we learn how to have relationships, navigate the environment, and become a full member of our tribe. Our early interactions stimulate neural growth, establish our neurochemical set points, and determine how well or poorly our neural networks develop and integrate—all this in addition to shaping our attachment schema, affect regulation, and self-identity. Through this process, both the wetware of our brains and the organization of our minds are always an encultured reflection of experience.

When I listen to clients talk about their childhoods, my mind wanders to Plato's *Republic*, where he outlined his vision for raising the elite guardians of his utopian community. One of his ideas was to make sure that the children were raised communally so as to counterbalance the idiosyncrasies of any particular set of parents. The benefit of growing up in extended multigenerational families and solid communities is exposure to a wide variety of people so as to average out the effects of any who are too unusual or extreme. It also provides extended bonding and attachment to grandparents, aunts, uncles, cousins, and neighbors. Isolated families do not usually create the best foundation for launching children into the world. Brains and minds are all too often shaped to adapt to parental idiosyncrasies assumed to reflect the social norm.

Having brains shaped by our childhoods is good news for some and bad news for others. Children don't have a say about the social world into which they are born and know of no other possibility. This is nature's way to ensure that we bond with those who promote our survival. Unfortunately, children with irrational parents grow up feeling anxious, confused, and distrustful of their own judgment or the judgment of others. Children with parents who are unwilling or unable to nurture them often grow up feeling unlovable and ashamed of their very existence.

ATTACHMENT BASICS

In every real man a child is hidden that wants to play.
—FRIEDRICH NIETZSCHE

The key figure in the field of attachment is the psychoanalyst Sir John Bowlby, who carefully observed interactions between mothers and their children. It's hard to believe that a century ago, this was a revolutionary concept. Fascinated by the delicate balance between bonding and exploration, Bowlby developed the concepts of attachment schemata, proximity seeking, and a parent serving as a secure base for exploration and growth. His work highlighted the importance of physical and emotional contact with caretakers for the development of secure attachments. He recognized something that we have come to take for granted: children thrive in the context of consistent and caring adults.

> *Neurofluency Principle 17*: At its core, attachment is the regulation of arousal via proximity.

At its primitive core, attachment is the regulation of fear and anxiety through proximity to caretakers. Children use their caretakers as a secure base from which to explore the world and, in the process, slowly learn to regulate their own arousal, anxiety, and emotions. Bowlby believed attachment schemata to be the summation of thousands of experiences with caretakers, translated by the brain into implicit predictions of how others will behave toward us. Attachment schema are implicit memories that persist into adulthood, impacting the choice of partners and the quality of our relationships.

One way to define secure attachment is the ability to tolerate separation from our attachment figures in a way that allows for continued exploration. We see this in the infant strange situation, where one-year-olds are left by their mothers in a room with a stranger. While concerned about their mothers' absence, securely attached children are able to stay regulated and engage with a stranger, greet the mother upon her return, and go back to playing once the connection has been reestablished. In contrast, children with insecure attachment are characterized by high levels of distress, a lack of exploration, and disrupted reunion behavior. Attachment schema also determine whether we are able to use relationships for emotional regulation and a sense of safety in the future.

THE NEUROBIOLOGY OF ATTACHMENT

The social brain is in its natural habitat when we are talking with someone face-to-face.

—DANIEL GOLEMAN

Evolution has selected for social animals to stick together. It accomplishes this by shaping their neurochemistry to drive togetherness. The conscious experience of these biochemical processes is the warm and positive feelings of being together and the pain and anxiety of separation; the pleasure of having our backs scratched, the joy of our team winning a championship. While we are observing the interplay of bonding and attachment between children and their parents, a multitude of powerful and complex neurobiological processes are being established within the children's brains. At the same time, relational experiences are being translated (via epigenetics) into the wetware of the social brain. Simultaneously, other structures that produce and regulate the biochemistry of attachment circuitry are shaping the implicit memories of connection that will become activated when in proximity to others.

A central neurobiological hub of secure attachment is the hierarchical network that includes (from top to bottom), the OMPFC, the anterior cingulate cortex, the anterior insula, and the amygdala.

The OMPFC is the primitive core of the prefrontal cortex that sits at the apex of networks that organize attachment and affect regulation. At the bottom end, the amygdala is intricately connected up to the OMPFC and down to many points in the lower brain that activate the body in response to positive and negative stimuli. Both the OMPFC and amygdala are in the business of appraising the value of what is around us and trigger our bodies to avoid spiders and snakes and to approach children in distress and piles of cash.

Neurofluency Principle 18: The core of attachment circuitry is embedded in the hierarchical networks that connect the OMPFC with the amygdala.

While the OMPFC evolved from the amygdala, a major difference between the two in contemporary humans is that the amygdala makes very broad, black-and-white approach-avoidance decisions while the OMPFC is more nuanced in its evaluations. Lying between the two, the anterior cingulate emerged along with maternal behavior in primates and is involved with nursing, play, feelings of empathy, and face recognition—all central aspects of maternal behavior. The anterior insula connects our bodily states to conscious awareness via the anterior cingulate and the OMPFC. This system processes the punishment and reward value of complex stimuli (parents and other environmental factors relevant to survival) and mediates emotional and visceral responses based on past learning.

Given that it is such an evolutionarily primitive structure, the amygdala is fully developed even before birth. In general, the parts of our nervous system that evolved earlier develop earlier during our life. What this means is that even before we are born, our amygdala is capable of triggering the body's fight-flight mechanisms and the cascade of biochemicals that cause panic attacks and compromise the body's immunological defenses. Young children are therefore totally dependent upon a parent's ability to regulate their anxiety for them by appearing when they are distressed, figuring out what they need, and returning the child to a state of calm and bodily equilibrium. If these experiences are largely positive and successful, the child tends to feel safer and more secure in the world, experience others as sources of comfort, and eventually learn to regulate their own fear through self-talk, memory of positive outcomes, and proactive problem solving.

But how do the brain and body learn to be secure? A major component rests in the amygdala-prefrontal circuitry via inhibition and modulation. You may notice that very young children have extreme reactions, both good and bad, to many situations. Their overwhelming joy at being handed an ice cream cone can almost immediately turn to abject despair if the ice cream falls to the ground. This extreme and rapid emotional lability is the amygdala at work with minimal modulation. Over time, the relationship between the amygdala and the prefrontal cortex modulates and shapes our emotional reactions. When therapists talk of an inner mother, a major biological component is the shaping of the amygdala-prefrontal system to modulate our arousal and emotions.

The ANS, with its two branches (sympathetic and parasympathetic), serves the body's homeostatic balance between activation and inhibition. When the amygdala is activated, the sympathetic branch of the ANS becomes activated as part of our fight-flight-freeze reaction. Sympathetic dominance of the ANS corresponds with anxious-ambivalent attachment patterns characterized by irritability, dependency, acting-out behavior, and a decreased ability to recover from stress. Such children experience difficulties with impulse control, hostility, and abandonment fear and are often diagnosed with attentional deficits and hyperactivity. In contrast, an ANS biased toward parasympathetic dominance might result in an avoidant attachment style, with a low level of emotional expression, physical activity, and eye contact. Proximity seeking, exploration, and positive interpersonal relationships are limited. These children are more likely to present as lonely, depressed, withdrawn, or unmotivated.

The ANS is a primitive system that works as a kind of on-off switch for activation or restoration. As we evolved into increasingly social creatures, this on-off switch became inadequate for dealing with the complexities of close and sustained relationships. A second network that is shaped by early experience has been called the social engagement system. Steven Porges has proposed that the vagus, or the 10th cranial nerve complex, has evolved in humans as an integrator and regulator of physiological arousal and social connection. The vagal system extends from multiple points within the body including the heart, lungs, throat, and digestive system and is involved in the regulation of their activity.

The second contribution of the social engagement system is to provide information from our internal organs to the muscles in our face. This system allows parents to watch the facial expressions of their preverbal children and get a real-time readout of their internal state. Think of the vagal system as a volume control that allows us to stay in proximity, deal with emotionally arousing situations, and dial in an appropriate level of relationship-sustaining arousal, activation, and emotion. If the polyvagal regulation of the social engagement system is underdeveloped due to insecure attachment, we may depend on the utilization of more primitive autonomic regulation (fight-flight-freeze) in relationships.

THE NEUROCHEMISTRY OF ATTACHMENT

When you massage someone, the levels of oxytocin go up in the brain, and oxytocin is one of the chemicals that drives attachment.
—HELEN FISHER

In addition to the social networks that crisscross our brains, a variety of neurochemicals (neurotransmitters and neurohormones) are used for communication and modulation of our social and emotional functions. These neurochemicals have long evolutionary histories and have been utilized in an increasing number of ways to regulate more complex relationships. They all have very powerful influences on our behaviors, emotions, and thinking, as evidenced by the "madness" of love and crimes of passion, and the incredibly powerful bonds in a wide spectrum of social settings. The social connections between romantic partners, parents and children, and members of teams, armies, and cults are all driven and modulated by social neurochemicals.

Endorphins

Endorphins (a form of opioid), which naturally reside in our brains and bodies, serve to reduce pain and create a feeling of well-being. Opioids shape early bonding experiences by promoting a warm sense of safety. For example, children express separation anxiety while mothers report feeling distress, anxiety, and sadness when separated from their children. Both are caused by precipitous declines in endorphins triggered by separation. This is one of evolution's strategies to keep parents and children as close as possible and to enhance social connectivity throughout life. The familiar runner's high is caused by increased levels of opioids in the different areas of the cortex. The amygdala, a key component of fear circuitry, has a high density of opioid receptors. It is believed that endorphins evolved because they allow us to more successfully fight and flee by decreasing both the physical pain and emotional distress associated with life-threatening experiences. During evolution, endorphins were used to enhance attachment and increase the emotional attractiveness of relationships.

Oxytocin and Vasopressin

Oxytocin and vasopressin evolved from molecules that control sexual behavior and egg laying in reptiles. In mammals, they have come to regulate proximity, romance, and social emotions. Oxytocin is released into a woman's bloodstream during labor, breast-feeding, and sex. Its main function is to drive procreation and maternal behavior while inhibiting aggression and irritability. In males, vasopressin facilitates pair bonding, attachment, and the maintenance of monogamy while its reciprocal relationship with testosterone contributes to its ability to decrease aggression in intimate and caretaking relationships.

Oxytocin and vasopressin play a role in broader social relationships. For example, when male chimps fight to establish dominance, the rest of the troop gathers to observe the outcome. When one chimp begins to realize that he's losing the fight, he may run to one of the female observers, grab an infant from her arms, and put it in the face of the alpha male. This raises vasopressin levels and decreases testosterone levels in the alpha, calming him down and allowing the beta to survive. The growth of oxytocin receptors is stimulated through epigenetic processes triggered by maternal attention. The touch, pressure, and warmth of another increases oxytocin levels, decreases blood pressure, and supports the protein synthesis necessary for neural growth and plasticity. This is likely why those with secure attachment appear to have well-developed and better-integrated brains. When subjects are administered oxytocin, they tend to be more generous, charitable, empathic, and more perceptive of others.

Dopamine

Dopamine is a key reward biochemical that motivates bonding, attachment, and social interactions. It is produced in the brain stem, travels up through the thalamus, amygdala, and OMPFC, and back down again. These systems of attachment that detect, store, and activate past events are modulated by dopamine. Interactions with caretakers are analyzed and stored based on their emotional reward value, then unconsciously applied to future situations. It is within this hierarchical network that attachment schemata are learned, stored, and modified by subsequent relationships—including psychotherapy.

It has been shown in rats that repeated separation from the mother decreases dopamine activity, exploration, and affiliative behavior while increasing reactivity to stress. Oxytocin has been found to block dopamine receptors, which prevents habituation (and eventual disinterest) to those we love. The metaphor of being addicted to love may not be a metaphor. The biochemical systems regulated by relationships are the same as those impacted by drugs like cocaine and heroin, and the experiences of craving, dependency, and withdrawal are similar in romantic separation and addiction.

Serotonin

Serotonin is an ancient neurochemical that first emerged in the gut to modulate peristalsis and other gastrointestinal activities. In social animals, it has evolved to be a modulator of sociality, aggression, and a sense of well-being, establishing the clear connection between relationships and eating. Serotonin has also been found to regulate mood, appetite, and sleep. It is more plentiful in individuals with secure attachment, and low levels have been found in people who are incarcerated. Medications that increase available synaptic serotonin levels, called SSRIs (selective serotonin reuptake inhibitors), are in wide use as a treatment for depression and anxiety.

EXPERIENCE-DEPENDENT NEUROCHEMISTRY

> *Every single brain is absolutely individual, both in its development*
> *and the way in which it encounters the world.*
>
> —GERALD EDELMAN

The cocktail of these five neurochemicals, along with other substances, is used in different combinations to drive sexual, bonding, parental, and affiliative behaviors from dyads to groups. The nuclei that produce these neurochemicals, the number of receptors, and their resting levels are all influenced by the nature of attachment interactions. We literally build our children's brains in positive and negative ways as epigenetic processes convert our interactions into the neuroanatomy and neurochemistry of their brains. When we think about an internal mother, a central component of this hypothetical inner person is the biochemistry that is triggered when we invoke her. The soothing abilities of an internal mother are connected to increases in endorphins, oxytocin, serotonin, and dopamine in attachment circuitry and other key neural structures that process arousal and fear.

Neurofluency Principle 19: Secure attachment reflects the ability to use others to successfully regulate arousal.

I've always been impressed by how many people report that their dogs were either crucially important in their development or serve as such good companions later in life. Dogs may be man's best friend because when we become attached to them, endorphin, oxytocin, and dopamine levels rise in both our animals and in us. A little morphine will even get a puppy's tail to wag in the same way as it does when another dog or familiar human approaches. Playful contact with our dogs provides us the added benefits of reduced heart rates, lower cortisol levels, and increased immunological functioning, not to mention the cardiac value of taking them for walks—a beautiful example of cross-species sociostasis.

The chemical cocktail of nonoptimal attachment will stimulate a mix of approach and avoidance, a tentative sense of safety and relaxation, and a higher baseline of arousal. The neurochemistry of insecure attachment leads to increased agitation, anxiety, and even fear. While we don't prescribe injections of endorphins and oxytocin, we do often suggest exercise and increased social interactions, which amount to the same thing. We do prescribe medications that directly impact serotonin and dopamine for all forms of anxiety and depression. Primarily, we leverage the sociostatic abilities of the therapeutic relationship to modulate the biochemistry of attachment, affect regulation, and well-being.

There is no doubt that early experience has a profound role in the development and functioning of the entire nervous system. Stress, stimulation, affection, and novelty all combine in shaping the many neural networks of the brain. In addition to all this is the challenge of integrating the various functions of the nervous system into a seamlessly functioning whole. The inconceivable complexity of this process allows for many mistakes, problems, and system hiccups. The brain is truly the Ferrari of the body, and many things can go wrong.

The insecure attachment schemata described by Bowlby, Ainsworth, and Main are characterized by suboptimal patterns of activation and neural network integration that are evidenced in patterns of thought, emotion, and communication. Insecure patterns are all reflective of emotional dysregulation, whether expressed as anxious engagement or withdrawal. The lack of success in establishing a secure attachment results in sustained states of arousal that impair neuroplasticity, neural growth, and optimal network integration. To my astonishment, the effects of these early experiences have been documented in how we communicate. Through a linguist's lens, we gain a window into early experiences and how they affect the building of our brains and our ability to communicate clearly with others. In Chapter 9, I describe in detail how this research can help us understand our clients' experiences, defenses, and inner worlds.

THE MAGICIAN

Jan was a 49-year-old man who came to therapy with the expressed desire to learn how to cope with his painful loneliness. Long desperate to be in an intimate relationship, he had already suffered through two failed marriages, a broken engagement, and innumerable short-lived romances. He announced during our first session that he had given up hope of finding his soul mate and needed to figure out how to cope with the loss of his dream. In stark contrast to his presenting problems, he spent most of each session regaling me with stories of his multiple current romances, his next intended seduction, and his disappointment with each potential mate. It seemed that once he seduced someone, the drive to be with her fizzled, and the clarity with which he saw their lack of compatibility became complete. He struggled with his constant disappointments and felt like he was losing the battle with feelings of hopelessness.

Jan would alternate between two states of mind; in the first he would explain that he was looking for someone intelligent, beautiful, successful, and able to join him in his busy and adventure-filled life. In the second, he would feel hopeless, lost, and depressed about most everything in his life. As I carefully observed these alternating states of mind, what initially stood out to me was that none of the women he talked about fit the description of what he was looking for in a mate. Despite this, he would expend a great deal of time, energy, and emotion pursuing a long list of women, first feeling close to them, and then becoming distant. In his conscious mind, his frantic dating was linked to his desires for sustained intimacy, but in reality, they seemed very much dissociated from one another. Of course, he found all of this very confusing and struggled with the hopelessness of his endeavor.

As our relationship deepened, I began to tentatively share some of my thoughts about the apparent contradictions between his goals and methods. In response, a perplexed look would come over Jan's face, he would stare off into the distance, and disconnect from me. He was a bright man, and I believed that his lack of comprehension had nothing to do with the complexity of the concepts. For some reason yet unknown to either of us, he needed to both fantasize about intimacy and engage in compulsive serial seduction. I came to believe that there was another level of narrative embedded in his systems of implicit memory that might help us to understand the hidden logic of this compulsive circular loop. As we continued to work together, I began to pick up on another track woven into his dating experiences. He expressed a desire to save many of these women from their unsatisfying lives. I suspected that this might be a piece of the deeper narrative we needed to discover.

When I could get him to change focus from discussing his dating life, I would ask him about his early family life and his relationship with his parents. He would begrudgingly give me a bit of information or a story or two but would reflexively go back to talking about his current relationship dilemmas. Bit by bit I was able to glean that his parents had gotten divorced when he was 6, after which his mother became extremely depressed and periodically nonfunctional. He would try to cheer her up by telling jokes or getting her to take him places that he thought she might enjoy. When he got a little older, he took odd jobs to earn the money to buy her gifts that he hoped might cheer her up. He was crushed each time she would accept his gift with an emotionless thank you and then indifferently set it aside. From time to time in our sessions, Jan would get in touch with how terrifying he found her distance and the desperation he would feel as he tried to rescue her from her despair. Each time, he would soon turn his attention back to dating.

The cycle of hope, approach, anticipation, and disappointment with his mother seemed to parallel Jan's dating experiences. It was disconnected from his wants and desires and may have been a way to continue to try and save his mother. This may have been the episodic traumatic memory in his implicit memory systems that guided his pattern of seduction, dating, and disappointment. What Freud called a repetition compulsion may simply be the brain's way of keeping old habit patterns alive. There was an addictive quality to Jan's compulsive dating behavior, and I began to wonder if it would also fit the model of addictions others develop to drugs, alcohol, shopping, and gambling. The anticipation of connection, paired with the biochemicals of reinforcement, might motivate Jan to stay engaged, similar to other addictions, where despite obvious problems, the habits are maintained and strengthened during each cycle.

I knew that Jan's brain and mind were expending a great deal of energy pushing these early traumatic memories out of consciousness. My hope was that touching on them for even a few minutes each session might move him toward integrating this unconscious narrative from childhood with the conscious processes of his current behavior. In other words, if we could simultaneously activate the deep and surface narratives in the safer context of our relationship, he might be able to engage more cortical involvement, allowing for insight and positive change. When I first started asking about his childhood, Jan couldn't understand the relevance of his relationship with his mother half a century ago. Gradually, he began to become open to the idea and sometimes even curious about the memories my questions would trigger. The process was slow as together we rode the roller coaster of his dating ups and downs and the occasional insight of his deeper motivations.

After about six months, Jan came into session eager to tell me about an experience he had the night before. He began, "I don't know if it was a dream or a daydream, but I was lying in bed next to one of my girlfriends and by the sound of her breathing, I could tell she had fallen asleep. I always feel relief after my date falls asleep, but this time I felt like I was hallucinating. I imagined slowly rising from bed so as to not disturb her, and looking in the mirror. I was only a little surprised to find that I was dressed like a magician—top hat, long black coat, the whole getup. I know it sounds weird, but in the dream, it seemed to make perfect sense. I took off my hat, turned it over, and took out the rabbit, petted it, and gave it a carrot. One by one, I removed the props of my act and laid them down on the table. I looked over at my girlfriend and felt satisfied that I had put on another good performance. I fell back into a chair, exhausted from what felt like a long and tiring performance."

"Wow," I said, "that is an amazing dream." Resisting my impulse to make an interpretation, I asked him what he made of it. "It hit me like a hammer," Jan told me. "My relationships are an act—the same act I put on for my mother. Instead of being taken care of like a son after my father left, I no longer had a mother. I had a child who used to be my mother. I wasn't ready at six to have a child, but I did the best I could to take care of her and cheer her up. None of the relationships I'm having now are about me or the intimacy I say I want. It's all about them, about saving them like I had to save my mother; so were my marriages and so are my relationships with women at work. The seduction isn't about sex. It's the adult version of making them laugh to distract them from their sadness for a while. At the end of the night, the audience goes to sleep or goes home and I'm alone again, like I was as a child. I never learned how to pay attention to my own needs. My entire life before was lived from the outside in. I was always on stage, always playing to the audience."

Now the work of learning how to take care of himself and getting what he needs could begin.

5

THE EXECUTIVE BRAINS

Humanity's troubles are due substantially to the fact that . . . we have Paleolithic emotions, medieval intuitions, and . . . godlike technologies, and that's a dangerous mix.

—E. O. WILSON

For most of the 20th century, executive functioning was thought to be a specific set of high-level cognitive abilities that included working memory, problem solving, and abstract reasoning. It was also believed that they were completely conscious processes primarily organized by (and housed within) the prefrontal cortex. This was certainly the go-to answer for exam questions when I was in school. The proof offered for this view was that damage to the prefrontal cortex resulted in a range of dysfunctions that undermined the victim's ability to think clearly and navigate the world. This view of executive functioning emerged primarily from the metaphor of the homunculus, a little person (or "mini-me") in our heads, who thinks and controls our behavior from a control panel located behind our eyes. It was believed that IQ was, more or less, a direct measure of both the intelligence and executive capabilities of our little person.

Thinking of intelligence through the keyhole of cognition is deeply grounded in Western culture, and the prefrontal cortex has traditionally been posited by comparative anatomists as the brain structure that separates us from other primates. These beliefs were more tied to our Judeo-Christian heritage than to any scientific evidence. This is why most executive function experts used computer analogies and flowcharts to explain how the brain works, completely disregarding the inputs from the body, emotions, and relationships. They are, in essence, stuck in the medieval notion that we are spirits inhabiting the material world.

Despite the power of this cultural and neurological bias, there were many problems with the top-down, prefrontal cortex view of intelligence. One was that significant prefrontal damage also resulted in deficits of emotional regulation, relational abilities, and social functioning. There are also plenty of examples to demonstrate that IQ doesn't map onto the quality of everyday functioning, relationship abilities, or worldly success. Educational systems driven by the cognitive model of intelligence left many students being told by their teachers that they would never amount to anything. Yet many of these individuals, who were miserable students in traditional settings, went on to make revolutionary discoveries and pioneer new industries. Despite this, teachers continued to judge new generations of students on old models of intelligence. Because the traditional model of executive functioning was held so strongly, the examples that contradicted its validity were treated as trivial exceptions rather than indications of its inadequacies.

Over the past few decades, findings in neuroscience and neurology have undermined some of these simpler assumptions about executive functioning. Increasing awareness of key issues related to culture and gender diversity have further shaken confidence in abstract, patriarchal, and imperialistic models of human intelligence. For these and other reasons, neurocognitive and intelligence testing are falling out of favor in education because of their diminishing validity. The fact that the world is now changing so quickly is making educators pause and reconsider their confidence in old methods of thinking and notions of intelligence. By the end of the 20th century, the notion of emotional intelligence captured the attention of scientists and the general public, while the popularity of mindfulness and other forms of meditation added to a growing appreciation of the importance of self-awareness and self-reflective capacity as important components of executive functioning.

As old dogmas about intelligence and executive functioning were crumbling, a devastating blow was dealt by Antonio Damasio when he demonstrated that judgment and decision making rely on input from regions of the brain that process somatic and emotional information. It turns out that, contrary to Descartes's belief "I think, therefore I am," somatic awareness and emotions serve as equal evidence of our existence. Dr. Damasio provided us with both a robust neurological model and the empirical evidence to prove it. This has led to an explosive expansion of sensorimotor-based educational interventions, somatic and emotion-centered forms of psychotherapy, and a general rethinking of both intelligence and executive functioning.

At this point in the development of our thinking, we have to take a fresh look at the scientific and clinical data that have been neglected for so long. We have to ask ourselves many questions: What is the role of emotion in intelligence? How might sensorimotor experience contribute to problem-solving abilities? How do implicit memories in the form of attachment schemata and affect regulation contribute to executive functioning? How does working in a group influence our abstract abilities, imagination, and innovation? These and hundreds of other questions await exploration and empirical research in the coming years.

THE COMPONENTS OF EXECUTIVE FUNCTIONING

Who asks whether the enemy was defeated by strategy or valor?
—VIRGIL

As we open our thinking to expanded notions of executive functioning, it seems safe to say that we should include the categories of emotional intelligence, self-awareness, and social intelligence in the discussion. Emotional intelligence would include such areas as one's ability to successfully navigate stress and exhibit emotional control in challenging situations. Self-awareness would be expressed in the ability to engage in self-reflection, strike a balance between self-care and caring for others, and be able to take responsibility for one's actions. Social intelligence would include understanding things from the perspective of others, and the ability to experience sympathy, empathy, and compassion. It is clear that these social and emotional abilities are not independent of one another, just as the components of cognitive intelligence such as attention, concentration, language, and memory are interdependent.

> *Neurofluency Principle 20*: We possess three executive networks, each with its own evolutionary history, developmental course, and functional specializations.

All three of these areas—emotional intelligence, self-awareness, and social intelligence, traditionally excluded from the conversation by cognitive scientists—have gained both scientific and cultural support. We certainly have to negotiate day-to-day survival; don't touch hot stoves, eat yellow snow, or walk too close to the edge of the cliff. But we also have to deal with many different people, be aware of our inner experiences, and keep our emotions regulated and in check. We have to manage ongoing relationships with ourselves and others as well as engage in self-care and caretaking. This more inclusive model of executive functioning accounts for many of the variables we have always recognized as relevant to successful adaptation, but were without specific tests or a theoretical model of executive functioning to assess or include them in our evaluation.

These other components of intelligence come into stark relief when assessing the skills of business executives. It is clear that traditional ideas of IQ, while important, don't necessarily correlate with success. Being the smartest person in the room and letting others know it has its place, but isn't usually the best leadership strategy. In the last decade, the tyrannical CEO has morphed from a cultural icon into a tragic character on his or her way to a heart attack. As businesses transition from family-run enterprises to multinational corporations, the patriarchal strategies of prediction and control are giving way to increasingly distributed models of decision making and feedback. What we are seeing is an emerging notion of intelligence and executive functioning as a set of cognitive, emotional, and social skills that are integrated in the way people treat others, know themselves, and drive positive and productive corporate cultures.

This is not an altogether new idea. In the 1880s, the infamous railroad worker Phineas Gage experienced prefrontal cortex damage that turned him from a responsible, organized, and god-fearing man into an irresponsible, emotionally erratic, and immoral drifter. The century of neurology that followed Gage's case also showed that brain damage could result in emotional dysregulation and antisocial behavior as well as a loss of abstract thinking. Thus, there was always some recognition that problem solving and emotional stability were somehow related. And given that fits of rage, anger, or fear seem to shave many IQ points off our functioning, the connection has long been recognized if not directly articulated.

Looking at the case of Gage, it is clear that he lost the ability to inhibit impulses and regulate emotions, which led him to be unable to lead men or organize his own life. Given that we are social creatures and much of our intelligence is demonstrated in social situations, we need to be able to regulate our emotions and impulses while being aware of and attuned to the feelings of others. This occurs all the time in business, where people rise to the top based on their technical expertise only to be undone by their difficulties managing others, emotional dyscontrol, or sexual impulses. It isn't enough to have good executive functioning based on old top-down information-processing models, because lack of affect regulation and unresolved trauma can cancel out intelligence and technical know-how.

MULTIPLE EXECUTIVE SYSTEMS

There is zero correlation between IQ and emotional empathy. . . .
They're controlled by different parts of the brain.
—DANIEL GOLEMAN

As in many explorations of brain-behavior relationships, we begin with the search for a single brain region or neural network to explain some complex function. We then come to learn that what we are looking for is far more complex than we anticipated. As our ideas about executive and neural functioning have expanded, so has our understanding of how our brains have evolved to navigate, adapt, and survive our physical and social environments. Pushing past old prejudices, it appears that we possess multiple executive systems, each with its own adaptational roles, evolutionary history, and developmental course. Keep in mind that whenever I mention individual structures in each of the executive systems, it is just a shorthand for the entire network.

We have a primitive executive system, with the amygdala and

many nuclei within our brain stems at its core, that we share with all other mammals and reptiles. Its role is to support our immediate survival by placing positive and negative value on the things around us. This results in us approaching things that support survival and avoiding things that are potentially dangerous. This system is a descendant of the most primitive chemical sensors in single-cell organisms that would lead them to approach or avoid things in the environment.

A second executive system (centered around the parietal and frontal lobes) is associated with the traditional idea of executive functions thought to be housed only in the prefrontal cortex. This P-F system combines the processing of space (parietal) and time (frontal) with memory for past cause-and-effect associations to allow us to navigate successfully through the physical environment. Whereas the first executive system might direct us to approach something, this second executive system organizes the strategies to get us there. The second system also contains mirror neurons that allow us to learn skills through observation and imitation of others.

As the cortex expanded and this second system evolved, it was able to leverage more and more neural complexity in the service of increasingly sophisticated problem solving. You could say that the first executive system allows us to remember that a coconut contains food when we are hungry and it is something to approach when we feel hungry. The second executive system will be in charge of finding, gathering, and storing the coconuts and breaking into them to get the food. Far down the evolutionary path, the second executive will figure out a way to make machines to do the job, bottle and preserve the milk, and get it to market.

Our third executive system, which we call the default mode network (DMN), becomes active when we are neither concerned for our immediate survival nor engaged with external tasks. In other words, when the first and second executive systems are not deployed, this third executive becomes active. This system was first called the default mode network because it became active when subjects lying in brain scanners were between experimental tasks. This reinforced the idea that the brain is always active, even when we are not dealing with threats to our survival or engaged in activities. But what do our brains do when we are not focused on external challenges and tasks? We learn the answer to this question if we pay attention to what happens to our stream of consciousness when we are resting comfortably without external distractions. We may daydream, reflect on ourselves, and think about others. The research seems to support that the DMN is active when we are having these experiences.

It has been found that this third executive system becomes active during self- and other-directed attention. It is thought to specialize in the experience of self-awareness, social awareness, and mental travel through space and time. It appears to be centrally involved in the aspects of social intelligence related to understanding, empathy, and compassion for others and ourselves. Think of the DMN

The Three Executive Systems

	Core Structures		
First	amygdala	approach/ avoidance	rapid evaluation of stimuli basic survival
Second	parietal frontal	navigation/ engagement	problem solving, abstract thinking
Third	DMN OMPFC and cingulate	internal processing social processing	self-reflection, imagination, daydreaming empathy, compassion, attunement

as the system we attempt to activate and communicate with in the process of insight-oriented therapy. We do this first by working to deactivate the first executive system through the development of a safe and trusting relationship. Next, we work to have clients orient away from an anxious focus on the problems they face in the outside world. And third, we help them shift their focus to the realities of the here and now—their thoughts, feelings, and the interactions within the therapeutic relationship.

The DMN has been found to be largely anticorrelational with the other two executive systems, which means that it is inhibited by both the amygdala-centric first executive and the parietal-frontal functioning of the second executive. In English, this means that when we are anxious, afraid, or preoccupied with some external task, it is far less likely that we will be either self-aware or empathic to others and often ourselves. This may explain why those with severe anxiety disorders have difficulty with empathy for and connection with others. It is also why, if our inner worlds are troubled and painful, we can engage in manic-type defenses, making long lists of tasks to keep us distracted from our negative thoughts and feelings. The fact that the DMN is largely anticorrelation, but not completely so, reflects the likelihood that the executive systems need to integrate and collaborate under certain conditions to attain certain goals. An example of this might be a simultaneous activation of the second and third executive systems to both have empathy for another's struggles (DMN) and figure out practical ways to help them (P–F).

MIRROR NEURONS

Gratitude is when memory is stored in the heart and not in the mind.
—LIONEL HAMPTON

Let's take a moment to focus on a component of the parietal-frontal executive system called mirror neurons. Mirror neurons connect sensory, motor, and motivational systems to help us both learn by observation and allow the behaviors and emotions of others to influence our own. These neurons activate either when we witness others engaging in behaviors (like using a tool or picking up an object) or when we engage in these actions ourselves. If you have ever found yourself looking up or yawning because you see others doing so, you've experienced mirror neurons in action. These reflexive imitation responses are based on our visual system automatically triggering our motor and somatic circuitry to synchronize our behaviors with others in our group. Reflexive imitation may have arisen for learning and group coordination during hunting, gathering, and migration. Mirror systems are suspected to be involved with many social functions including the evolution of gestural and verbal language. Mirror circuits support other social functions including emotional resonance, attunement, and empathy.

Imitation is a central form of cognitive and social learning. Via mirror neurons, our motor systems are actually able to practice from simple observation. This is why the use of visual imagery is so central to sports psychology. The repetitive imagining of a successful ski run or batting a ball shapes neural networks in visual and motor circuits that allow us to better perform them in space and time. Chimpanzees observing other chimps fishing in anthills using long blades of grass will almost immediately go and find a blade of grass and an anthill of their own in which to go fishing. Imitation via mirror neurons is also a powerful tool in psychotherapy and education.

Many studies have shown that therapists and clients will imitate each others' behaviors during session, and the more they like each other, the more imitation will take place. The facial expressions, gestures, and posture of one will activate circuits in the other that support resonance and attunement. In these and other ways, mirror neurons may bridge the gap between sender and receiver, helping us understand one another and enhance the possibility of empathic attunement. Thus, our internal emotional state—generated via automatic mirroring processes—can become our intuitive theory of the internal state of the other. All of this nonverbal communication across the social synapse between client and therapist may represent the biological basis for the finding that the quality of the therapeutic relationship is the most important variable in therapeutic success.

Mirror neurons have so far been found in association areas of the frontal and parietal cortices where networks converge to process high-level information. It is because of this privileged position that they are able to bridge observation and action. When we engage in imitation, we are using the same space-time construction to re-create what we are observing. These systems contain maps of other people and the space around us, as well as our own musculature, survival needs, and strategies for attaining goals. The discovery of mirror neurons and the systems they connect have helped us to understand an important aspect of how our brains link together in thoughts, behaviors, and feelings. This leads us to a discussion of the integration and cooperation of the parietal-frontal executive with the DMN.

THE EXECUTIVE SWITCHBOARD

The greatest weapon against stress is our ability to choose one thought over another.

—WILLIAM JAMES

With three executive systems, our brains need ways to direct our attention and select the appropriate system to be in control for the needs of the moment. The ability to instantaneously shift our focus to any potential danger is both the most primitive and most essential for survival. For most animals, this involves an orienting response and the immediate triggering of a fight, flight, or freeze reaction. This will occur regardless of whether they are eating, attending to their young, or relaxing in the sun. The quality and speed of this reaction have been honed by evolution through the selective survival of those who react the fastest and in the most adaptive way. This executive switchboard, referred to as the salience system, is automatically and unconsciously at work every waking moment. It works with and through the amygdala to enhance rapid reactions to threat.

Neurofluency Principle 21: Optimal executive functioning requires integration and balance among the three executive systems.

This means that we are constantly vigilant for external or internal cues of meaning or threat. A commonly cited example of this saliency system at work is the cocktail party phenomenon, which occurs when we are having a conversation with one person and actively filtering out all of the background conversations and extraneous noise. Yet, if our name is mentioned by someone across the room, we not only hear it but orient toward the person to gather more information. The fact that our names jump out from the din of conversations that surround us demonstrates that the saliency network is on constant alert slightly below consciousness awareness. As we became increasingly social animals, the ability to hear our name mentioned must have had survival value. And we are especially interested in gossip, especially if it is about us or one of our rivals.

At a third level, our brains need to not only attend to important things, but not attend to what is irrelevant to the task at hand. In the absence of a clear and present danger, we must selectively attend to those things that have greater reward value such as food, potential mates, and the behavior of the higher-ranking individuals in our tribe. This selective attention and sustained focus allow us to maintain engagement and focus on the things we are working on that are relevant and necessary. Problems with this function most often show up in those described as having attention deficit disorder. They have a difficult time both staying focused on the task at hand and not orienting to the movements and sounds around them. Perhaps the opposite phenomenon occurs when people become so engrossed in what they are doing that they don't notice they are hungry, ill, or even in danger.

THE SALIENCY NETWORK

Success in life is founded upon attention to the small things.
—BOOKER T. WASHINGTON

The saliency network of the insular and cingulate cortices is involved in integrating bottom-up bodily information with top-down cognitive processing in the service of directing our attention. If the connection between the cingulate and insula is disrupted, such as in alexithymia and autism, one may be unable to identify or label either bodily sensations or emotions. When we are engaged in meditation or self-reflection, we rely on cingulate and insula involvement to provide us with an experience of what is going on in our bodies and the emotions associated with them. And when we are trying to make a decision, this network contributes to the ability to understand subjective preferences and pay attention to gut feelings. These somatic contributions to higher thought are reflected in the fact that the cingulate-insula circuit shows more activation during risky and emotional decision making as well as when we experience insights into a problem we are working on.

This same network guides our behavioral reactions to the external world, especially to other people. It seems that this saliency network serves to direct the focus of our attention to either the inner world, the outer world, or the integration of the two, allowing for emotional resonance and empathy. This process also provides the foundation for our ability to attune and identify with others. In support of this idea, this circuit becomes activated when we see others in physical pain, fearful, or being treated unfairly. It also becomes active when we are experiencing other social emotions such as resentment, guilt, and embarrassment. The fact that our emotions are a blend of thought and bodily sensations is highlighted by the activation of the salience network along with the painful (abandonment and sadness) and joyful experiences (laughter and being in love).

As we mature, the salience circuit shows greater participation in everyday functioning and is increasingly influenced by cognitive instructions, expectations, or the consequences of outcomes. While younger children show activation mostly in the frontal and then parietal lobes during executive functioning, there is an increasing participation of the salience network during adolescence and adulthood. Based on its functions and developmental trajectory, it is safe to assume that its healthy maturation contributes to self-regulation, self-reflective capacity, and attentional capabilities.

It is likely that this saliency network is also involved in regulating the joint activation of the second and third executive systems when we are confronted with problems that require problem-solving and abstract abilities regarding challenges in social relationships and within our own lives. One good example of this might be in the difference between intelligence and wisdom. Intelligence is most likely the result of parietal-frontal processing when we are communicating sophisticated information about a technical or intellectual problem. Wisdom is different in that it is information tailored to an individual's experience, which both requires empathy for them and is grounded in caring. I imagine that when I am trying to communicate wise advice to someone, both my second and third executive networks need to be engaged to allow me to organize my thoughts and present them in a connective and compassionate manner.

THE EXECUTIVE SWITCHBOARD IN ACTION

Mindfulness helps you go home to the present.

—THICH NHAT HANH

When my son started preschool at age 3, my task was to drop him off each morning on my way to work. This meant that in addition to getting myself ready in the morning, I would be helping my wife get Sam washed and dressed, fed, packed up, and on his way. This would take place simultaneously with my showering, drinking coffee, brushing my teeth, getting dressed, and making sure I had packed everything I needed for work. All of these things needed to be accomplished about 20 minutes earlier than my usual schedule to allow time to drive to his school, park, take him into school, sign him in, store his supplies for the day, and settle him in so he wouldn't be upset by my leaving him behind; simple enough.

Most parents recognize some version of this routine we are equipped for via our frontal-parietal executive system. This number two executive allows us to simultaneously sequence multiple tasks, keep an eye on the clock, alternate between putting on our shoes and changing diapers, while remembering to brush our own teeth. (I would, however, occasionally show up at work with only half of my face shaved, or a diaper bag instead of a briefcase, so my executive system did fail me from time to time.) With my number two executive system mostly in control, Sam and I would exit the front door, briefcase in one hand, Sam's tiny hand in the other, and walk slowly down the pathway to the car. When we would arrive at the back door of the car, I would put down my briefcase and open the door so he could jump up into his booster seat. The next steps were to buckle him in, walk around to the back of the car, put our stuff in the trunk, walk around to the driver's door, get in, and drive to his school. Sam had other plans.

The opened car door and the sight of his booster seat seemed to trigger a desire for conversation. So instead of getting in, he plopped down on the curb and began to ask me questions about my work, the color of the sky, or how the wind managed to be invisible. As an older father, I had plenty of time to think about having a child and looked forward to conversations like these. The problem was that we were on a tight schedule and these were better questions for bedtime talks or weekend strolls. I wasn't in a relaxed state of mind but in my "get to work" mode—very frontal-parietal of me. The fact that Sam was blocking my progress triggered a stress response that created a picture in my mind of the dirty looks I would get from the saintly ladies of Montessori.

Being thwarted by Sam and the thought of dirty looks triggered my first executive system to sound the alarm. The voice in my head that usually said "what cute questions" was drowned out by the irritation and impatience driven by my anxiety—"Get in the car!" In this state of mind, which contained little self-awareness of my internal state nor any empathy for Sam's, getting him into his car seat became a power struggle, which included a flurry of flailing arms and legs. The same thing happened the next day and the next; I realized that I woke up dreading the whole uncomfortable ritual. On the night of the third day, I reflected on these conflicts during a quiet moment with my third executive system online and engaged.

What was going on here? What was I missing? Was there a better way? I questioned my dedication to the schedule and lists of tasks and wondered why it triggered so much agitation in me. Thinking back to my father, I remembered how irritable and impatient he always seemed to be and how scared and sad it would make me. There was never time to relax and always pressure to move to the next thing. The result was that I felt unseen and unimportant—Had I become that guy?

With this memory, and the emotion and empathy for Sam it engendered, it became perfectly clear that taking time to talk with my son was both more important and better for both of us than getting to school or work on time. In reflecting back on his gestures and facial expressions in the mornings, I realized that he did look a little anxious. I wondered if going to school was stressful for him and if he needed a few more minutes of transition time. I decided to try to leave the house 5 minutes earlier the next morning and sit and talk with him when he hesitated at the car door instead of urging him forward.

The next morning, I opened Sam's car door, and he sat down on the curb and started talking, waiting for the struggle to begin. When I sat down on the curb next to him, a quizzical look appeared on his face for a moment. He then went on happily talking and asking questions for about a minute until he finally said, "Let's go, Dad. We're gonna be late." The thing we all need most is to be seen and heard, yet our brains evolved to get things done. The ability to remember to be a human being in the midst of human doing is the key component to mindfulness and essential for optimal executive functioning.

During her groundbreaking attachment research, Mary Ainsworth sent observers into homes to watch natural interactions between mothers and children. One of the things she noticed in the interactions between securely attached children and their parents was the nature of the parents' availability. These parents who were doing various things around the home remained open to interruptions by their children. Unlike the parents of insecurely attached children, who would either avoid or intrude on their children's activity, these parents would be able to shift their focus to the child without difficulty or distress. They would put what they were doing aside and give their total attention to their child, usually for a brief period of time. The child would soon have enough, "fill the security tank," and head back to play. The parent would then smoothly return to previous activities.

Although I didn't think of it when I first read the attachment research, it now seems clear that parents of securely attached children possess highly tuned salience and executive systems. They are able to shift their attention as needed, keep their multiple priorities in perspective, and, as a result, optimize their attunement to their children. They shift focus in ways that allow them to be neither neglectful nor overinvolved with their children; neither missing in action nor a helicopter. Contrast these parents to those of insecurely attached children, and we see many examples of those who are unable or unwilling to shift from their tasks and direct their attention to their children. We also see those with inadequate emotional regulation and dominant first executive systems who are unable to change attention from their own inner distress and unresolved trauma to be appropriately available for their children. A fluidity of attentional focus and the ability to activate the DMN in response to children's needs are important components of parenting. Although I often fail, I try to sit down on the curb and listen whenever I can.

6

NEURODYNAMIC INTEGRATION

Communication . . . is not just part of the game, it is the game!
—OSCAR MUNOZ

From the beginning of gestation, neural networks responsible for metabolism, movement, emotion, and thinking begin to learn, connect, and integrate. This process continues after birth, continues through development, as we mature, and into old age. Neural growth and maturation require oxygen, glucose, and protein synthesis along with human interaction, environmental stimulation, and new challenges throughout life. Stacking blocks, playing peekaboo, and crawling from place to place may seem like simple activities, but they are both high accomplishments and the training grounds for skills development. As we learn to run, play soccer, and vote, neural networks continue to grow in size, complexity, and connectivity. Hiding in plain sight are the same integrative processes at play as we build relationships, join groups, and come to identify with far-flung communities like Cubs fans, Independents, and Americans.

Because we are taught to emphasize comparisons and distinctions, it's difficult for us to see ourselves as a small part of the superorganism of the human species. This may be why we struggle to accept concepts like evolution and climate change that require detecting long-term patterns instead of the differences and distinctions of our immediate experience. What if the interconnectivity and integration of neurons and neural systems are a basic strategy that extends to our bodies, families, and cultures?

The ideas I present in this chapter expand the venerable biopsychosocial model to include the perspectives of development and the existential experience of self. I propose that these five ways of understanding human experiences are interdependent and that each can be leveraged to help our clients. I argue that our psychology, sense of self, and identity emerge from and depend upon the quality of neural and social development, and the integration of neural networks and social relationships that precedes it. This is all based on the fact that our early relationships influence our biology in ways that shape the infrastructure of our brains. These initial processes establish our affect regulation and attachment schemata, which provide us with an intuitive sense of the safety of the world and our acceptability to others. It is upon these earlier foundations that our internal worlds, our sense of self, and our social identities are established.

A GOVERNMENT OF SYSTEMS

The theory of evolution by natural selection is the only theory capable of explaining the existence of organized complexity.

—RICHARD DAWKINS

To understand living systems, especially ones as complex as the human species, it is essential to appreciate what an intricate structure a billion neurons are able to create over a hundred million years. Within neuroscience, the term "connectome" is used to describe the mapping of all the connections of the brain of a particular species. To date, only the connectome of the roundworm (nematode) has been completed. The ongoing human connectome project is currently mapping the 90,000,000,000 neurons, 100,000 miles of white matter tracks, and 15,000 neural pathways of our brains. It focuses on the density of connectivity among brain regions, whether or not their activations are correlated, and which functions are served by each.

The current model of the human brain, like our social systems, is made up of a government of hierarchical systems that must communicate, cooperate, and integrate with one another in order to perform its many functions. Each system has to have internal integration, proper integration with other systems with which it cooperates, and so on up the levels of complexity. The stepwise process of system integration eventually gave rise to emergent functions such as imagination, consciousness, and culture, which require neural, psychological, and social integration. In the process, the social and psychological processes made possible by our biology are now able to create a feedback system to influence and regulate the brain. In other words, now the brain, relationships, and the mind have an interactive, collaborative, and integrative relationship. A central aspect of this process is the ability of brains to link together to influence one other. Our brains, just like our governments, become distorted when communication breaks down or becomes dysfunctional.

Consider human attachment: First, our early interactions shape the neuroanatomy and biochemistry of our brain, which in turn influence our emotional regulation and our self-esteem, which then determines our ability to relate to others. Biology, psychology, and relationships are woven together during development into a living thing that creates the possibilities of human experience. Attachment is a small piece of the whole person that connects biology, psychology, epigenetics, and social relatedness.

Higher-order processes, such as complex language, abstract reasoning, and imagination, all rely on the evolution of the social brain and the emergence of culture. These functions that could not exist in a species of unconnected individuals. This essential fact points to the necessity of exploring the human brain within its natural social context. Neural and social integration are parallel and interwoven processes that rely on one another for their mutual development.

FROM PHRENOLOGY TO NEURODYNAMICS

Truth is neither to be found in simplicity nor in the multiplicity and confusion of things.

—ISAAC NEWTON

At its inception, Western neurology followed in the footsteps of phrenology, the "science" of personality assessment via an examination of the bumps on the head. While this may seem frivolous today, it does represent the dawn of associating areas of the head with behavior, a strategy neurologists and neuroscientists follow to this day. When I was in training, I dutifully learned that visual processing was the sole domain of the occipital lobes, expressive language resided in Broca's area, and the transfer from short- to long-term memory was the sole purview of the hippocampus.

Neurofluency Principle 22: Optimal neurodynamics, like healthy psychodynamics, requires integration and communication among the brain's government of systems.

This general approach, referred to as localization, seeks to discover brain-behavior relationships associated with certain areas of the brain. The importance of this pursuit was amplified during the 20th century by the importance to surgeons of establishing a general sense of the location of brain damage before opening a patient's skull. Prior to the availability of present scanning techniques, clinical neurological examinations and neuropsychological assessment were relied upon for this kind of topographical information. While this straightforward location-function orientation works acceptably well in simple animals and for some aspects of basic tasks in humans, it begins to break down for more complex functions like intelligence, abstract thinking, and social connectivity. These higher-order processes require the interconnection and participation of multiple complex neural networks that are distributed throughout the brain.

The conceptual leap from localizationism to the consideration of complex systems has brought us to a new approach called systems neuroscience or neurodynamics. Neurodynamics is the exploration of the anatomical and functional connectivity of broadly distributed systems. We recognize that optimal functioning of these systems requires integration, coordinated activation, and a logical relationship between their basic functions, evolutionary history, and specific contributions to higher level processes. Put in a slightly different way, the components of broad networks need to connect, communicate, and coordinate to support the functioning of higher-level functions.

Freud had the idea of neurodynamics more than a century ago. In a monograph titled *The Project for a Scientific Psychology*, he drew simple diagrams of neural systems that he thought might be associated with defense mechanisms. He believed that neuroscientists would someday be able to explain the biological substrate of clinical phenomena like avoidance, denial, and dissociation. The lack of scientific knowledge at the time led him to suppress the publication of this monograph. Freud's project is still alive and well, and we are creeping ever closer to mapping complex patterns of brain-behavior relationships.

PATTERNS OF INTEGRATION

> *Every science consists of the coordination of facts; if the different observations were entirely isolated, there would be no science.*
>
> —AUGUSTE COMTE

In past writings, I have discussed what I call axes of integration, the great neural superhighways that allow information to travel horizontally (between the left and right sides of the brain), vertically (between the cortex and the brain stem), from front to back (from sensory areas in the rear to association areas in the front), and inside out (from the center of the brain to the outer surface). While a general appreciation of this broad topography is important, don't become overly attached to it. These broad concepts can become a roadblock to a more sophisticated understanding of the complexity and deeper levels of integration. There is no way around the fact that complexity is complex.

Left-Right

Most vertebrates are divided along the body's midline, creating the need for connecting and coordinating the left and right sides of the brain and body. The complexity of left-right integration has grown more challenging in humans and other primates as the cerebral hemispheres and the subcortical structures they work with have become increasingly differentiated from one another. The most likely explanation is the exchange of redundancy for increasingly diverse neural topography. This differentiation allows for the increasingly high-level functions required for complex socialization and group coordination. The limits of head size dictated by the size of the birth canal also contribute to the swap of redundancy for lateral diversity.

Neurofluency Principle 23: Laterality, or the differentiation of the hemispheres, is one of the brain's many evolutionary adaptations.

It is thought that the organization, structures, and functions of the right hemisphere represent how both sides were earlier in our evolution. The left hemisphere is thought to be the experiment that contains those elements that differentiate us from other primates, especially along the dimensions of language, logic, and self-awareness. The right hemisphere specializes in visual process and extreme emotional states (terror and shame), and could be considered more primitive and uncivilized. In Freud's terms, the right hemisphere could be characterized as the more primal, selfish, and id-like hemisphere. The two cerebral hemispheres communicate primarily via the white matter tracts of the corpus callosum and a number of smaller cortical and subcortical fiber bundles that connect the two halves of the brain.

The right hemisphere specializes in visual and emotional processing while the left handles the semantic aspects of language, positive social interactions, and our conscious ability to experience time. The inhibition of the more self-centered right hemisphere by the left may have allowed for the development of large, sustainable social groups. Our ability to act in politically correct ways while harboring very opposite thoughts likely reflects the two parallel modes of processing allowed by the modulation of the right hemisphere.

The traditional biases seen in many cultures against left-handedness may reflect an intuitive understanding of the left hand's (right brain) relationship to the dark, primitive aspects of our nature. The French word for left (*gauche*) and the Italian (*sinestre*) and all their tasteless and evil connotations may reflect the deep history of the march to becoming civilized. Of course, the inhibition of impulses is also made possible by top-down networks connecting the basal ganglia and the amygdala with the prefrontal cortex. Damage to this top-down circuit can lead to both antisocial and asocial behavior. This is a prime example of the coevolution of left-right and top-down neural networks.

Language is the first and best-understood example of lateral specialization. We all know that Broca's area, located in the left frontal lobe, is directly involved with the sequencing and organization of the grammatical aspects of language. What is often overlooked is that a parallel area in the right frontal lobe contributes the tone, cadence, and emotion of spoken language—an aspect of language we sometimes react to more strongly than the specific words. It is common for people to say, "I'm not mad about what he said. It's the way he said it."

When the region parallel to Broca's area in the right hemisphere is damaged, or if the white matter connection between them is damaged, people's speech becomes mechanical and stilted, like a robot from a 1950s science fiction film. This is a good example of a failure of integration. In addition to these two frontal areas in both cerebral hemispheres, language production also receives contributions from the motor areas further back in the frontal lobes (front-back) as well as from top-down circuits connecting to the basal ganglia and cerebellum that contribute to the sequencing and coordination of smooth, complex motor movements of the lips and tongue. Saying words requires considerable neural processing and integration across multiple neural axes.

Most generally, psychological and physical health are associated with neural integration, and illness is related to disruptions of integration or functional dissociation within and among neural systems. Conceptualizing psychological syndromes in this way can help us connect them to neurobiological processes, treat them, and describe them to clients in basic scientific terms. Whenever network integration is developmentally inadequate or disrupted due to physical or psychological trauma, deficits become apparent in either particular abilities or larger-scale functions.

Applying this to imbalances in laterality, a bias toward left-hemisphere processing can result in an over-inhibition of emotional processing, while a similar bias toward the right can lead to extreme emotionality, magical thinking, or even auditory hallucinations. Damage to the right hemisphere can compromise our ability to interpret facial expressions, hand gestures, and tone of voice. Many studies have shown that an imbalance of left-right activation in the prefrontal cortex can lead to depression (right bias) or mania (left bias). Inhibiting the right prefrontal cortex through the application of disruptive magnetic charges to the surface of the skull above it has been shown to be a beneficial treatment for depression in some clients.

The OMPFC along with the anterior cingulate and insular cortices are the first cortical regions to develop and are all larger in the right hemisphere. Richly connected with subcortical networks of learning, memory, and emotion, these right-biased structures are densely connected with the body, modulating vagal tone and HPA functioning. These connections reflect the role of the right OMPFC as the executive center of attachment, intimate social relationships, affect regulation, and higher-level input into bodily homeostasis. These systems are built during childhood in an experience-dependent manner through the attunement and connections of the right hemispheres of parent and child. This is in stark contrast to the dorsal-lateral prefrontal cortex (DLPFC), which is biased to the left hemisphere and more densely connected front to back with the sensory and motor systems of the cerebral cortex. These systems have evolved to negotiate playing by the rules of the group and the broader culture. This is probably why we extend our right hand (left brain) in greeting and reserve our left for other purposes.

Inside-Out

This leads us to a clumsy and semiconvincing shift to inside-out integration. Although the OMPFC and the DLPFC specialize in top-down and front-back integration respectively, they are also part of an inside-out system that serves our ability to balance our attention to inner or outer experience. While the DLPFC (as a component of the second executive system) is attending to external tasks, the OMPFC must successfully modulate the first executive system of the amygdala. If the OMPFC fails in this role, the DLPFC will be inhibited with declines in focused attention and cognitive abilities.

Another consequence of a failure on the part of the OMPFC to adequately regulate the amygdala is the inhibition of the default mode network. The DMN, which runs along the center edges of the brain (inside) is in dynamic tension with the cortical structures along the outside of the second executive system of the frontal and parietal lobes (outside). This inside-out dimension is characterized by neural processing of the experience of the body, the self, and our connection with others (inside) and our interactions with the environment via sensory experience and motor behavior (outside).

The ability to toggle back and forth between the second (frontal-parietal) and third (DMN) executive systems is an important aspect of healthy functioning that allows us to shift between an inner and outer focus in our processing. We need the ability to combine cognitive and emotional information, our own perspective and the perspective of others, and our knowledge with empathy for compassionate interactions with others (wisdom). This inside-out balance was demonstrated during Mary Ainsworth's early attachment research. Raters observed mothers of securely attached children smoothly shifting from the tasks they were engaged with to reorienting to and attuning with their children. When their children no longer needed their attention, they would return to play, and their mothers would return to their tasks. This is inside-out integration in one of its highest and best uses.

Top-Down

The top-down axis is characterized by the many cortical–subcortical–brain stem networks that activate and direct our actions in our social and physical worlds. This axis embodies the interconnectivity and integration of our arousal, primitive drives, motivations, and motor impulses, with cortical guidance and inhibitory control. The top-down dimension is characterized by circuitry involved with cognitive processing, language, and conscious awareness (top) and those dedicated to physiological and emotional processes (bottom). Key structures to consider are the prefrontal,

frontal, and parietal cortices (top) and the limbic structures of the hippocampus, amygdala, and hypothalamus (bottom).

A top-down circuit, especially important for psychotherapists, is a dense bidirectional pathway that links the OMPFC and amygdala. This circuity feeds physiological and emotional information up to the cortex, which is gathered from much of the brain and body and processed by the amygdala. The downward tracks allow the OMPFC to regulate the amygdala and its output to the autonomic nervous system. A good analogy might be a squad of soldiers trained to fight and survive (amygdala and autonomic nervous system) and a general who is an expert strategist, who continues to keep an eye on the entire battlefield, update his strategy, and adjust long-range goals (OMPFC).

> *Neurofluency Principle 24*: Top-down networks, involved in excitation, inhibition, and motivation, guide processes of attention, navigation, and attachment.

The OMPFC-amygdala circuit is likely the neural system that serves as the core of the attachment schema. The amygdala is fully matured by seven months of gestation, while the cortical systems that will come to modulate and inhibit it take many years to develop. During the first year of life, the OMPFC-amygdala circuit stores our early experiences with caretakers, shaping our earliest expectations concerning the value of proximity to others in regulating our arousal and fear. Later in therapy, as we develop a secure attachment with our clients, this circuit is likely modified by the relationship, allowing clients to be more open, trusting, and neuroplastic in utilizing the therapy for positive change.

Front–Back

Front–back integration is generally characterized by the weaving together of sensory and motor information (back to front) with guidance systems that direct purposeful movement through time and space toward a specific goal (front to back). An interesting example of front-back integration lies in our ability to recognize faces. Visual information passes from the eyes back to the thalamus and then on to the back of the occipital lobes. Vision is then constructed from its component parts and fed forward to sensory, motor, and executive systems. Our brains contain three different visual processing streams specializing in (1) identifying what we are seeing, (2) locating it in space, and (3) determining how we will engage with it. When it comes to recognizing and interacting with others, all three are required for normal functioning.

Faces contain some of the most important information for human survival. Moments after birth, primitive reflexes guide us orient to and focus on the faces of those around us. This simple beginning leads to a lifetime of looking into the faces of others to find if we are safe, valued, and loved, or undesirable and worthy of shame and ostracism. By the time we are children, seeing someone, recognizing them, reading the meaning of their facial expressions, and initiating interactions is so effortless that we take it completely for granted. Yet this automatic ability requires the participation, cross talk, and integration of a wide array of neural systems. Its complexity and its widespread distribution throughout the brain make it a good example for understanding neurodynamics.

Because faces are so important, the occipital lobes have a specialized region called the fusiform face area. It is here that information about shape, contrast, geometry, and the other components of vision are combined to form our ability to recognize a right-side-up face. The hippocampus and temporal cortex interact to compare this information to faces we have seen in the past and with the amygdala to determine if we will have a positive or negative reaction to the face based on past experience. To read facial expressions, the amygdala is again brought in to determine the social and emotional value of their expressions. Naming the person, if that is required, will recruit additional memory circuits and the language systems of the left hemisphere.

It is self-evident that facial recognition and engaging with a friend, enemy, or stranger calls on sensory, emotional, and memory networks. These systems have evolved to be so complex and sophisticated that what we think of as sensory systems have in reality become perceptual systems. In other words, by the time sensory information becomes available to conscious awareness, it has been integrated with memory and emotion in ways that shape our experience far beyond the information provided by our senses. This is certainly the case in implicit biases and prejudices of all kinds driven by the evaluative input of the amygdala into the visual processing stream. Research has shown that higher base rates of amygdala activation, as found in individuals with anxiety and borderline disorders, result in a bias toward interpreting neutral facial expressions as either angry or fearful.

WHEN INTEGRATION FAILS

I have not failed. I've just found 10,000 ways that won't work.

—THOMAS EDISON

As we have used facial recognition as an example of systems integration, let's consider one of the ways in which its integration can break down. In a phenomenon called Capgras syndrome, individuals come to believe that people very familiar to them (spouse, children, or old friends) have been replaced by imposters. Capgras syndrome is most commonly seen in dementia, epilepsy, and schizophrenia, although in rare cases it has occurred on its own. The illusion of imposters is grounded in a disconnect in the sensory-emotional processing of face recognition. It begins with the proper recognition of familiar faces when they are compared to a patient's memory—for example, she recognizes the person as looking like her husband.

The breakdown lies in the lack of integration of this information with the usual amygdala activation.

In Capgras syndrome, patients recognize familiar faces but don't experience the emotions usually paired with recognition. This doesn't lead them to think there is something wrong with their face recognition systems, though. They try to find some external attribution for what is happening. Most often this is called a delusion of imposters, where victims come to believe that incredibly accurate replicas of their family and friends have been substituted for those they know and love. The more they try to figure it out, the more they realize the money and technology required to pull off such a thing must be the work of the government, the mafia, or some evil genius. I've had elderly dementia clients brought to my office by a son or daughter, who express gratitude for the ride and surprise at both these strangers' generosity and how much they resemble their own children. Despite all the evidence that they are their children, they just can't believe it's possible. When I ask them how they know this is not their child, in one way or another they all say something like, "Don't you think I'd know my own child?"

Research has shown that those with Capgras syndrome do not have damage to neural networks involving facial recognition. They are aware that the imposters are dead ringers for their real relatives. The problem is rooted in the fact that the feeling of familiarity, the emotional component of recognition, is absent, so while the people around them look familiar, activation of the emotions of love and attachment is missing. This suggests that the socioemotional networks including the amygdala are likely involved, becoming dissociated related to changes in brain functioning. Capgras syndrome may, in some ways, be the opposite of a déjà vu experience, when something new is paired with a feeling of familiarity. Déjà vu is likely a random firing of familiarity circuits in an unfamiliar setting. The frequency of déjà vu experiences is greater in the presence of brain disturbances and correlates with a decreased number of neurons in the hippocampus.

We can expand this concept of neural integration and balance to multiple forms of emotional illness, interpersonal difficulties, and diagnosable mental illnesses. When neural systems charged with different functions lack adequate communication and regulatory balance, we see the emergence of symptoms for which people seek treatment. Too much anxiety inhibits functions like attention and empathy; too much task focus increases attention while inhibiting empathy; overactive empathic processes can impair cognitive processes related to judgment and problem solving. As we learn more about neurodynamics-behavior relationships, we will likely see the emergence of new and more effective treatments across the range of psychological functions.

AM I SMART OR NOT?

Common sense is a genius dressed in working clothes.

—RALPH WALDO EMERSON

From first grade through high school, I was a highly erratic student—meaning that I was either an A student or someone struggling to pass the final to avoid failing or getting left back. Having a father extremely generous with his criticism, I assumed that I was basically stupid with the occasional good fortune of having a teacher who took pity on me. It was only when I became an adult that I realized that I was a real A student in classes where I loved the teacher and felt that the teacher cared for me. When I felt a teacher didn't like me, all students, or humankind in general, learning became a struggle instead of academic play. I now know that our ability to learn is based on neuroplasticity. I also know that neuroplasticity is enhanced by the neurochemistry of secure and caring relationships. Caring for and connecting with students is not optional for teachers; it is part of what makes you a successful teacher. Therapy is no different. Although our classroom most often contains only one student, the quality of the relationship remains the leverage to stimulate brain change and positive outcomes.

Thinking in terms of integration, the systems that govern our brains are woven together in interactive and mutually regulating networks. Systems dedicated to cognition, emotion, and sensory and motor experience can become disconnected and limit our experience, our abilities, and our capabilities. The same dissociation can occur in the classroom and the consulting room if we develop a slavish focus on just one aspect of a client's experience, identity, or life. Understanding without emotion is a booby prize, as is emotional experience in the absence of cognition. Both, along with our bodies, relationships, history, and culture all need to be seen, heard, respected, and made part of the whole. Our fathers' unintegrated and unconscious anger at their fathers is passed on to us in many forms. Our teachers' attachment issues become the foundation of classroom culture. Our therapists' unresolved traumas contribute to the challenges and limitations of our therapeutic work.

7

LINKING WITH OTHERS AND
THE EMERGENCE OF THE SELF

*Our brains have been designed to blur the line between self and
other. It is an ancient neural circuitry that marks every mammal
from mouse to elephant.*

—FRANS DE WAAL

Freud believed that life's purpose is "to love and work," and I agree.
Carol Gilligan expressed the same sentiment in her notion of a care
perspective in female development. Erik Erikson's theories of development were based on the notion of generativity via our contributions to others. We associate the name of Jesus with love, Mother
Teresa with service, and the Buddha with compassion. These wise
women and men point past the superficial distinctions that separate
us, to the truth of our interconnectivity. The health of our brains,
minds, and relationships depends on our ability to resonate, communicate, and integrate with others.

In Chapter 6, we explored how neural and psychological connectivity and dissociation result in positive and negative adaptation. In this chapter, we focus first on how our brains and minds
are able to link together to form couples, families, and tribes. We

will then examine one possible explanation for the neurobiological mechanisms of the experience of self-identity and self-awareness. Although most of us assume that we first develop a self and then form relationships, I am going to propose that we first form relationships from which the individual self later emerges.

WING TO WING

It is not only fine feathers that make fine birds.

—AESOP

Earlier this morning, my son and I gazed upward at a flock of geese heading south for the winter. As we mused about the reason for their V-shaped formations, I shared that I had read that the wing-to-wing strategy allows them to fly with less effort by using the air currents created by their neighbors. Sam volunteered that maybe it allowed them to keep better track of each other. I think he may be right because I know this is why fighter pilots use this pattern. As we stared at wave after wave of these splendid migrants, I noticed that each group was itself shaped like a giant bird and wondered if this might help to keep potential predators at bay. It is much easier to grasp how schools of fish, flocks of birds, and herds of animals are shaped to serve the survival of the group than it is for us to grasp why we interact the way we do. Perhaps our focus on individuals blinds us to all the evidence for interconnectivity all around us.

Sam asked a good question: "How do geese know to fly in the V pattern?" I replied, "They probably just follow what they see the group do, and it triggers instincts within them that have been shaped for a million years." I suggested that he think about the way people instinctively treat each other differently based on size, gender, and color and organize to form groups of all kinds. We have

leaders and followers, couples, teams, and families, saints and bul-
lies, wise women and foolish men. "We look around and do what
other people do to fit in and survive." That seemed to make sense
to him, and he said, "I guess it just comes naturally." After a while I
said, "Maybe birds fly wing to wing for the same reason that fathers
and sons sit next to each other, look up at birds, and ask why they
fly in a V."

From the beginning of mammalian evolution to the highly
social animals of today, natural selection has developed strategies to weave individuals into groups. The shape and color of
our eyes, our complex facial expressions, and our ability to blush
when we violate social norms are all ways we automatically and
unconsciously communicate our feelings, thoughts, and intentions to one another. All forms of human messaging rely on neural networks to receive, interpret, and transmit information back
and forth across the social synapse. These systems allow parents
to know what's going on inside of their children, poker players to
gain an advantage over their opponents, and emotions like exhila-
ration and panic to spread through a crowd, triggering celebrations
and stampedes. Scores of instincts, reflexes, and other primitive
mechanisms inherited from our mammalian ancestors support our
ability to connect and automatically exchange information with
others of our species.

The foundation of our connectedness comes from the earliest attunement of right hemisphere to right hemisphere with our
caretakers. It is during these interactions that our deepest and
most basic sense of the safety of the world, our lovability, and our
self-esteem are formed. This process is reflected in the psychodynamic cliché that a child's first reality is his or her mother's unconscious. Through biochemical exchanges before birth and primal
emotional and visceral attunement during the first years of life, a
mother teaches her child to be in a world as she experiences it, via

both conscious and unconscious communication. Central to our present focus is our ability to attune to and resonate with our clients during therapy to become a functional unit that parallels the parent-child relationship, a phenomenon Robert Langs called the bipersonal field.

The existence of the bipersonal field, and the fact that our conscious and unconscious minds link and communicate during therapy, means that the therapeutic relationship is influenced by the therapist's unconscious wishes, needs, and unresolved traumas as well as training, strategies, and conscious intentions. This is the primary reason why therapy for therapists is so important to expand their self-awareness. A client may be none the wiser, but all of a therapist's gestures, words, silences, and interpretations are refracted through the prism of our own intense inner emotions. It is almost certain that the quality and direction of therapy will be strongly influenced unconscious and unprocessed emotions.

MIRROR NEURONS

There are two ways of spreading light; to be the candle or the mirror that reflects it.

—EDITH WHARTON

You will recall that our second executive system, centered around parietal-frontal systems, organizes patterns of behavior within space and time that allow us to navigate our day-to-day worlds. Both the parietal and frontal lobes contain what are called mirror neurons, which fire both when we observe another engaging in an action and when we engage in that same action. Mirror neurons are not unique to humans; other primates and even octopuses have them. Mirror neurons probably first evolved to support imitative learning and the coordination of group behavior. They allow us to learn through observation by linking our sensory and motor systems with our reward circuitry for goal-directed behavior through time.

A classic example of imitative learning is ant fishing among chimps. If a chimp who knows how to fish finds a long blade of grass and slides it into the top of an anthill, other chimps will watch with curiosity. When, after a minute or so, the chimp pulls out the blade of grass, now covered with ants, and eats them, the other chimps will get all excited about capturing their own lunch. As the observers watched the fisher-chimp, their sensory systems were linked with their motor systems, and they were (in a sense) internally practicing the fishing behaviors. When a reward was added, the sequence and timing of the fishing behaviors were linked with reward and motivation, and before you know it, they all knew how to fish. The phrase "monkey see, monkey do" also applies to chimps, apes, octopuses, and humans. If you've spent any time with young children, you can see this played out a hundred times a day, because it is the primary way children learn how to navigate their worlds.

As we evolved into increasingly social-emotional creatures, these mirror systems were used to support emerging abilities like attunement, resonance, sympathy, compassion, and empathy. While we can learn to fish and boil an egg through observation, mirror neurons also support our emotional connection to others by creating an internal model within us of what the other is experiencing. When we see someone laughing or crying, grieving or playing, mirror neurons will stimulate the same motor movements, postures, and expression within us, which, in turn, triggers our emotions. This is why we experience emotions as contagious, why depressed people are often shunned, why celebrity suicides trigger copycats, and why we all want to hang around positive people.

Research has shown that when people feel safer with and like one another more, the amount of mirroring imitation of facial expressions, movements, and postural shifts increases. This interpersonal dance enhances a sense of connectedness and increases openness to learning from another. This is likely an unexplored but significant mechanism of change in therapy and why clients always correlate liking their therapist with beneficial therapy. When a client feels safe and comfortable, and likes her therapist, she takes the therapist inside or introjects her sensory, motor, and affective circuitry. This is how we become part of one another and likely contributes to the physical aspects of the grief we experience after a significant loss. Just as neurons link, integrate, and grow, so do humans. Our ability to integrate with others supports learning, psychological development, and physical health because all levels of the biopsychosocial matrix are interwoven and interdependent.

THEORY OF MIND

Who sees the human face correctly: the photographer, the mirror, or the painter?

—PABLO PICASSO

Because social animals need to both cooperate and compete with others for survival, the ability to form predictions of what others might be about to do is an invaluable adaptational tool. The ability to strike before you are hit, run before the other begins to chase you, or grasp something to eat before someone else gets it enhances your chances of survival. This ability has been dubbed theory of mind (TOM), the ability to generate an automatic inference about what others know and don't know, what their motivations might be, and what they will likely do next. Considerable research has focused on the development of TOM and deficits of this ability in autistic individuals. You have probably already made the connection between TOM, mirror neurons, and the parietal-frontal executive system. TOM rests on our ability to make cause-and-effect connections in time and space using our knowledge of the physical and social worlds.

Picture this: A young chimpanzee was headed down a path, followed by the slower members of the troop, when she came upon a banana placed there by an observing researcher hidden from view. The primatologist reports that when the young chimp saw the banana, the first thing she did was freeze in her tracks. The second was to look around to see if any of the other chimps had seen her or the banana. Surmising that she was the first and only one to see it and hearing her troop mates getting closer, she gave the scream for snake, which sent all the other chimps scurrying up the closest tree. Seeing this, she sat down next to the banana, picked it up, peeled it, and ate it with great enjoyment. This is using TOM to outsmart others to achieve reward.

TOM is not a theory in the usual sense, as we usually think of a theory as something we mull over and arrive at after prolonged thought. It is akin to attachment schemata, which are unconscious predictions based on past experiences that lead us to have automatic expectations of the value of others in meeting our needs and regulating our anxiety. The chimp in the banana scenario doesn't have an elaborate theory of what is on the minds of all of her troop mates, but she does have a love of bananas combined with innumerable experiences of all of their behaviors related to bananas, the importance of what is seen, relative distances, and knowing what happens when you scream "snake"!

Many years ago, I was at a conference in Norway where most everyone was impressively multilingual. I, like most Americans, am not, a fact well known by Europeans. I have a vivid memory of being in a large conference room hearing many simultaneous conversations in a variety of languages. As I walked through the room and passed two different groups engaged in conversation, one after the other switched from French or Norwegian to English and then switched back after I passed. I was so impressed by this that I asked the conference organizer about it. She told me that it was a sign of respect; neither group wished me to experience not understanding what they were saying. I was not only struck by their courtesy but also by the fluidity of their language changes based on their theory of my mind.

Figuring out how to outsmart rivals may be the original impetus for speculation about what makes others tick. It is easy to imagine that these TOM abilities, when combined with bigger brains and greater processing capacity, would eventually lead to things like personality theory, the novels of Jane Austen, and psychoanalysis. One of the many definitions of psychology is the study of the prediction and control of behavior, which also happens to be a great definition of TOM. Although many of us revel in gossip and consider ourselves experts in analyzing others, we possess little or no capacity to self-reflect or have self-insight. The obvious conclusion is that having a theory of mind of others is an ancient and automatic process, while self-reflection and insight are relatively recent evolutionary developments that are learned over time.

Before you can develop complex aspects of self-awareness, you have to first develop a self. Spoiler alert—I suspect that our sense of self is essentially the application of our primitive TOM capacities to ourselves. Whether self-awareness is a positive evolutionary development is open to debate. While having a TOM of others provides us with a survival advantage, having a TOM of ourselves creates an adaptational challenge. For example, the word for depression in Zimbabwe is *kufungisisa*, literally, "thinking too much." For many people in psychological distress, their minds are not their friends, and many of them state, "I am my own worst enemy."

THE CONSTRUCTION OF THE SELF

*The self is not something ready-made, but something in
continuous formation through choice of action.*

—JOHN DEWEY

What is the self and from whence does it arise? These questions
have long baffled Western philosophers, theologians, and neuroscientists. Having studied all three disciplines, I can say that none
has come up with a satisfactory explanation. In my view, Buddhist
philosophy has the most compelling argument to date; in a nutshell,
it is that the experience of the self is a construction of the mind in
interaction with our bodily processes, senses, and the physical and
social worlds. The resultant activations create behaviors, memories,
perceptions, and the collection of thoughts we come to identify as
the self. Surprisingly, all of it is in line with current neuroscientific
knowledge.

Two pieces of knowledge that earlier Buddhist philosophers
lacked was an understanding of evolution and the social nature of
the brain. This led them to understand the mind as arising spontaneously from within as opposed to an adaptation for group and
individual survival. While this doesn't invalidate their perspective,
it does allow us to understand the workings of the mind, the emergence of self-awareness, and the creation of the self in a broader
adaptive context.

Neuroscientists have a fairly good idea of how each of the
component parts of experience (referred to as aggregates in Buddhism) arises. We understand the mechanisms of motor behavior
and memory, how the sensory systems work, and how all of this
information is sent upward to the association cortex for higher-
level processing. All of the contributors to our conscious experience outlined in Chapter 3 are also central components of how

the brain constructs awareness. We are pretty sure that multiple areas of the cortex are required for conscious awareness, although how this occurs exactly is still being explored. How do we come to be able to reflect on our self, think about ourselves as we think about others, and make conscious choices that allow us to alter our thoughts, feelings, and behaviors? Most neuroscientists who consider this question posit some mechanism related to brain wave activation or some as yet undiscovered master mechanism. However, I think we may have already discovered the mechanism, and it is hiding in plain sight: it's the same mechanism that creates a theory of mind of others.

As humans evolved increasingly sophisticated imagination, language, and abstract thinking, we were also called upon to engage in more complex social interactions, with expanding expectations and responsibilities. Perhaps there was no survival advantage to having a separate sense of self for Paleolithic humans. But as societies grew more complex, inward-facing TOM may have become associated with the idea of a separate self to serve more precise identification, assignment of specific roles and status, and greater organizational demands. As tribes expanded and combined into chiefdoms, city-states, and nations, the number and nature of relationships we had to navigate grew exponentially. We had to learn to deal with strangers without becoming terrified and learn to navigate multiple social settings on a daily basis. As we passed through different social settings each day, the ability to establish and maintain an identity and a consistent sense of self without relying on the sociostatic feedback from a small tribe may have become a survival advantage.

Neurofluency Principle 25: Our experience of the self is a construction that builds on our primitive TOM for others, and is augmented by our abstract and imaginative capabilities.

It is likely that the automatic TOM mechanism we inherited from our primate ancestors was gradually expanded to perform this new function. Instead of being limited to predicting the motivations and intentions of others, it was turned on the self to develop a theory of our own minds. The ability to do this is not automatic, as is evidenced by the vast number of individuals who are able to reflect on others in great detail but have little or no sense of themselves or the ability to take responsibility for their own behavior. The circuits responsible for TOM could serve as the infrastructure for self-identity and eventually self-awareness. This may account for the considerable overlap between the patterns of neural activation during tasks focused on either TOM or autobiographical memory. It may also be why the DMN becomes activated both when we are reflecting on our own internal state and when we experience empathy for or thinking about others.

We all begin to develop TOMs early in life and only come to construct an idea about our self-identity during childhood and adolescence. This supports the idea that the ability to spontaneously generate a TOM is evolutionarily ancient. Before that, our experience of ourselves was likely an amalgamation of our symbiotic connections to others. This symbiotic reality still exists but is usually excluded from the conscious narratives of self. (This may be why we are surprised by the regressions we experience when we rejoin our biological families later in adulthood.) The essence of early self during development is a set of behaviors, motivations, and predilections we associate with our names and our interactions with others.

What is called the illusion of the self in Buddhism may begin with the mind's everyday organization of attributes we associate with our name and our relationships to others. If this is true, we don't need any special neural mechanism; all we need is the ability to use the imaginary idea of the self and attribute our memories, habit patterns, and preferences to it and give it a name. If this is true, the self is a specific example of TOM applied to ourselves. To restate this in a slightly different way, the sensorimotor reward systems that gave rise to a TOM of others, combined with our ability to imagine, came to form the perception of how we see and experience ourselves.

If the mind is capable of creating imaginary worlds, poetry, and the theory of relativity, it is certainly able to construct an idea of a self from the component parts available to us. The experience of the self is woven into a social illusion shared with those around us. Buddha came to see this clearly around 2,000 years ago. The conscious experience of self is organized around a story created by the mind. There is nowhere to find the self in the brain, and the self requires no special neurobiological qualities. We've had the necessary wetware for 50,000 years. We are a story, told first to us by others, and then repeated to ourselves in a million different ways, until the self becomes "self-evident." This is one of the ways in which family and cultural myths simultaneously shape and trap us, making positive change so elusive.

The wonderful thing about the narrative of the self is that stories can be edited. All forms of therapy, religious cults, and the military leverage the power of narratives and our need to have one to serve their goals. The challenge for our clients is to get to the point where they can comprehend this reality and rewrite their narratives in ways that serve as more adaptive blueprints for thought, emotion, and action. Coming to see all of the things you once thought of as objective reality to be a subjective fabrication is difficult and sometimes impossible to grasp. It is made especially difficult by our primitive tribal loyalties to the myths of our families, whom we are loath to betray.

LEVERAGING SELF-AWARENESS IN PSYCHOTHERAPY

The more self-aware an animal is, the more empathic it tends to be.

—FRANS DE WAAL

What happens in our brains during self-reflective moments in therapy, when we are not being defensive, telling stories, or voicing habitual complaints about others? What is happing in our brains when we are open to looking at ourselves as others see us or absorbing feedback in a nondefensive manner? What's happening when a powerful interpretation hits home? We know that when clients shift into this state of brain and mind, they show dramatic changes in posture, tone of voice, breathing patterns, and facial expressions. The reflexive and compulsive thinking stops and they fall into the vastness of the present moment—where change is possible. During these moments, we shift from being human doings to human beings. What might be happening in our brains that allows and supports this state of mind?

In 1929 Hans Berger, the inventor of the electroencephalograph, noticed that the brains of his subjects remained active when they were at rest between experimental tasks. This curious finding was largely ignored for 70 years, until researchers using brain imaging techniques noticed the same phenomenon. These researchers found that a set of structures along the midline of the brain, including portions of the prefrontal, temporal, and parietal cortices, along with the cingulate and hippocampus, the DMN became active when subjects were outwardly at rest. The DMN was subsequently found to be a functionally coherent system that becomes activated when subjects are engaged with tasks related to self-awareness, social awareness (thinking and feeling about others), and mental perception and cognition (memory scene construction, mental time travel, and imagination).

Working together, the regions of the DMN appear to weave together a conscious experience of the physical self with autobiographical memory and an ability to imagine the future. This may serve the function of grounding our experience of self within the flow of time. This experience of self, integrated with the mechanisms that organize TOM, is the likely neural substrate of the construction of self-identity and (later in development) self-reflective capacity.

A key to understanding this DMN executive system is that its activity is primarily anticorrelational with both the amygdala and frontal-parietal executive systems. This means that when we are anxious, frightened, or preoccupied with a task, the DMN is largely inhibited. When the DMN is activated, the other two executive networks are inhibited until a signal from the salience network indicates a possible threat or a novel stimulus. Safe and quiet moments throughout life allow for building and utilizing an internal space for retreat from the outside world for self-reflection and imagination free from impingement. We do our best in therapy to create, nurture, and utilize this safe internal space where clients can see beyond their symptoms, assumptions, and narratives to imagine different worlds and ways of being. This is likely why the sociostatic mechanisms at play in the bipersonal fields created within therapeutic relationships can be such a powerful matrix of change.

Research suggests that the anticorrelational nature of the DMN with the other two executive systems isn't always complete. In other words, there are conditions under which the two or three executive systems may combine for improved task performance. The medial prefrontal regions are capable of inhibiting the amygdala along with task-oriented networks to allow the posterior cingulate cortex and parietal lobes to provide us with a platform for internal mentation and a three-dimensional workspace. This allows us to internalize and manipulate images, play out interpersonal scenarios, and process emotions without interference. It also offers us the possibility of experiencing time travel through the juxtaposition in working memory of the present, past, and ideas about the future. What we call mind wandering and daydreaming may be both the soil of creativity and the background processing that helps us function in the world.

Tasks like psychotherapy may require a more subtle balance of internal and external focus in order to monitor, facilitate, or influence cognition. Cooperation between the frontal-parietal network and the DMN may be essential for maintaining a focused, internal train of thought. This point of interaction between internal and external processing may be an avenue for the influence of autobiographical memory on current experience—a central neural mechanism underlying projective processes and other influences of the past on the present. DMN participation during outside interactions (frontal-parietal) may also be responsible for a client's ability to simultaneously experience a transference reaction and be aware that it is happening.

The nascent DMN has been detected as early as two weeks after birth, but it only forms into a coherent network around age 7, when most children begin to have a sense of being a separate being, independent from their parents. The DMN remains immature through childhood but becomes functionally coherent during early adulthood. At the same time, the medial and dorsal regions of the frontal lobes also shift from being correlational to anticorrelational with one another as we learn to better separate internal and external experience. Women with early life trauma exhibit decreased functional connectivity within the DMN. In fact, DMN connectivity in adults with childhood maltreatment parallels patterns observed in healthy 7- to 9-year-olds, strongly suggesting that trauma impairs the DMN's development.

I suspect that a key component of PTSD is the sustained inhibition of the DMN, cutting victims off from connection with themselves and the group mind. Psychological, social, and neural integration are interrelated and interdependent processes upon which normal healthy functioning depends. Proper inhibition and coordination among our three executive systems are required for us to stay connected with others, achieve psychological integration, and have a sense of wholeness and connection to ourselves.

A FRIGHTENED CHILD

Love involves an unfathomable combination of understanding and misunderstanding.

—DIANE ARBUS

Although the parallels between the neurological and psychological are not a precise fit (and there is much still to learn), we know enough now to say that they are connected in meaningful ways. It is clear that psychological health depends upon the development of different abilities and that optimal functioning requires their communication, coordination, and integration. The best example is optimal executive functioning, which necessitates the integration of cognitive, social, and emotional abilities. The opposite state, found for example in PTSD, is a reflection of the inhibition and dissociation of multiple psychological abilities, which undermines both functioning and well-being.

Long before I began to think about the notion of neural integration, I lived through an experience that I believe has helped me to understand dissociation. When I was a child of 10, my parents went through a contentious divorce. Although largely sheltered from much of the acrimony and fighting, separation from family, financial insecurities, and moving from a safe suburban neighborhood to a frightening urban one were some of the consequences I had to face. These stressors, combined with my mother's anxiety, depression, and agitation, completely shook my world. I found myself barely able to get to school (navigating the dangers of my new neighborhood) or to pay attention once I got there. I simultaneously suffered from head and stomach pain, certainly psychosomatic in origin. My ability to focus in school and any motivation to learn were nonexistent. There was little fun, no sense of a future, and what little energy I was able to muster was invested in coping with anxiety and getting through the day.

With my stress at an all-time high and my emotional reserves on empty, I was unlucky enough to overhear an argument between my parents. The screaming, invectives, and crying had the effect of pushing me over some emotional edge. Something in me snapped, and I remember falling on my bed, physically shaking, my mind empty of thought and unavailable to me to use. My head was spinning, surrounded and overwhelmed by sights and sounds beyond my control. It was as if I had been given a hallucinogen. Many years later in the midst of an emotional therapeutic session, I was catapulted back to this experience with all of its sensory, emotional, and cognitive memories. I was once again the 10-year-old, overwhelmed with terror, and without the words to explain or even describe what was happening to me. Both my therapist and I watched helplessly as the scene unfolded around me and within me in real time.

For the last four decades, I have heard stories of childhood abuse from victims that have brought me to tears, broken my heart, and nearly crushed my faith in humanity. What I personally experienced during my difficult times was nothing compared to what many others have had to endure. I can only imagine the devastating impact of sustained sexual and physical abuse I have helped clients to work through. Despite its relative insignificance, I believe that my experience allows me a small personal window into the much broader realm of trauma and dissociation. The inhibition of thinking, the sensory flooding, and the physiological activation I went through have been described by many of my clients. Years later, when I read Freud's definition of trauma as the experience of a "surpassing of the stimulus barrier," I thought of this moment in my life as a possible example of what he might be referring to. I didn't know what a stimulus barrier was, but I did know that something inside me, something that had allowed me to hold myself together, had broken.

Speculations about hypothetical psychic processes that Freud and others needed to rely on a century ago are rapidly being replaced by neural structures and neurodynamic processes. We now know that the neurochemistry of sustained stress and traumatic experiences distorts our perception and cognition in ways that support our immediate survival. On the other hand, if these neurochemical states are sustained, they diminish our reality testing and functional capabilities. The endorphins that allow us to tolerate pain and imagine we are out of our bodies as we are victimized also impair our memory, problem-solving abilities, and social connectedness after the threat has passed.

The high state of arousal I experienced activated my first executive system to the point where my second and third executive systems seemed almost fully inhibited. I was unable to understand or even process what was happening to me, had no way to regulate my body or my emotions, and felt completely disconnected from others. I had indeed surpassed a stimulus barrier. Trauma is a dramatic example of the breakdown of both psychological and neurological integration.

Despite the robustness of our nervous systems, we are especially vulnerable to failures of neural and psychological integration. This is primarily due to the brain's staggering complexity and the trade-offs evolution has made during the many twists and turns of natural selection. The many opportunities for neural dissociation, triggered by the challenges of adaptation, can result in a wide array of psychological distresses. Our vulnerability to dissociation is based on the history of how our brains evolved to perform so many specialized functions and how those functions came together to construct conscious experience.

PART II

Applying Neuroscience in Your Clinical Practice

8

NEUROSCIENCE AND PSYCHOTHERAPY

*One of the ultimate challenges for biology is to understand
the brain's processing of unconscious and conscious perception,
emotion, and empathy.*

—ERIC KANDEL

Just a few decades ago, most psychotherapists practiced within a single theoretical orientation and only interacted with like-minded others. Therapists organized more like religious sects than professional guilds, and teachers competed to convert students to their personal belief system. As the years have passed, the practice of psychotherapy has become increasingly eclectic and open to new theories and treatment models. As part of its expansion, the field has come to embrace neuroscience as a relevant and even necessary addition to our knowledge base. And because neuroscience is now being included in clinical discussions, we are expected to be fluent in the basics of brain-behavior relationships.

It is important to begin with the understanding that there is no neuropsychotherapy or any specific form of therapy that the neuroscientific research supports over another. All of the major schools of therapy—CBT, psychodynamic, client-centered, dialectical behavior therapy (DBT), humanistic-existential—help some of the people some of the time. From a neuroscientific perspective, when any therapy works, it is because the therapist has managed to stimulate plasticity and positive change in a client's brain.

BECOMING NEUROFLUENT

> *I am always ready to learn although I do not always like being taught.*
>
> —WINSTON CHURCHILL

The question I'm asked most is, how do we integrate our knowledge of neuroscience into the conceptualization, assessment, and treatment of our clients? In other words, how do I become fluent in using the concepts and language of neuroscience in my clinical practice? At a theoretical level, I am interested in the relevant neuroscience issues with all of my clients in the same way that I am in their cultural background. I assume each of my clients is unique and ask them many questions so they can educate me about how they experience themselves, the world, and the therapeutic process. I'll spend time having clients educate me about their culture and do my best to adapt what I do to their experience. In the process, I also want to develop an idea of how a client's brain was shaped early in life, how this client processes information, and get a general sense of the nature of his or her neural development and integration.

Neurofluency in Clinical Practice 1: Although there is no neuropsychotherapy, all forms of therapy rely on stimulating neuroplasticity in order to be successful.

Of course, neuroscience and culture go hand in hand because the brain, as a social organ of adaptation, is built through experience, and all human experiences occur in the context of a specific culture. Knowledge of culture and neuroscience always influences my understanding of client histories, the adaptive value of their symptoms, and the totality of their experience. Addressing issues of culture, and especially cultural differences between client and therapist, is central to the establishment of a positive therapeutic relationship and working alliance. For one client, cultural background might become a central issue in therapy, while being of little consequence for another. The same is true for brain functioning. Issues of both diversity and neuroscience may lead to strategic changes in language and tactics.

Additionally, sharing with my clients how our brains work and how we can use this knowledge in assessment and treatment provides us with a nonshaming way to explain their symptoms and how to work together to develop strategies to change them. Neuroscience can also serve as a common language among health care providers from different disciplines who may not work within a psychological framework. The key here is to be open to new ways of thinking, different ways of understanding, and new strategies for healing.

Given that the inclusion of neuroscience in clinical conceptualization and decision making is a relatively recent development, few of us have had clinical supervision that included any systematic consideration of the brain. However, everyone practicing today has been exposed to the biopsychosocial model and hopefully incorporated it into their thinking. I'm always amazed to listen to case presentations that completely ignore any consideration of the possibility that a client's psychological symptoms may be the result of coexisting physical illness, the side effects of medication, or the consequences of social and economic injustice and repression. This kind of limited thinking is a catastrophic consequence of professional silos and the segregation of knowledge.

Neurofluency in Clinical Practice 2: All forms of psychotherapy can be successful if the strategies and tactics employed
stimulate neuroplasticity in the service of positive change.

Despite the lack of an established formula for this new clinical
synthesis, there are some relevant precedents from rehabilitation
medicine and neuropsychiatry that begin to point the way. Practitioners in these two fields have always had to consider the brain,
the mind, and social relationships in assessment and treatment.
When clinicians work with victims of traumatic brain injury, specific functional deficits are taken into account in the selection and
delivery of treatment. Challenges in language comprehension, for
example, will impact the nature, speed, and type of treatment they
receive. On the other hand, seizure disorders and the medications
used to treat them have their own social, emotional, and cognitive
sequelae that influence the nature of treatment.

Neurofluency in Clinical Practice 3: Neurofluency parallels cultural sensitivity by highlighting aspects of our clients' experience that fall outside of a narrow psychological
framework.

Closer to home, we have discovered that some mental disorders
thought to be purely psychological have considerable neurobiological correlates. For example, there is solid evidence that borderline
personality disorder and complex PTSD correlate with significant
changes in brain development and neural functioning. The changes
that parallel the cognitive, memory, and emotional symptoms of the
illness likely means that the psychodynamics and neurodynamics of
these disorders are interwoven and interdependent. The reason why
targeted interventions like DBT and EMDR have been so successful with many of these clients is that they compensate for the dif-

ferences in brain functioning of their specific client populations. It is in the same way altogether possible that the more we learn about our clients' neurodynamics, the better we will be at shaping more successful forms of therapy.

THE CONVERGENCE OF THE SCIENCES

The only thing that will redeem mankind is cooperation.
—BERTRAND RUSSELL

At first blush, you may find the remarkable convergence of psychotherapy and neuroscience a bit surprising. After all, many of us are first attracted to psychology as a rejection of the hard sciences, preferring to relate to people rather than lab rats and hard facts. These distinctions are, in many ways, an artifact of cultural biases and the fractured organization of university departments. Most people either never knew or have forgotten that Freud began as a neurologist, and his master plan was to create a scientific psychology that connected the brain and mind. You may also be surprised to find that our exploration of neuroscience leads us directly into the fields of evolution and epigenetics. These deep connections are the impetus for the growing convergence of scientific disciplines that have until recently remained segregated.

Neurofluency in Clinical Practice 4: Techniques like progressive relaxation exercises and EMDR can be used as adjuncts to any form of psychotherapy to promote affect regulation and memory reconsolidation.

As the biologist Theodosius Dobzhansky wrote, "Nothing in biology makes sense except in the light of evolution." We are learning that in order to more deeply understand what is happening in psychotherapy, we must include other fields and ways of thinking in our own. It is now fair to build on Dobzhansky's statement with such postulates as "nothing about the impact of early parenting makes sense except in the light of epigenetics" or "nothing about PTSD makes sense except in the light of the integration of neural networks." This makes it necessary for us to accept the notion of consilience. Consilience is a countermovement to the traditional segregation of academic disciples. It's based on the belief that the sciences have an underlying unity and consistency that can be explored and comprehended through many perspectives and strategies.

Again and again, I've been impressed by how much research in biology and animal behavior affords us deeper insights into human experience. It can help us see some of the blind spots that are embedded in our language, culture, and egos. One of my favorite examples has to do with the parallel between the growth of neurons and individual social animals. Just like people, individual neurons are involved in a Darwinian struggle for survival. It is the core evolutionary strategy of diversity, overproduction, and adaptation through natural selection that shapes the brain to adapt to its social environment as species to adapt to their natural habitats. The brain is its own ecosystem, with millions of neurons that struggle to survive just like animals in a jungle or on the savannah.

We are born with far more neurons than we need, and those which are able to communicate, coordinate, and form a bond around some function—finding our mouth with our thumb, learning a new word, or associating the sound of footsteps with the appearance of a familiar face—are stimulated by one another and survive. The excitation and stimulation received within the electrical network of the nervous system is what keeps neurons alive. Therefore, connection equals life, and lack of connection means death. This is why individual neurons do not exist in nature, at least not for long. You can keep them alive in the laboratory if you simulate the excitation they would receive from other neurons. Ostracism by other neurons, due to a lack of cooperative fit in functional relationships, leads to cell death (apoptosis) in a kind of neural Darwinism.

This process allows a decrease in the number of neurons to be the measure of brain development. It may sound like a paradox, but as our brains enlarge, the actual number of neurons decreases. The space cleared by the removal of dead neurons allows for the growth and increased connectivity of those that survive. Our brains grow larger because those neurons that survive grow larger and larger. This adaptational process of neuronal death is called apoptosis, while normal loss due to illness or physical trauma is called neurosis. Inadequate apoptosis leads to individuals with abnormal brain development and is one of many neurodevelopmental abnormalities found in autism.

Neurofluency in Clinical Practice 5: Connectivity is a central process of biological life, from neurons to all social animals—connection equals adaptation and survival.

If you watch a neuron under an electron microscope, you see it expending its energy reaching out its dendritic arms in what appears to be a desperate search for connection. Neurons are social creatures, and connection is their first order of business. With a little anthropomorphism, they remind me of a drowning person who is flailing to reach the hand of a rescuer. And it is a desperate situation—failure to connect leads to an exhaustion of the neuron's energy reserves and certain death. Survival is a race against the clock during early critical periods for neurons. For neurons don't only look like people drowning—they also look like young children when they realize that they are alone and faced with a stranger. There is a deep sense of danger and a full-body reaction to this life-and-death dilemma.

THE DRIVE FOR CONNECTION

A flower cannot blossom without sunshine and man cannot live without love.

—MAX MULLER

In these parallel processes, we witness evolution's strategy of connectivity from individual neurons carried up the scale of complexity to individual social animals. Just like neurons, infants rely on their ability to attach first to their caretakers and subsequently to the social world around them. Humans, like neurons, are social creatures who strive to become a part of a functional unit called a family. In many subsistence cultures, orphaned children and older people are put to death because their resource needs are a threat to the survival of the tribe. As societies gather or lose resources, those who can't contribute are either taken care of or expelled. In both the brain and in the family, part of the calculation of the value of a neuron or an individual is predicated on their contribution to the survival of the whole.

Can we truly say that humans have a social process parallel to apoptosis? Do we contain a similar self-destruct mechanism triggered by the absence of sustained connection with others? The answer might be yes. A century ago, orphanages had such high death rates that physicians replaced nuns and social workers in leadership positions in an attempt to identify the cause of so many deaths in otherwise healthy and cared-for children. Assuming that the deaths were based on infections, physicians further separated children from one another and kept their handling by the caring staff to a minimum. Unfortunately, children continued to die at such rates that admission forms and death certificates were filled out during intake for the sake of efficiency. It was not until early attachment researchers suggested that the children be held, rocked, and allowed to interact with one another that survival rates in orphanages and other facilities began to improve.

Neurofluency in Clinical Practice 6: Although they may manifest as depression, anxiety, fears, and phobias, most human problems result from difficulties in bonding, attachment, and sustaining connection,

During World War II, René Spitz studied children who had been removed from the rubble of the bombing of London and brought to orphanages in the countryside. He documented how the infants went through a period of protest when they would cry out and jump in their cribs, trying to get their parents to return to them. After this period of flailing protest, they would slowly settle down, lose energy, and develop a vacant stare. The same pattern was discovered by another researcher who studied children who were hospitalized for long periods and only allowed parental visits one hour per week. Initial periods of agitated protest were followed by calm, listlessness, and eventually indifference to others in their surroundings. Spitz called this catastrophic reaction to abandonment "anaclitic depression," and a similar process is now described as reactive attachment disorder.

Watching the films of these children during the protest phase, shaking the bars of their cribs, writhing and screaming, reminded me of neurons desperately trying to connect with other neurons. Human creatures, especially very young ones, depend on connectivity with others for the kind of stimulation that builds and sustains the brain and body. Without connectivity, both human children and neurons die. To some degree this phenomenon continues throughout life. We see the evidence for this in the countless studies that demonstrate the correlations among social connectivity, physical and mental health, and longevity. We see it in the pain of solitary confinement, losing face among our peers, or the punishment of exile from home and family. Suicidal thoughts and behaviors, perhaps the clearest expression of a self-destruct program, are often triggered by feelings of separation, abandonment, and other forms of social loss. The sense of being alone in the world is both emotionally and physically painful and makes us desperate to reestablish connection. While neurons can't experience psychological pain, I believe the anguish we experience during separation has a direct evolutionary through-line from apoptosis.

Neurofluency in Clinical Practice 7: Early learning shapes implicit memory systems that guide all subsequent conscious thought, feelings, and behavior.

When neurons fire together, stimulate one another, and wire together, they derive the necessary energy for survival, growth, and expansion. In parallel, we know that human contact stimulates neural circuits to grow, drives gene transcription, and builds our brains. The vital importance of early interactions to the building of the brain helps us to explain the death of institutionalized children who are deprived of physical and emotional connection. What Spitz labeled as anaclitic depression may parallel apoptosis at the human level—essentially running out of energy in the absence of reciprocal stimulation. Evolution has shaped attachment as a life-or-death situation for both neurons and humans. Attach and you will survive; don't attach and you will be eliminated. Many children and adults suffer from severe anxiety triggered by separation, abandonment, and loss.

THE CONSTRUCTION OF CONSCIOUSNESS

Memory is the fourth dimension to any landscape.

—JANET FITCH

The brain is not a unitary structure but a complex system of systems, each with its own evolutionary histories, developmental trajectories, and functional responsibilities. This understanding of the brain allows us to grasp both the brain's complexity and its vulnerability to neurodynamic disruptions. A great deal of mental distress can be understood in the framework of a deficit of neural connectivity among networks that are supposed to integrate their functioning to perform higher-level tasks. This is reflected in the area of memory by the fact that there isn't only one form of memory but many different kinds all working at the same time. Different systems of memory can be integrated with each other, disconnected (dissociated) from one another, or activated simultaneously (to our great confusion, as during flashbacks).

For example, if you are riding your bike next to a friend while talking about a test you are both in the process of studying for, you are simultaneously utilizing multiple memory systems. You are using a procedural memory system that contains the motor and vestibular learning of riding a bike, probably from earlier in life. You have emotional memory networks that store your early competitive experiences with your siblings that get triggered and make you work harder to get a higher grade than your classmate. Both of these memories are implicit, which means they are stored and activated without access to language or conscious awareness. You may not remember learning how to ride a bike, and you may deny being competitive with your friend, and really believe it. Depending on our level of self-knowledge and level of insight at the moment, we are more or less aware of all of the streams of memory impacting and shaping our moment-to-moment conscious experience.

If a memory is associated with fear, its activation will trigger a physiological reaction and perhaps even a fight-flight-freeze response. If we are consciously aware of the memory being triggered, we call it an intrusive memory related to a past trauma. If we are not consciously aware of the memory that triggers the fear response, we call our reaction a panic attack. These are often more frightening because they seem to appear from nowhere without cause and make us feel completely out of control. If we can at least connect our fear with a real danger, we worry a lot less about whether we are going crazy. Another way of saying this is that the amygdala can function either integrated with or dissociated from conscious awareness. When our brains are dissociated and the amygdala becomes activated, we become terrified, but we don't know why.

One of the amygdala's many jobs is to generalize from frightening experiences in the past to situations in the present it interprets as similar. What trauma experts call flashbacks, or what Freud termed regression, are amygdala–activated implicit memories of prior similar experiences designed to set off a fight-flight-freeze reaction for protection in the present moment. Direct eye contact triggers amygdala activation in all primates because of the potential threat signals it may contain.

Neurofluency in Clinical Practice 8: The amygdala's most primitive function is to remember every negative and dangerous experience we have ever had and be on the lookout for anything that even vaguely resembles what has caused us distress or fear in the past.

Many people with social anxiety avoid eye contact at all costs because they find it so dysregulating. Therapists can also be avoidant and even frightened of conflict and anger. The intimacy of therapy triggers their fear systems and leads them to avoid or even be blind to areas that they need to explore with their clients for fear of making them angry. We all have to face the struggle of challenging our clients when it is appropriate to do so. If we avoid confronting our clients on important issues, the therapy can be converted into a friendly regular meeting that the client thinks is really therapy. This may well be the most frequent form of countertransference.

Because so much of conscious awareness depends on memory, the fact that we have evolved many systems of memory allows for the possibility of psychological and neurological dissociation. At the psychological level, there can be a dissociation between our thoughts, feelings, behaviors, and conscious awareness. We can engage in "motivated forgetting," when we choose not to remember things that are too painful or distort memories to make them more acceptable. Adults who were sexually abused as children have frequently been found to forget it happened or remember it as happening to someone else. Some exceptionally painful memories can be repressed and emerge decades later, or never at all. At a neurological level, neural networks involving somatic experience and conscious awareness can be disconnected or noncommunicative and make it impossible to be aware of what's going on in our bodies and emotions (alexithymia). This is parallel to how our right and left cerebral hemispheres can become surgically disconnected and result in two different experiences of self.

BELIEFS TRUMP FACTS

> *The human mind evolved to believe in the gods. It did not evolve to believe in biology.*
>
> —E. O. WILSON

A clear lesson from neuroscience, as well as the fields of social psychology, political science, and economics, is that our brain and mind have not evolved to perceive the world accurately. Just as our visual system has evolved to process only a narrow range of light frequencies, and our ears are shaped to hear only certain frequencies of sound, our brain and mind have been shaped to organize reality in ways that help us adapt to the world. This is why we tend to think of our friends as better than others, why we blame others for our own mistakes, and why all of our children are above average. We minimize our faults, amplify our strengths, and deny unpleasant realities because these distortions protect us from despair and hopelessness. Some even consider depression to be the result of a deficit in appropriate denial.

> *Neurofluency in Clinical Practice 9*: Our minds have evolved to believe rather than to rationally assess information. Beliefs organize individuals in groups and lead them to behave in ways which (they believe) will support the survival of their tribe.

It is clear that the human brain has been shaped by evolution for belief rather than a rational evaluation of available information. It is likely that emotionally driven cognition is more supportive of group cohesion and strongly contributed to the survival of tribes back into prehistory. This is why the birth of science and the scientific method are seen as so important in the history of civilization. Although civilization has progressed over the last few thousand years, the fundamentals of the human brain have not. Politicians know that the average voter is far less interested in the facts than they are in a clear and simple solution they can believe in; good guys and bad guys, us versus them, and a wall to keep "them" out.

Being human, therapists fall into all of the usual human traps. In the face of the complexity of human experience and the rigors of psychotherapy, many find a one-size-fits-all orientation and come to believe it explains everything. Like sinners gone to Jesus, therapists come back from weekend seminars on any one of a thousand therapies and feel like they've found the secret to mental health. Yes, there is even a placebo effect for therapists when it comes to believing that therapies work. This all goes back to our emotional need to believe in something to make us feel more confident, less anxious, and less lost in a complex world. This is the primitive brain-mind at work within us "civilized" creatures.

Among its many distortions, the human mind creates the illusion that normal conscious experience is of the present moment and contains all of the information required to make choices and navigate the world. A key aspect of everyday experience is that we are free agents, making decisions based on the information available to us, and that we possess free will. It is upon these illusions of separateness, autonomy, and free will that society is organized and upon which our systems of education, government, and justice are based.

As we peer deeper into the brain-mind, we learn that an increasing amount of what we do, feel, and think is the result of reflexive and highly automatic processing. We learn from both the psychoanalysts and the neuroscientists that our experience of and behaviors in the world are heavily influenced by early childhood experiences. Attachment research teaches us that early relationships establish unconscious schemata in implicit memory that determine how to behave in intimate relationships. Social psychology has empirically demonstrated thousands of ways in which our perceptions and decision making can be influenced by subliminal messages, while thousands of cases in the neurology literature have shown how the loss of a group of neurons in a specific brain region can lead a man to mistake his wife for a hat.

Freud was an explorer of how traumatic early experiences, when inadequately resolved, resulted in thoughts, feelings, and behaviors that impeded the adult's ability to love and work. He wasn't interested in resolving every trauma or curing each neurosis; his aim was the pragmatic goal of allowing sufferers to regain connection with others in positive relationships and to be generative in their endeavors. Freud would say that we do have free will but that our free will is limited by unconscious processes that distort our perceptions, limit our vitality, and keep us from living up to our potential.

Advertisers have exploited the limits of our free will by manipulating us with advertising strategies that leverage our primitive drives for sex, status, and success to sell their products by pairing them with symbols of these things. A tall bottle of beer is juxtaposed with the face of a beautiful young girl whose mouth has been modified to look inordinately open, or the ice cubes in a glass of whiskey have been drawn to contain images of reptiles. Cigarettes are smoked by a cowboy or a cartoon camel to lure in young consumers. The Freudian unconscious and the implicit memory systems targeted by advertisers share the ability to influence our experience and actions without us knowing. In Freud's case, it results in early trauma having a prolonged effect on us, while in the case of advertising it makes us vulnerable to manipulation in ways that may not be in our best interest.

Neurofluency in Clinical Practice 10: A core principle of psychotherapy is that our freedom to make choices depends on our awareness of the biases embedded in our implicit programming.

A growing understanding of how much of our experience is illusory will hopefully lead us to be more humble about what we think and believe. We can never be certain that what we believe is objectively true because beliefs are more akin to probability statements than facts. This is even more true for what we believe about ourselves, because our investment in appearing better than we are will distort both our perceptions and our judgments. Another area of concern is eyewitness testimony in the courtroom. So much of our legal system relies upon trustworthy witnesses of crimes—yet we know how distorted our memories become, especially in highly emotional situations, which is exactly what witnessing a crime is. Another key issue has to do with implicit prejudice in both policing and the criminal justice system. Saying and even believing you are not prejudiced doesn't hold up in experimental settings. Implicit biases determine how we judge others, whether we feel they are capable of a crime, and whether an ambiguous object in someone's hand is a weapon or a can of soda.

What is free will and free won't? Free will is a mix of reality and illusion that is difficult to tease apart. We have learned that it is impossible for a human not to have reflexive and spontaneous thoughts and urges. As long as we are mammals, we will possess these drives. It does appear that we are capable of becoming conscious of these thoughts and feelings, inhibiting the reflex to act on them, and employing a decision not to act on them if they are inappropriate. Saddled with Paleolithic brains better suited for tribal life on the savannah than a diverse and pressure-filled city, we need to take more responsibility for how we use them. We have to be smarter than to think we know the correct answers for everything and that what our brains and minds reflexively dish up into consciousness is either accurate or to the benefit of ourselves and those we live with. It is this skeptical and curious stance from which psychotherapy can be most effective.

THE UNSPOKEN CONNECTION

> *To listen well is as powerful a means of communication and influence as to talk well.*
>
> —JOHN MARSHALL

Evolution has shaped our brains into very complex social organs consisting of a government of systems that need to develop and integrate for optimal functioning. Their very complexity leads them to be extremely vulnerable to breakdowns in communication, regulation, and integration. Fortunately, neural complexity also provides us with a means of healing via interpersonal relationships; psychotherapy is one of these relationships. Although the focus in training is mostly concerned with what is said in psychotherapy, a case can be made for the equivalent value of what is silently enacted within the relationship.

Because the social synapse has a broad bandwidth including many unspoken and unconscious levels of communication, we are able to both receive and send messages that assist mutual sociostatic regulation. In the same way that different clients lead us to feel very differently from one session to the next, we also can create a state of brain and mind in our clients that can influence therapy in both positive and negative ways. Our posture, tone of voice, facial expressions, hand gestures, the pace of our breathing—to name but a few elements—are automatically transmitted across the social synapse. These signals are processed and interpreted by our clients' mirror neuron, autonomic, vagal, and attachment systems—to name another few—that are unconsciously processing their experience in the session. If we are aware of the signals we are sending, we can use them in ways that can impact our clients' ability to regulate their affect, experience trust and vulnerability, and listen and benefit from the relationship.

If therapists only pay attention to what they hear and how they should respond, they will miss at least half of the available information they are receiving and most of their ability to impact change in their clients. In the decades I've spent learning and teaching therapy, it has always been the case that therapists who can only focus on the words spoken in therapy have little access to their own inner worlds and the experience of their bodies. As I see it, this is one of the many failures of psychotherapy training that overall decreases the efficacy of treatment. Being a neurofluent therapist doesn't just consist of knowing the science; it also requires applying the science in the room with your clients.

The science shows that we are social animals, millions of years in the making, and that science and language have only arisen in the last nanosecond of human history. We need to be aware of the primitive ways in which we link to and influence one another and leverage this knowledge to the advantage of our clients. When we are agitated, uncentered, angry, or dysregulated in any way, we bring all of this energy into the consulting room with us and make it part of the session, whether or not we are aware of it or believe it to be taking place. A parallel to this lack of insight are the parents who come in to ask for help with their dysregulated children or teens and believe that the fights, affairs, and estrangements that are a part of their relationships don't impact their children. They don't want to believe that their children resonate with their emotions even if they never fight in front of them. In the exact same way, therapists want to believe they can keep their personal conflicts and emotions out of the session. The problem is, humans just don't operate that way.

9

NEUROSCIENCE IN CLINICAL ASSESSMENT

The human brain produces in 30 seconds as much data as the
Hubble Space Telescope has produced in its lifetime.

—KONRAD KORDING

As therapists, we've been trained to listen to our clients' words and to speculate on their deeper meanings and symbolic value to try and make connections to presenting symptoms and struggles. We pay attention to what our clients are able to talk about, how they talk about it, and what is excluded from their conscious awareness. We observe the process of our interactions in the form of transference, attitudes, gestures, postures, and facial expressions. And we are curious about their beliefs and attitudes about themselves and other people, as well as how adamantly these beliefs are held. The bottom line is that everything is potentially important information for us to consider.

As time has passed and I've learned more about the nervous system, I can't help but also wonder what is going on in my clients' brains. In this chapter, I explore various areas of research that inform making educated guesses about how our clients' brains have developed and organized. These ideas and methods are not meant to replace other forms of assessment, but to allow us to use the research to generate and test hypotheses based on our clinical experiences.

THE ABILITY TO MODULATE AROUSAL

There are some things you learn best in calm, and some in storm.

—WILLA CATHER

First and foremost, it is important to get a sense of a client's physiological arousal, which is a reflection of the activation of the amygdala and the circuitry designed to modulate it. We know that these core circuits affect everything from physical health, to learning, to attachment. Clients' resting level of arousal and their ability to modulate affect is a window to their genetic heritage and early developmental experiences.

Benefiting from psychotherapy requires considerable emotional regulation in client and therapist. The modulation of arousal in both parties is necessary for optimal connection, attunement, neural plasticity, and positive change. I have had clients who are so agitated that they can't remain seated, stay focused on one thought, or keep track of our conversation. Many have suffered with such high levels of arousal for so long that they have learned to hide it from others and are no longer aware of it themselves. The only visible clues for the therapist might be distractibility, physical agitation, or reports that they are unable to sleep or focus on their work. We can't necessarily rely on their reports of anxiety because they may no longer label it as such.

If you use positive visualization, yoga, or meditation in your practice, you may find that these practices don't seem to work with agitated clients. I've found that for many clients, directing them to clear their minds or focus on their breathing opens a Pandora's box of agitation, fear, and uncontrollable thoughts. Sitting quietly removes the distractions that they depend upon to stay ahead of the anxiety and fear that haunts them. The demons unleashed in any quiet moment are far worse than their usual state of anxiety and agitation. These clients often report negative and even frightening experiences after taking recreational drugs or opioid-based pain killers. The fact is, clients with anxiety and affective disorders, manic defenses, or early histories of stress and trauma sometimes have brains that are so biased toward arousal that their minds lack the leverage to calm their brains.

Neurofluency Assessment Principle 1: Assessing and understanding your clients' level of arousal and their ability to modulate it is central to all forms of psychotherapy.

Clients with a high baseline level of arousal (first executive system activation) will also have chronically inhibited second and third executive systems. It is these two systems that we have to access to use therapeutic techniques that require abstract thought, problem solving, and self-reflective capacity. With higher-level executive functioning essentially unavailable, these individuals can find themselves in exile from any soothing connection with themselves or with others. For some of these clients, useful psychotherapeutic work requires beginning with medication that successfully lowers arousal to the point where their cortex can participate in the treatment. Others are sometimes able to combine lifestyle changes such as aerobic exercise, diet, and social interactions to down-regulate their arousal. The important thing to know is that successfully addressing hyperarousal must precede addressing nonemergency psychological issues.

A helpful way to assess (and potentially treat) a client's ability to regulate arousal is to use a simple biofeedback device that measures galvanic skin response (GSR). You can buy one online for around $75. It looks like an old computer mouse with two silver strips on top and measures subtle changes in secretions of the sweat glands tied to autonomic arousal. The basic idea of biofeedback is for clients to use the tone to learn to recognize their tension and more easily achieve relaxed states of body and mind. Use it yourself to get comfortable with how it works, the experience of the tone, and changes you are able to achieve in your own arousal. You can do the relaxation techniques that work for you and monitor how well your physiological arousal matches your conscious experience of relaxation.

If you decide to use it with clients, have them lie down and get as comfortable as they can. Next, have them rest their nondominant hand on the GSR device so that their index and middle fingers rest on the two silver strips. Once they find a comfortable position and can rest their hand on the device without movement, adjust the tone to a moderate level. Start by having them become alternately tense and relaxed for five seconds at a time so that they can experience the tone change with their level of tension.

Neurofluency Assessment Principle 2: The ability to attain and sustain a moderate level of arousal is necessary for neuroplasticity, learning, and positive therapeutic change.

Clients usually find the experience of biofeedback interesting and take on the challenge. Session by session, they learn how their breathing, muscle tension, and thoughts impact their bodily tension. I sometimes use it myself between clients to help me recenter and become more relaxed, especially after a difficult session or during some life challenge. Most of us are able to learn to lower the tone over a 10- or 15-minute session. Clients often report that they are surprised by how much more relaxed they are able to become. Some even order one for themselves to use at home and work. By assessing your client's ability or inability to benefit from the GSR device, you are learning about the neurodynamics of their executive systems. Most specifically, you are learning whether they are able to leverage their second and third executive systems to downregulate and inhibit the first (amygdala) executive system.

In contrast, clients suffering with various anxiety disorders are unable to change the tone of the biofeedback device no matter how long and how hard they try. There could be many possible explanations such as medical conditions, medication side effects, or how many energy drinks they had for breakfast. Regardless of the reason, it usually indicates that contemplative techniques will likely fail. In my experience, clients like this often need some sort of biochemical intervention that downregulates amygdala activation before they are able to benefit from insight-oriented therapy.

POLYVAGAL TRANSITION

If you must break the law, do it to seize power.

—JULIUS CAESAR

At the next level of arousal regulation is the social engagement or polyvagal system, discussed in an earlier chapter. Porges hypothesized three states of arousal: (1) dorsal vagal (withdrawal, shame, shutdown); (2) sympathetic (activation, motivation, fight-flight); and (3) ventral vagal (approach, connection, self-reflection, attachment). Clients locked in despair and immobilization are disconnected from their power, anger, and assertiveness. Stuck in this dorsal vagal state, they try to move directly to a ventral vagal state (approach and connection) but find it too frightening. They will suffer with immobility and intense shame, not about anything they have done, but about their very existence.

In order to attain connection, they need first to learn how to activate their sympathetic nervous system, experience anger, discover their power, and learn to manifest it in constructive and contact-full ways. We all need to have access to our strength in order to feel safe enough to be truly close to others. Many of us, including most therapists, are frightened by our anger and power because of past experiences of rage at the hands of others. Because of this, many try to form relationships with themselves and others while avoiding any strong feelings.

These clients often suffer from difficulty establishing and maintaining boundaries, and engaging in self-care, and come with a long list of unexplained physical symptoms. The therapeutic challenge is to help them shift from playing possum to being activated, assertive, and in touch with their own power. The therapeutic relationship requires the attainment of both sympathetic and ventral vagal states for attunement and connection. Because plasticity and learning depend upon a sense of safety, shifting from a dorsal vagal to a ventral vagal state of arousal is essential for a positive outcome in psychotherapy and incorporating these gains into one's life.

Accomplishing this shift requires careful therapeutic work in combination with experiments in living focused on self-care and being assertive in the face of those we find threatening. For many people, engaging in martial arts, competitive sports, and other physical challenges serve as an interim step between depression and reconnection with the social world. It's important to teach your clients that anger in the service of attachment and protection (of both yourself and your loved ones) is the somatic foundation for developing psychological boundaries. We may need to first be able to establish boundaries in three-dimensional space as a precursor for the psychological boundaries we later develop in interpersonal relationships.

RIGHT-LEFT HEMISPHERIC PARTICIPATION

Is the brain, which is notably double in structure, a double organ,
"seeming parted, but yet a union in partition"?

—H. MAUDSLEY

After speaking with someone for a while, most of us will become aware if that person is speaking from a purely intellectual or mostly emotional perspective. When faced with a totally rational speaker, we become aware of an emotional reaction akin to being held at a distance, our bodies being shut out of the interaction. We have the urge to ask questions about how the speaker feels about what he is talking about or how he feels about anything. We have to fight to pay attention, not get bored or angry. We know there is something wrong, even if we don't know what it is. This type of communication likely reflects an underlying dissociation of emotions and an inhibition of neural networks that process the emotional aspects of communication. Our best guess is that these systems are biased toward the left frontal cortex.

> *Neurofluency Assessment Principle 3:* The level of integration and balance between the right and left hemispheres is different for each of us, and imbalances in their functioning and cooperation can be reflected in attitudes, defenses, and disconnections between emotional and cognitive processing.

In the opposite direction, speakers who are highly expressive can overwhelm us with a series of emotionally-charged stories. Our bodies react to these with a defensive stance as we try to protect ourselves from the onslaught of emotions by backing away, stiffening up, or trying to impose some sort of logical framework on the speaker. We try to help these clients compose themselves, in other words, organize their fragmented emotions into a coherent narrative. From an attachment/coherence perspective, these speakers would most likely fall into the anxiously attached group and have a neurodynamic characterized by greater amygdala (first executive system) right-hemisphere bias, while the overintellectualized clients in the previous paragraph would fall into the avoidant group and be characterized by blocked or inhibited right-hemisphere activation and be guided primarily from the task-oriented second executive system.

Communication styles biased in either of these directions reflect a lower level of neural integration of the logical, linear, and modulatory skills of the left hemisphere with the emotional and nonlinear processing characteristics of the right. Most forms of therapy address these imbalances by helping clients to become more inclusive of the functions that have been minimized or excluded from consciousness. In these situations, the client relies on the therapist's integrated brain to guide their own integration.

NARRATIVE COHERENCE

Talking much about oneself can be a means to conceal oneself.

—FRIEDRICH NIETZSCHE

Creating coherent narratives—telling stories that are understandable and relatable—is one of the brain's highest accomplishments. It requires the successful development and integration of many neural circuits from all regions of the brain dedicated to cognitive, emotional, motor, and social skills. Because the process of creating narratives is so complex, it is also fragile and vulnerable to stress and trauma during development. This is why the coherence or incoherence of a client's speech may contain valuable information about early life, attachment relationships, and brain development. Think for a moment about what is required of the brain to engage in coherent communication:

1. Expressive and receptive language networks of the left hemisphere to understand and organize verbal communication

2. Emotional language centers in the right hemisphere to provide tone, prosody, and feeling through our words

3. A theory of mind of listeners that takes into account what they know, what they don't know, and what they are able to understand

4. Mirror neuron systems that aid in attunement and connectivity, and allow us to monitor the listener's facial expressions, gestures, postures, and reactions to our words

5. Well-developed and integrated executive systems that allow us to modulate and inhibit emotional and cognitive distractions from without and within (first executive), organize linear and meaningful discourse (second executive), and be aware of ourselves and our listeners (third executive).

6. Healthy temporal-hippocampal memory networks that allow sufficient explicit and autobiographical memory storage and retrieval

Some speakers habitually make reference to people and situations of which I am unaware but don't offer me the necessary information. Others go off on tangents, linking multiple stories and side plots that leave me confused, indifferent, or emotionally numb. Consider for a moment that the ways in which discourse fails to be coherent provides us with clues about our clients' developmental history and neural functioning that is unavailable to conscious autobiographical memory. In other words, these failures of comprehension on our part may provide clues as to how their brains were shaped from the earliest moments of life and the kinds of social conditions they first adapted to. Mary Main and her colleagues developed the Adult Attachment Interview, which consists of a series of open-ended questions about childhood relationship experiences.

Neurofluency Assessment Principle 4: Generating understandable narratives is a complex achievement which
reflects the development and integration of many cognitive,
emotional, and executive neural networks.

Instead of examining the content of the responses, they used a
linguistic measure of coherence that rated how easy or difficult it
was for the listener to understand and believe the stories. This analysis takes into account the integration of emotional and experiential
materials, gaps in memory and information, and the overall quality
of the presentation. Coherence analysis was based on Grice's maxims, which are (1) quality: be truthful, and have evidence for what
you say; (2) quantity: be succinct, and yet complete; (3) relevance:
stick to the topic at hand; and (4) manner: be clear, orderly, and
brief. Main and her colleagues found that individuals with secure
and insecure attachment schemata produced different types of narratives, which reflect the interwoven nature of psychological, social,
and neurobiological development.

Secure Attachment/Coherent Narratives

Parents of securely attached children created coherent narratives with
more vivid and detailed memories. The emotions they expressed
and adjectives they used were congruent with and supportive of the
content of their stories. They presented a realistic and balanced perspective of their parents and childhoods and were able to express
negative feelings without being emotionally overwhelmed. This
type of coherent presentation in an adult client usually means that
their current difficulties are more likely the result of experiences
after childhood and they are likely to have solid development and
integration of the six neural systems described above. Their issues in
therapy are usually around relationship challenges, stressful experiences, or specific blind spots related to their personality style.

As they grow, securely attached infants engage in self-talk and become self-reflective. These processes of mind that require the second and third executive systems allow for increased affect regulation, cognitive oversight, and coherent discourse. The cognitive, emotional, and neural integration these abilities reflect make us better able to process stressful and traumatic experiences and benefit from therapy. Not surprisingly, parents' emotional insight and availability to themselves appear to parallel their emotional availability to their children. My sense interacting with these folks is that their three executive systems are all online and well integrated.

Avoidant Attachment/Incoherent Narratives

A second group of parents, those who tended to have avoidant children, had narratives characterized by significant gaps in memory for important events during childhood. The memories they did have were often constructed based on family photographs and stories told by others. My assumption is that this group suffered from chronic stress during childhood, which interfered with (1) the consolidation of episodic memory, (2) the development of temporal-hippocampal memory systems, and (3) their third executive system. Their dismissive attitude toward their children and relationships in general likely paralleled their experiences with their parents.

Such people's defenses tend to be forms of denial, avoidance, and intellectualization, and they stand firmly in their left hemispheres and are often analytical and emotionally distant. Interacting with others creates considerable discomfort, and they often experience relationships as a burden. Transference will focus on a lack of trust in the therapist's abilities and motivations, as they rely heavily on their personal rules to navigate relationships and often have a strong negative reaction to those who don't. The lack of recall and black-and-white thinking of the dismissing parent likely reflect blocked and unintegrated neural coherence.

Neurofluency Assessment Principle 5: Clients who lack significant detail in autobiographical memory tend to have dis-
missive/avoidant attachment styles, experienced high levels
of arousal as children, and experience challenges in their
emotional functioning.

Anxious Attachment/Incoherent Narratives

A third group, described as anxious or enmeshed, tended to produce disjointed, tangential, and emotion-driven narratives. It was as
if they were unsettled by their own words. There was an absence of
self-awareness, monitoring what they were saying, and keeping the
perspective of the listener in mind. It is likely that their chronically
high levels of anxiety result in inhibited second and third executive systems and lead them to have difficulty problem solving in the
outer world and to experience a disconnection from themselves and
others. They exhibit a lack of clear boundaries between the past and
present, and continue to be preoccupied with their parents.

As clients, these individuals have difficulty maintaining interpersonal boundaries and produce a flood of words that can often make
conversation impossible. The initial challenge facing the therapist is
to discover a way to help them decrease their arousal and anxiety.
The next challenge is to get them to talk less and say more, to think
as well as feel, and help them refocus from the past to the present.

Neurofluency Assessment Principle 6: Clients with narratives that are overinclusive and tangential often have anxious attachment schema and have difficulty regulating their
emotions.

Disorganized Attachment/Incoherent Narratives

The last group had highly incoherent narratives that were disrupted
by both emotional intrusions and fragmented information. Their
narratives were characterized by an overabundance of unfiltered

content. It appeared that their emotional dysregulation resulted in pressured speech that led them to say things that further dysregulated them. The content of their childhood narratives spoke to unresolved trauma and grief, consistent with their inability to organize their narratives while under the stress of recalling their childhoods. Of all of the groups, these individuals demonstrated the most vivid connection between early stress, the development of executive function, and the ability to generate coherent narratives.

Overall, this research highlights the transfer of attachment schemata across generations and the ways in which the coherence of adult narratives reflects early stress and brain organization as well as attachment schemata. In essence, narrative coherence can be thought of as parallel to neural coherence. To whatever extent this assumption holds true, findings from these studies are all potentially applicable to the assessment of our clients' brains and minds in psychotherapy. While the content of explicit memories is highly malleable and vulnerable to distortion, the memories of our early life, embedded within our neurobiology, are highly resistant to change. The nature and quality of our discourse may be one of the best and most accurate retrospective measures of early experience.

EARLY ABUSE AND LANGUAGE IMPAIRMENT

> *Every word, facial expression, gesture, or action on the part of a parent gives the child some message about self-worth.*
>
> —VIRGINIA SATIR

Epigenetic research suggests that early trauma and abuse can have a negative impact on the development of receptive and expressive language systems. This may correspond to reports of learning difficulties and impairments in occupational and relationship functioning based on missed cues and misunderstood communications. It may also lead people to have difficulties benefiting from talk therapy, especially if their verbal abilities are far below their other intellectual skills, making the language deficits easier to miss.

With clients like these, you may have to be especially careful in the choice of words, the pacing of your speech, and monitoring their facial expressions for signs of not comprehending what you are saying or drifting off. People with receptive language difficulties often fill in the blanks of what they miss and say that they understand you when they don't. Having frank process conversations about your ability to track one another in therapy can open the door to deeper disclosure as well as helping you work together to overcome this challenge to communication.

Neurofluency Assessment Principle 7: Clients who have experienced trauma and sustained stress may experience difficulties in both receptive and expressive language.

In addition to the impact of early stress on neurodevelopmental development, current stress can lead to the inhibition of Broca's area, resulting in a transient aphasia or the classic speechless terror of PTSD. These data suggest that difficulties in fluidity of speech and comprehension can be indications of early stress and trauma as well as a client's current state of arousal.

POLITICAL AND PARANORMAL BELIEFS

> *It's always been of great survival value for people to believe they belong to a superior tribe.*
>
> —E. O. WILSON

Politics and the paranormal have always occupied regions of my mind distant from my interests in neuroscience. Given how contentious both of these issues can become, it seems clear that they are tapping into something ancient about how our brains are wired. Beginning with our political views, a number of studies have explored the neurobiological differences of those with conservative and liberal ideologies. Thus far, studies have shown that liberals have more gray matter and demonstrate greater activation in their anterior cingulate cortices in decision-making settings, whereas conservatives have more gray matter and increased activation in their right amygdala, and a larger left insula.

Neurofluency Assessment Principle 8: People with conservative and liberal political beliefs have differences in neuroanatomical activation and patterns of thinking that may be helpful in understanding, communicating, and treating our clients.

Based on these differences, you would predict that conservatives would experience greater risk aversion and feel more frightened by strangers and the unknown. Research from social psychology has shown that conservatives are more structured (black and white) and persistent (less influenced by new information) in their thinking. Political strategists know about these tendencies and use them during campaigns. Higher amygdala activation inhibits functioning of the third executive system, which would correlate with decreased theory of mind, decreased sympathy and empathy for those who make conservative people anxious (evil people, terrorists, immigrants, etc.), and being more responsive to calls for protection against external threats (greater military strength and more border walls). By contrast, with their greater anterior cingulate activation and the caretaking role it plays, liberals are more responsive to political messages of fairness, inclusion, and turning enemies into friends.

Thus, a client's political leanings can give us an idea of the relative balance of their three executive systems, their self-reflective capacity, and their ability to tolerate ambiguity and the unknown. This information can assist in choosing structured versus unstructured interventions. Conservatives are likely to benefit from more specific and directive forms of therapy, while liberals may be better suited to insight-oriented and relational approaches. Conservatives may also require longer periods of relationship and trust building at the beginning of therapy but may be more connected and committed once the relationship is established. Beneath the tough-talking hawk may lie a fear of danger from the unknown, while liberals may have more trouble with establishing personal boundaries, codependency, and adequate self-care.

Turning our attention those who report paranormal experiences and beliefs, I have had many clients who frequent psychics and believe in astral projection, time travel, and telepathic abilities. Although none have been psychotic, all suffered from symptoms of anxiety and depression, and reported chronic early stress and childhood traumas. Because of this fairly consistent pattern, I've come to see paranormal beliefs and practices as potentially informative about the impact of stress and trauma during a client's development.

The biochemistry of traumatic stress during childhood results in the developing brain having a larger and more active amygdala, smaller and less competent hippocampi, and higher resting levels of cortisol, adrenaline, dopamine, and endogenous opioids. These changes lead to greater levels of fear and anxiety coupled with decreased reality testing and problem-solving skills. These factors lead victims to be guided primarily by their first executive system and the primary process thinking of childhood. As they develop, they are also more likely to accept and create paranormal explanations to make sense of their exaggerated, distorted, and overwhelming experiences.

None of my clients who had strongly held paranormal beliefs

associated them with their childhood challenges. A man I saw for social anxiety believed that he could travel through time. He also told me that his mother beat him every day from the time he was an infant until his 14th birthday, when he asked her to stop. "Sure! I thought you liked it," she replied. Another client, a woman in her 30s with a firm conviction of her telepathic abilities shared with me that when she was 8, she was sitting on the sofa next to her baby brother when she heard a gunshot and then saw the TV explode. When she was able to focus on her brother, she could see that the bullet that had come through the wall and destroyed the TV had also shattered his tiny head. As an adult, she suffered from anxiety, panic attacks, agoraphobia, and a conviction that she could read minds and predict the future.

Neurofluency Assessment Principle 9: During development, trauma and sustained high levels of stress create imbalances in neuroanatomical and biochemical development that make victims more vulnerable to perseveration of the magical thinking of childhood and to paranormal experiences and beliefs later in life.

The symbolic value of escaping abuse by traveling through time and maintaining psychic connection in the face of overwhelming loss are clear. While defenses take many forms, I think that paranormal beliefs and experiences reflect underlying brain development and may provide us with a window to a client's past. Keep in mind that in many cultures, paranormal explanations for events may be more socially influenced and may not represent evidence of early trauma. However, early trauma occurs across all cultures, and clients' adherence to paranormal explanations may still hold valuable information about their early history.

SELF-REFLECTIVE CAPACITY AND AN INTERNAL WORLD

In the madness, you have to find calm.

—LUPITA NYONG'O

Self-reflective capacity is a complex evolutionary and developmental accomplishment. It requires a theory of mind, awareness of one's emotional and somatic state, and the ability to see ourselves as others might—a kind of self-objectification. It also relies on our ability to regulate our emotions enough to tolerate seeing ourselves without the filters and defenses that calm our anxieties. Having an internal world means a number of things. The first is that we have a continuous sense of self through time. As we grow older, we retain a sense of continuity with our past selves. The second is that we are able to still our minds and bodies for periods of time and experience a sense of coherence in the present moment. The third is that we create and are able to access an internal imaginary world to use as a strategic retreat from everyday life to consider our lives from a bit of a distance. At its essence, it is the ability to be self-possessed and self-aware, and to become the CEO of our life.

As someone who developed these abilities early in life, I naturally assumed that self-reflective capacity and an inner world were universal. It took me years to realize that many people never developed them because they grew up surrounded by people who either never had them or who never thought to share them with their children. Still others live in exile from themselves because of the effects of stress, trauma, or brain damage. A sense of an inner self is not something we are born with, but is created over many years. It begins with growing up within a family and culture that treats you as if you have an internal world by demonstrating curiosity about what you are thinking, feeling, and experiencing. We often see that the children of narcissistic parents enter adulthood with little sense of self but an elaborate sense of others. This is shaped by caretakers who have no curiosity about their children but instead see them as extensions of their own needs.

Neurofluency Assessment Principle 10: The ability to create, visit, and revisit a safe and quiet internal world can be a source of affect regulation, self-identity, imagination, problem solving, and creativity.

Clients who don't have a sense of self usually experience crushing shame that they attempt to control through perfectionism or obliterate via distractions and addictions. They are often unaware of how they feel about things, what they like, or what they want to do. They have learned not to have an opinion, be assertive, or leave a mark of any kind. These clients often come to therapy because of depression, anxiety, and physical illnesses, locked into dorsal vagal states. Instead of being self-reflective, they live in the heads of others and think of themselves as they fear others think of them. The neurodynamics of this clinical presentation, like many others, rest in the dominance of the primitive executive system, which hinders the development of the other two executive networks that are required to cultivate reflection and internality. The second executive needs to be able to competently navigate the external world to allow for the luxury of disconnecting from the world. The third executive is then free to develop a sense of self and an inner world.

You can assess whether clients have an internal world by what they say and don't say about themselves, their relationships, and their daily experiences. Those who live outside of themselves have externally biased motivations and concerns, and don't address subjective experience when describing their relationships and careers. I'll often ask clients what they are thinking about when they are silent during a session, or ask them a question like, "When you're alone on a quiet Sunday afternoon, what thoughts cross your mind?" If they say something like, "That never happens," I usually press a bit and ask the same question in a few different ways. You will see that they have to stay active and distracted to avoid becoming anxious and depressed and will often lack the capacity to be alone.

If you come to realize that a client seems devoid of subjectivity and lacks an internal world, and you think having one might be helpful for her to have these abilities, you may want to try and help her build one. I usually start with some kind of focused body work to increase self-awareness. I then work with her to build an imaginal safe space to retreat to and relax. Whether this proves helpful depends upon her ability to manage the anxiety and fear it will uncover, her imaginal abilities, and your creativity in finding a way to engage in this experiment in living.

10

BUILDING A CASE
CONCEPTUALIZATION

Medicine is a science of uncertainty and an art of probability.
—WILLIAM OSLER

Although the biopsychosocial model has been around for many decades, the biological component has been poorly developed in psychotherapeutic training and practice. In case reports, it is usually limited to a section titled Medical History focusing on physical illnesses, medication use, and known neurological damage—essentially the same as a half-century ago. Compare this to the contributions diversity studies have made to case conceptualizations and treatment over the same period. Issues of cultural background, acculturation, and the possible psychological impact of prejudice and injustice have become essential components of a good case conceptualization.

My hope is that the biological aspects of the biopsychosocial triad—the contributions of evolution, brain development, neuroscience, and genetics—will gain a broader understanding, appreciation, and integration into the field of psychotherapy. If this way of thinking is to take hold, there is much exploration and experimentation ahead. A key piece will be to see how we can integrate what we know of brain-behavior relationships into the psychological and social concepts we understand and use every day. Before we focus on a deeper exploration of the biological aspects of psychotherapy, let's review the broad focus of a case conceptualization into which the science can be integrated. I'm assuming that this has already been a core aspect of your training, so I present the barest of outlines here as a context for expanding the biological component we are focusing on.

TEN STEPS TO A BALANCED CASE CONCEPTUALIZATION

1. **Orientation:** A case conceptualization is grounded within a theoretical orientation (CBT, psychodynamic, humanistic/existential, etc.) that organizes your understanding of your client within theories of mental health, mental illness, and theories of positive change that emerge from your chosen conceptualization.

2. **Target problems:** Target problems will include your client's presenting problems, difficulties with other symptoms reported by your client or demonstrated in sessions, and other challenges that may be the focus of treatment.

3. **Biological issues:** This is where your neurofluency comes in and focuses on brain development and integration, the production and coherence of language, the quality and balance of executive systems, and potential neurodevelopmental issues related to trauma, neglect, or chronic anxiety. Also included here are the traditional biological considerations including medical issues, medication side effects, and history of brain damage.

4. **Psychological issues:** This includes symptoms, defenses, coping strategies, core beliefs, attitudes, spiritual beliefs, meaning, sources of inspiration, resiliency, areas of strength, and so on.

5. **Social issues:** Includes things such as social skills, engagement, and support, attachment style, culture, acculturation, family dynamics, prejudice, social attitudes, and so on. It might also be helpful to the client to have others (spouse, friends, siblings, parents, etc.) involved in assessment and treatment.

6. **Assessment:** What do I need to know that I could use help to find out (psychological, cognitive, neuropsychological, and medical evaluation)? What more can I learn from the information already available to me (see Chapter 11)?

7. **Collaboration:** What other professionals and nonprofessionals (if any) should be enlisted to the treatment team? These could include relatives, sponsors, teachers, coaches, religious advisors, other therapists with specialties, friends, and so on.

8. **The relationship:** This might include transference and countertransference reactions based on the client's and therapist's personal histories, or therapist-client differences such as race, personality, culture, attitudes, age, gender, and so on.

9. **Treatment goals:** These are the shared goals—short, middle, and long term—agreed to by the client and therapist. The therapist can also articulate other goals to be discussed with the client after the initial treatment goals have been reached.

10. **Strategies and tactics:** Strategies are the overarching therapeutic logistics for treatment. For CBT these would include uncovering and modifying negative core beliefs, while for a Gestalt therapist they could include expanded awareness across thinking, feeling, and sensing. The tactics would be the specific intervention techniques utilized in implementing your strategy. A CBT therapist might use the tactics of rational questioning of a negative core belief, while the Gestalt therapist might use the empty chair technique to expand a client's awareness to include another part of his or her experience.

Once you take all of these factors into account, the next step is to consider how each of the categories may affect the others. For example, a client with intellectual defenses and a considerable bias toward left-hemisphere processing may feel more comfortable with a cognitive-oriented therapy but may benefit more from a somatic form of treatment. A somatic treatment would create more anxiety but would have the opportunity of expanding the client's awareness and the integration of neural systems responsible for affect and cognition. As another example, if you are seeing clients from another culture, your assessment may include learning more about their background and the meaning of their symptoms within their culture as opposed to administering psychological assessments that may not be appropriate for them. You may need to collaborate with professionals who understand how to embed your client's symptoms in a culturally appropriate context. Culture builds the brain, and the mind emerges from both.

THE BIOPSYCHOSOCIAL TRIAD

People are very complex.

—DANIEL KAHNEMAN

Thinking of the brain as a social organ of adaptation, we can frame the biopsychosocial model as a developing brain, built by relationships within a culture, which results in the emergence of mind and psychological experience. If we think about fleshing out a biopsychosocial model in the context of psychotherapy, we have some common assumptions about the psychological and social aspects based on a century of theory, research, and practice. The social aspects of experience focus on multigenerational family history, attachment relationships, cultural context, and ongoing social embeddedness and support. The psychological consists of personality, core beliefs, self-esteem, defenses, coping strategies, and symptoms. The biopsychosocial nature of being human means that all three of these columns are interwoven, so don't be surprised if you find your mind sliding across categories. That just means you're paying attention. The following table is a brief list of some aspects of a client's life within each category.

Some Biopsychosocial Aspects of a Client's Life Included in a Case Conceptualization

Biological	Psychological	Social
Arousal and affect regulation	Symptoms	Family history
	Core beliefs	Attachment schema
Self-reflection and empathy	Coping strategies	Family dynamics
Executive integration	Defenses	Social embeddedness
Narrative coherence	Symptoms	Social support
Traumatic adaptation	Self-esteem	Culture and acculturation
Social status		

THE BIOPSYCHOSOCIAL MODEL IN ACTION

In complexity are the fringes of beauty, and in variety are generosity and exuberance.

—ANNIE DILLARD

The task at hand is to begin the process of determining what ideas we can get about a client's brain within the context of our clinical interactions, and how it might help us improve diagnosis and treatment. Instead of talking about these issues in theory, I want to describe my work with my client Michael. I'll present him to you as I might bring a case to supervision. Along the way, I will share the clinical and scientific principles that help guide my thinking and how I weave them into my ideas about assessment, case conceptualization, and treatment. In line with what we have already discussed, I approach my work with Michael from a general psychodynamic perspective while adhering to Rogerian principles to set the tone of the therapeutic relationship.

As I listen and get to know Michael, I will be thinking within a developmental framework, exploring associations among his childhood experiences and his present adaptation, behaviors, and symptoms. I will be thinking in terms of his attachment history, how his early experiences shaped his brain, and how these early experiences shape how he perceives and interacts with his world in the present. In addition to listening to the content of what he is saying, I will be assessing the interpersonal processes within the transference to see how his past experiences with authority get played out in our relationship. I'll also be listening to the coherence of his narratives to get a sense of the development and integration of his executive systems and which functions may be impaired.

In addition to the challenges I will present within our relationship, I will cocreate experiments in living with him, with the goals of decreasing anxiety, stress, and negative arousal, thus increasing his neuroplastic abilities and setting the stage for positive change. Think of experiments in living as a shorthand for the ways in which a client takes the work of therapy out into the world to generalize and solidify its positive effects. These experiments consist of engaging in new behaviors, ways of thinking, and other activities that have been avoided out of habit, anxiety, or lack of knowledge. The goal of these experiments is to give clients experiences that expand their behavioral repertoire and teach their brains and minds that their anxiety and avoidance are unnecessary for survival in their current lives.

MICHAEL

The hand that rocks the cradle is the hand that rules the world.

—WILLIAM ROSS WALLACE

When we met, Michael was a 30-year-old, single male trainee in a master's-level psychotherapy program, one of eight students in a weekly group supervision. Of otherwise average appearance, he nonetheless stood out from his peers for not wanting to stand out at all. His slouching posture and avoidance of eye contact made it seem that he was trying his best to stay off everyone's radar. He was deferential to a fault, apologized at every opportunity, and gave the impression that he would prefer to be completely invisible. Liked by some and tolerated by others, he seldom volunteered information about himself or stayed around to socialize after class, stirring speculation by his imaginative peers about his secret life as a Russian operative.

It soon became clear that he was struggling in his clinical work. He had difficulty keeping clients and trouble treating those who stayed with him. We had plenty of helpful technical suggestions for Michael, but it was clear to all of us, including Michael, that his challenges weren't technical in nature. While he was very good at understanding his clients' problems and formulating a treatment plan, he found it difficult to speak at all with his clients. Watching the videos of his sessions was torturous for all involved, and Michael shared that he dreaded every session. It was painfully clear that he needed to address his emotional difficulties if he was ever to become an effective therapist.

It seemed clear that Michael's problems as a therapist centered around his terror of his clients. He was so frightened, in fact, that he could hardly speak when sitting face-to-face with them. When words did come, he sounded so confused that one of his professors thought he might be suffering with a thought disorder. Michael had shared with the class that his mother had been diagnosed with schizophrenia, so this was a possibility to consider. But with his thinking so clear in his academic work and with no other symptoms of psychosis at age 30, my initial hypothesis was that his speechlessness was a kind of transient aphasia caused by fear and hyperarousal. It sounded more like a posttraumatic reaction disrupting his usually good cognitive processing rather than a thought disorder or psychotic process, a theory grounded in neuroscience research.

In addition to his difficulty speaking, Michael also found himself utterly confused. While he was as intelligent as anyone in his class, his ability to think abstractly or solve problems seemed to abandon him in the consultation room. He described the experience to be as if his brain had turned off, making it impossible for him to think about what to do or remember what we had discussed in supervision. The inability to speak or engage in higher-level thinking can be related to the ability of our fear circuitry to inhibit executive networks and language regions of the cerebral cortex. The amygdala sits at the apex of our primitive executive brain, which controls our fear response to stress and danger, both real and imaginary. This primitive executive has the ability to inhibit another executive network—the parietal-frontal executive—on which we rely for language, problem solving, and higher-level thinking. This is why what we have learned can become unavailable to us during a test if test anxiety triggers our amygdala and inhibits our cortical networks.

One day after supervision, Michael approached me with exasperation. He couldn't understand why he knew what to do when we discussed it but couldn't remember anything in sessions. "If I didn't know better, I'd think I was having a stroke," Michael said. "Bruce [another student overflowing with psychodynamic interpretations] suggested that I'm sabotaging my career because I don't think I deserve to succeed. What do you think?" After a pause I replied, "It's altogether possible, but the life of the mind is complicated and difficult to account for with a single cliché." Michael smiled with appreciation. He slowly came to trust me during our supervision sessions and, following graduation, requested that I see him as a client in psychotherapy. Even before he started treatment, I had already begun to develop hypotheses about what was happening in Michael's brain and how it might be interwoven with his behavior. In this chapter, I describe my initial therapeutic interactions with Michael and discuss my thoughts and case conceptualization as they evolved.

THERAPY BEGINS

> *The little child that peeped in at the door and then drew back and was never seen again.*
>
> —WALT WHITMAN

During our first sessions, I learned that Michael left home for college at age 18. While a successful student, he described himself as a "social failure" who couldn't feel comfortable around others. His few attempts at friendship fell flat, and he came to believe that he was an essentially unlikable person. By his sophomore year, he fell into a daily routine of isolation and described his college experiencing as "sleepwalking" for four years. He had very few memories of college. In fact, he found it difficult to share detailed memories about much of anything from his past. It was clear he wanted to, but when he tried, he told me that his memory banks were mostly empty.

At 30, Michael had yet to have an intimate relationship and was uncertain about his sexual orientation, or whether he had one at all. His only sexual experience was with a prostitute during college, which he found so unsettling that he came to question his attraction to women. After graduation, he resisted his parents' suggestion to return home and moved to Los Angeles. After many unsuccessful job interviews, he signed up with a temp agency and was eventually hired for a full-time clerical position. For five years he continued "sleepwalking" through his daily routine when he realized that he was going nowhere and decided to go back to school. He eventually enrolled in the therapy training program where I was a professor. Michael told me, "At the very least, becoming a therapist might help me figure out my parents." The thought of going to therapy himself didn't occur to him.

As I got to know Michael, I found out that his mother stayed at home with him, and his father was an engineer in the oil business. Michael described his father as a man who lived by the rules. He left for work the same time every morning (7:45 a.m.) and arrived home at exactly the same time every afternoon (5:25 p.m.). As Michael's mother would tell him, "You can set your clock by that man!" Michael then said something about his father that broke my heart: "He never let having a son get in the way of his work." It was during college that Michael came to realize, "I'm living my father's life. Whatever is wrong with him is wrong with me. No wonder no one likes me!"

Michael had no memory of his father expressing feelings or talking with him about anything but work. They only saw each other during meals, after which his father would go to his desk and work until he went to bed. His mother, usually preoccupied with chores and various projects, would occasionally talk "at" him for hours. Michael described these talks by saying, "I almost never understood anything she said. I just sat there like a frozen robot. I was afraid to move or say anything for fear that she would get upset and never talk to me again." She apparently gave him the silent treatment for days if he upset her in any way. It's not surprising that Michael decided to become a therapist; by the time he started his training, he already had decades of reading and responding to the thoughts and feelings of two troubled people. The image of a frozen robot stuck in my mind, and I wondered if that's what Michael experienced when face-to-face with his clients.

A PAINFUL HISTORY

Trauma is a fact of life. It does not, however, have to be a life sentence.

—PETER LEVINE

For most of his childhood, Michael's family moved around the Middle East, following his father's work. Although they lived in many houses, what he remembered most is that they lived "behind walls," and that it was always "hotter than hell." It was behind these walls where Michael grew up with no siblings, peers, or family friends. "My mother was too embarrassed to have friends, and my father couldn't imagine why you would want any." Michael's isolation was vast; beyond his parents, there was essentially no contact with the outside world. Their strange and isolated universe contained his only points of reference for reality.

Particularly painful to learn about was the family's daily routine during his childhood. After his father left for work, Michael's mother would gather up his toys, bring them into her room, and lock the door behind her. He could hear her talking to someone but could never make out what she was saying. Michael would spend the entire day alone without toys, television, or anything to do. These were the hours during which he was supposedly being homeschooled by his mother. A few minutes before his father came home each day, his mother would emerge from her room and put Michael's toys back in place. When he arrived, she would excitedly describe all the schoolwork they had done and the games they had played together. Michael spent his evenings in bewildered silence, sad, confused, and not knowing what to believe. He once tried to tell his father what happened during the day, but he was punished for lying and his mother didn't speak to him for a week. Michael told me, "My father was so weird himself, he couldn't see how crazy she was."

Although his mother only had a few serious psychotic episodes requiring hospitalization, she consistently suffered with symptoms associated with schizophrenia. Besides whatever delusional beliefs and hallucinations guided her daily rituals, Michael witnessed her tangential, pressured speech and withdrawal from the world on a daily basis.

Michael described to me how desperate he was to find some comfort during his eternally long days. Sometimes, despite the blistering heat, he would go outside and lie under the car to break up the monotony of being in the house. Without access to his actual toys, he would make toys out of objects from around the house and think up games to pass the time. He knew from experience that if his mother discovered a toy he had made, it would be included in her toy roundup each morning, so any toys he made had to remain a secret. His resiliency and creativity in the face of such soul-crushing conditions amazed me.

As we talked about his childhood during our third session, a gentle smile came over his face. When I asked him if he could share with me why he was smiling, he replied, "I'm thinking about a brick," and continued to look wistfully at a scene in his mind's eye. With a devilish grin, he began to describe how he tricked his mother by making a doll out of a brick. "I'd get a small towel from the bathroom and a magic marker from the kitchen drawer and bring them to the backyard. I would take one of the bricks that lined the walk and clean the dirt off. Then I would take the magic marker and draw a face on it, wrap it in the towel, and make believe it was a doll." As Michael described his doll-making method, the tone of his voice, the words he used, and his facial expressions shifted to those of a young boy. This image was locked into his early memory and seemed a true window to the innocence of his childhood.

Michael told me that he would rock and talk to his "baby" for hours, giving it what he so badly needed. "I would tell him he was safe and that someday everything would be okay." Somehow, having this doll to take care of gave him a feeling of efficacy and a sense of a future that would someday be better than the present. This appears to have been a central part of his coping strategy; deny his own needs, take care of others, hold on tight—very tight—and wait for something better. Each afternoon, he would tell his baby to go to sleep and promise he would see him soon. He would then unwrap him, place him back face down along the path, and return the towel and marker. His mother was never the wiser. "My father had his schedule, my mother had hers, and I had mine." His relationship with this brick doll would become a metaphor for both his challenges in forming human relationships and his incredible survival instincts.

BUILDING A CASE CONCEPTUALIZATION WITH THE BRAIN IN MIND

> *The important thing in science is not so much to obtain new facts as to discover new ways of thinking about them.*
>
> —SIR WILLIAM LAWRENCE BRAGG

With what we know thus far, we can begin to form a case conceptualization. It includes the hypothesized causes of mental health and mental illness, and the mechanisms of action in the healing process from a particular perspective. As a psychodynamic therapist, my conceptualization will revolve around Michael's developmental challenges, suboptimal adaptations of thinking, feeling, relating, and behavior, and the symptoms that have resulted.

At the center of Michael's presenting symptomatology was his reaction to his clients in the consulting room. While his difficulty with clients was extreme, it was obvious from his behavior with his peers that it was far from an isolated problem. There was little doubt that he suffered with some form of social anxiety, poor social skills, and what looked like a dismissive/avoidant attachment style. While there were no obvious cultural issues to consider, he seemed very out of step with his peers, and I had noticed during supervision sessions that he often missed references from popular culture. It was as if he were unacculturated to what everyone assumed to be his own culture. In some ways, he lacked a culture and a cultural identity, rather than having a secret life.

Psychological

> *You gain strength, courage, and confidence by every experience in which you look fear in the face.*
>
> —ELEANOR ROOSEVELT

A psychodynamic conceptualization attempts to associate negative emotional experiences in childhood with what is considered to be their symptomatic expression in adulthood. From this framework, the nature of Michael's early history stands out as both unusual and extreme. The avoidant attachment we see during his adulthood is most likely a perseveration of his early adaptation to the combination of distant, dismissing, and bizarre interactions with his parents. He had almost no positive socialization with peers or adults, and it is clear that he experienced a great deal of anxiety in his interactions with both his parents, especially his mother. It makes sense, as a working hypothesis, to think of his panic-like reactions when sitting face-to-face with clients as a form of countertransference triggered by implicit memories of his difficult and stressful talks with his mother. His conscious goal of becoming a therapist was likely driven by his need to heal his mother, heal himself, and learn to connect with others within the safe confines of the therapeutic relationship.

His developmental history, which had shaped the networks of his implicit memory, remained fixed. In essence, his early experiences shaped the architecture of the brain systems he now relied on to comprehend and navigate the world. Although we may list his panic symptoms along with his anxiety, depression, and relational problems separately on an intake form, they are part of an interwoven developmental process. Because all of these symptoms exist within the interactive matrix of his moment-to-moment experience, comprehending them all as mutually reinforcing is integral to understanding and helping Michael.

Biological

> *The biology of mind bridges the sciences—concerned with the natural world—and the humanities—concerned with the meaning of human experience.*
>
> —ERIC KANDEL

For Michael, we can start with the working hypothesis that any and all of his regulatory systems may function in a less than optimal manner. His retreat from the world may be a general avoidance strategy to keep his arousal at a manageable level. Keeping his own counsel, avoiding socializing with his classmates, and even his reported sleepwalking through his college years may all reflect behavioral strategies to compensate for his biological and psychological vulnerabilities.

For the biological component of the biopsychosocial model, he was in general good health, was not on any medication, and reported no medical illnesses. We have to consider the potential genetic risk of schizophrenia and possibly autism but currently lack enough support for either of these being a significant concern. I have already mentioned a couple of biological processes that may be relevant, including the inhibition of language and executive function under stress, and autobiographical memory deficits associated with a dismissive attachment style. The relevance of these factors to treatment may include (1) interruptions of language fluency as an indication of increased arousal, (2) difficulties in applying what is discussed in therapy to experiences outside of therapy, and (3) complex challenges in the transference relationship.

A neurodynamic framework examines how the brain is built during infancy, childhood, and adolescence in the process of adaptation to our social and physical worlds. The biological and neuroanatomical consequences of these adaptations continue into adulthood, determining the nature and quality of experience. In Michael's case, early attachment challenges likely resulted in a spectrum of epigenetic processes that impacted biochemical set points, the development of social brain systems, and the balance and integration of his executive systems. For example, Michael likely suffers from higher than normal levels of adrenaline and cortisol, which make him more likely to react with anxiety and fear in stressful situations.

Michael's panic reactions to his clients were his brain's attempt to protect him from the pain of human contact. The timing gap between the fast and slow systems helps us to understand why so many of us continue in old, ineffective patterns of behavior, despite conscious efforts to change. The fact that so much of our conscious experience is based on unconscious brain processing makes us extremely vulnerable to misperceptions and misinformation that our minds assume to be true, leading us to behave in repetitive and stereotyped patterns.

From Michael's perspective, the conditioning grounded in his early experience led to the perpetuation of the fear and isolation of his childhood—except that it was no longer being imposed on him as a dependent child. He was now creating his suffering himself while being an autonomous adult. (This type of insight isn't only the domain of Buddhism. It would fit well in rational-emotive therapy, CBT, and many others.) His brain and mind were remembering his pain from childhood and re-creating it in the present. This fooled him into experiencing others as dangerous to him as his parents once were. Whether you call this intrusive memory, ignorance, or suffering, the result is the same. Michael was being controlled by a reality that no longer existed. In Buddhist terms, he was suffering from an illusion. A neuroscientist might say that he was being fooled by unintegrated implicit memories. A CBT therapist would describe it as being controlled by an inaccurate core belief.

11

NEUROFLUENCY IN PSYCHOTHERAPY

The historic ascent of humanity . . . may be summarized as a
succession of victories of consciousness over blind forces—in nature,
in society, in man himself.

—LEON TROTSKY

Among other things, psychotherapy is a delicate blend of human connection and scientific exploration. In the process of establishing a warm, trusting, and supportive relationship, we gather information, generate and test hypotheses, and develop interventions to support positive change. While our heads contain information and ideas related to the science of what we are doing, communication with our clients is framed within the context of wisdom. Information is made up of facts and ideas; wisdom is information wrapped in understanding and empathy, to nurture, develop, and heal.

As we transitioned from supervision to therapy, the nature of my relationship with Michael gradually settled into this new therapeutic frame. He was no longer concerned that being open and honest would negatively impact his career, and I was relieved from the obligation of evaluating his clinical performance. This allowed me to shift entirely to a position of warmth, support, and unconditional positive regard. Within the privacy of the consulting room, we moved ahead.

WORKING THROUGH

All the world is full of suffering. It is also full of overcoming.
—HELEN KELLER

My time with Michael was long, difficult, and very rewarding. Because his defenses tended to be more intellectual, he was suspicious of psychodynamic theories and emotional expression and was much more open to CBT terminology and interventions. Early on, we began our work with techniques and strategies focused on relaxation and affect regulation. I began by using biofeedback (described in Chapter 9), then moved on to visual imagery and breathing techniques. While the surface focus was to help Michael stay regulated when sitting across from a client, these techniques also served the immediate function of helping him be more present, emotionally available, and better able to benefit from therapy. During our sessions, we would reverse therapist-client roles for 5 or 10 minutes at a time so he could practice pairing relaxation techniques and thinking clinically.

During some of our sessions, I played a hybrid therapist-supervisor role, getting him to shuttle back and forth between affect regulation and cognition—feeling and thinking, right and left hemisphere, cortex and limbic system—to increase his functional neural integration. This worked well as we processed his anxiety symptoms in the context of a biological understanding of how his arousal impacted his ability to problem solve, think abstractly, and connect with others. The explanation of the three executive systems was central to our work at that time. As he learned to apply these techniques with his clients, he found that he was increasingly able to access knowledge to think about his clients during his sessions. He found these incremental successes inspiring, and he began to have hope that he could also change in significant ways outside of therapy.

A month into my work with Michael, it became clear that he struggled with depressed thoughts, hopelessness, and a lack of motivation. In consultation with a psychiatrist, he was placed on an antidepressant called Wellbutrin. This particular medication was chosen because of its positive impact on serotonin and dopamine to lift both mood and energy. After a couple of weeks, Michael reported a 25% improvement in his depressive thinking, but he was most impressed with his increased energy and motivation. While many clients balk at taking medication, I often express my belief that medications are an opportunity to re-regulate the biochemistry of our brain, which may have not been correctly established and regulated during childhood. The challenge with most clients is to get them beyond the cultural assumption that their problems are the result of a character flaw and that they need to get better without medication. After Michael experienced positive results, I remember him saying, "I guess there is no sense suffering for the rest of my life for what I had to survive in childhood."

His greater sense of efficacy in his work and new experiences of success with his clients created some confidence that his career had finally gotten on track. The fear and anxiety associated with his clients resolved faster than I had expected, and he reveled in using what he had learned to develop strategies and select tactics in his clinical work. The next area of focus was expanding his social life, for which we used similar focusing and relaxation skills—like positive visualization and centering breathing exercises—to help him stay cortical in one-on-one and group situations. We added some mindfulness and somatic focusing exercises to help activate and develop his third executive system so he could begin building a greater awareness of his body and a healthy internal world. He slowly was able to utilize time alone as a source of familiarity and safety that he could use for self-soothing when he experienced the return of fearful memories of challenging situations in his current life.

It was after these blocks of work that he began to ask about whether it would be a good idea for him to process some of the trauma from his childhood. His successes at work and his optimism about his professional future seemed to serve as a source of confidence to take on other challenges. As he became a better therapist for others, he realized that he had someone inside himself who could help him overcome his fears from the past and in his everyday life. Part of his strength and courage came from learning that he had developed definitive boundaries against intrusions by his parents. It also led him to the realization that he had what it took to face the emotional challenges of revisiting his childhood and rescuing the frightened and isolated child that still lived with him. During this part of therapy he participated in EMDR sessions with another therapist to activate and reprocess some of his traumatic memories. This proved helpful to him and provided important content for our work together.

As the months passed, Michael developed a growing awareness of the difference between his vulnerable past and his increasingly autonomous present. I helped him to understand that his fear and anxiety were his amygdala's way of protecting him from the dangers it was certain still existed all around him. To work on this directly, Michael and I created a series of experiments in living. Experiments in living are challenges to the client to test new ways of thinking, feeling, and behaving based on insights uncovered during therapy. For Michael, these experiments include things like expressing his feelings, stating his needs, and promoting his own interests. Because he had already experienced success with experiments like these as a therapist, he had some confidence that they would work with acquaintances and potential friends.

Michael's experiments included exposing himself to connection with others, forcing himself not to run away, and eventually to be emotionally present. Sometimes we would again switch roles, and I would play someone he would meet at work or at a party while reminding and encouraging him to learn the relaxation skills he had learned. These exercises allowed him to begin to keep his cortex online in social situations and build on his success with clients. He had to act as if he felt he was an interesting conversation partner until he could see whether people would keep up their end of the conversation. He had to regulate his anxiety about someone starting to talk at him (like his mother), and never letting him speak or walking away. I taught him ways of disengaging from a conversation, which we practiced again and again in therapy, combined with lots of laughter. I helped him learn to take the messages of danger from his brain as a possibility instead of an inevitability and to have inner discussions with his brain, sometimes telling it, "Get lost!"

It would be a gross understatement to call Michael insecurely attached. You could even make a case for describing his attachment schema as disorganized. Michael was flooded by the traumatic implicit memories of his childhood when sitting across from his clients. The extreme arousal they caused hijacked his brain to an earlier place and time, inhibited his problem-solving abilities, and cut him off from himself and other people. His friendships remained superficial and perfunctory, despite his deep desire for connection, to protect himself from the irrationality, rejection, or indifference he was taught to anticipate.

Michael's decision to become a therapist was partly motivated by his need for intimacy within a relationship that would be safe for him—where he would be justified in exerting some control. Even the ability to limit interactions with others with a 50-minute stop point was appealing—he was not sure he could impose such limits outside of the structure of therapy. He hoped that the ground rules of therapy would provide him the safe boundaries that he didn't have with his parents. Michael confided in me that he hoped that the relationships he could form with his clients would help him to feel less alone and more connected to "the human race." Not an unusual countertransference reaction, but his was extreme.

Children who have parents who are unable to parent them can, as adolescents and adults, become very caring toward others. In the shadows lurk the remains of their childhoods in the form of low self-esteem, perfectionism, and a sense of deprivation. They don't feel they deserve any care or attention and find it impossible to accept care from others. At a neurological level, there is a disconnection between networks that organize the skills involved in caretaking and those dedicated to self-awareness and self-identity. People with this style of dissociated caretaking fit, among other things, the profile of what has been called the cancer-prone personality. Oncologists note that one of the most challenging aspects of treating these clients is getting them to express what is bothering them and asking for the help they need. These individuals are attracted to the helping professions, where they have the opportunity to parlay their childhood defenses into a career.

BECOMING A SKEPTIC OF YOUR BRAIN AND MIND

We know so little about one another. We embrace a shadow and love a dream.

—HJALMAR SODERBERG

Although many years had passed since Michael saw his parents on a regular basis, he still lived in the world they had created for him.

Although the brain remains plastic throughout life, early experiences have a disproportionate influence in shaping our implicit memory systems. Another way to think about this is that our brains are shaped to survive in our original environment. When Michael left his family, he no longer needed to employ the same defenses, but he was too frightened to stop. Michael, like many others, spent a great deal of effort to escape negative situations only to discover that his brain and mind re-created them everywhere he went.

Based on this early programming, his mind laid out his past in front of him, microsecond by microsecond, disguised as the present. Because the brain accomplishes this within the half second of neural processing prior to conscious awareness, he was unable to see the world in any other way. Instead of seeing that he was surrounded with many possibilities of real connection with others, his brain used anxiety and fear to keep him from any contact that wasn't absolutely necessary. It even made him fearful of his clients. All of his experiences left him befuddled. How could he have studied so long and done so well in his classes, only to go blank when his learning was supposed to be applied? He was left crippled with feelings of worthlessness and shame despite the fact that he had never done anything to hurt anyone.

One of Michael's many challenges was to learn to see the feelings, thoughts, and behaviors associated with his family structure as traumatic memories instead of accurate information about the present situation. This is what I mean by becoming a skeptic of your own mind. He might not have possessed the free will to stop the impulsive thoughts and feelings, but he could develop the ability to observe the churnings of his brain and learn to employ free won't. This might take the form of self-talk in which he reminds himself that his thoughts and feelings are memories and do not pertain to the current situation. Or it might be noticing his bodily impulse to leave the classroom immediately after a lecture, inhibit it, and hang around and talk to one or two other students. Whatever the strategy, the first step will be for him to learn to remember that these impulses are memories triggered in inappropriate situations.

We are not born with knowledge of our internal world; we learn about it through experience. When we grow up with people who share their inner experiences and ask us about ours, we learn to attend to and articulate our inner experiences. Michael had no such help. He became aware of his inner world the way many other traumatized children do, through the painful introspection born of loneliness, fear, and desperation. In one of our early therapy sessions, I asked Michael to close his eyes and imagine being in the room with a client. I could see his body immediately stiffen. Then I told him to imagine making one of the interpretations to his client that we had discussed during supervision. Michael's body froze and he quickly replied, "I'm frightened. I can see my client yelling at me, telling me I'm stupid, storming out of the room or giving me the cold shoulder." When he opened his eyes and looked at me, I could see both the fear on his face and his heart pounding in his chest. At some level, Michael knew that the likelihood of any of these things happening was extremely low. But regardless what his conscious mind knew, his brain and body reacted as if he were in danger.

Early in our relationship, Michael told me, "I was afraid my entire childhood of what my mother would do next. I thought that every word I said to her was potentially dangerous." At this point he couldn't make the connection between those experiences and what he called his "therapy panic." Months later, after I had made a few interpretations focusing on the connection between the fear of his mother and his clients, he said, "When I'm doing therapy, I want my clients to stay calm. When I think of saying anything, I'm always afraid it will make them angry. I sit and stare at them, frozen, like I sat and stared at my mother. My mind goes blank and all I can feel is a pain in my chest." He had finally made the connection that would come to help him to distinguish between his traumatic memories and his present reality, and invoke free won't.

Human beings are incapable of random behaviors, yet the many dilemmas Michael faced made no sense based on his present reality. This made Michael, like most of the rest of us, confused when he behaved in irrational ways. All of our behaviors are patterned based on our genetic histories and past experiences, and it is from this deep internal logic that we navigate our day-to-day lives. It is only when we uncover and come to understand these usually hidden narratives that our behaviors become both logical and predictable. We all have a deep narrative, the story our minds have constructed from the past, that we use to perceive, analyze, and make decisions in our lives. The degree to which this logic is unconscious and irresistible is the degree to which we lack free will.

An important component of psychotherapy, for both client and therapist, is learning to become aware of our assumptions, suspicious of our beliefs, and skeptical of our conclusions. This is a tricky proposition because we depend on our beliefs to give us the illusion of certainty in a confusing and often frightening world. In Michael's case, his early experiences organized his attachment schema, behaviors, and beliefs in ways that locked him into a state of chronic disengagement. In a similar manner, therapists can get stuck in patterns of thinking that can lead them to miss obvious symptoms, questions, and interventions. One of the many reasons a safe therapeutic relationship is vital is to create a space safe enough that a client no longer has to cling to their defenses to feel protected. One of the reasons why it is vital for a therapist to engage in considerable self-exploration and therapy is to develop the courage to not have to be right. Both client and therapist have to feel safe enough to explore, be curious, and be uncertain together.

When Michael first described his mother hoarding his toys, I became infuriated and had fantasies of breaking down the mother's door to retrieve his toys and give them back to him. I pictured setting up cameras and recording her behavior as proof to his father. At first, I kept these imaginary acts to myself because he was still embedded in the worldview of his family. Months into our relationship, when I felt he might be able to benefit from what went on in my mind, I told him about my rebellious fantasies. My strategies to "bust" his mother made him laugh and cry. He was surprised by my anger, bristled at first, and jumped to defend her. But it didn't take long for him to realize how normal my reaction was and how he had buried his anger to protect her. "I never thought of getting angry because I was so afraid of how she would respond. I needed her to hold it together because she was all I had." I told him that perhaps he needed to experience my anger first in order to feel safe to express his own. It is in interactions like this that the therapist's humanity is most needed and most useful. Not all countertransference reactions are necessarily negative.

A POSSIBLE CASE CONCEPTUALIZATION

> *Intuition will tell the thinking mind where to look next.*
>
> —JONAS SALK

Circling back to Chapter 10, let's consider how I might organize some thoughts for an initial case conceptualization based on what I've shared about Michael.

1. Orientation

My orientation is primarily psychodynamic and my interpersonal stance is within a Rogerian framework. Given that Michael's primary struggle is with interpersonal trauma, I think of a secure therapeutic relationship as the foundation from which he can become more aware of his feelings and thoughts about intimacy. The goal is for him to use these insights to create experiments in living outside of therapy. Because he has such powerful issues around trust, I will have to be especially vigilant to remain present, congruent, and as truthful as I am able. It will be important for me to be very sensitive to nonverbal signs of discomfort, watch carefully for indications of distance, and be sure to identify and own my own mistakes.

A considerable aspect of my approach will also consist of psychoeducation. In helping Michael to change his deep narrative, I will work to help him understand how the brain has evolved, how it develops, and how memory works. He needs to learn that he isn't mentally ill, but he has been navigating life with a brain and mind that have been shaped to survive in a very abnormal environment. He has to come to accept that many of the loyalties and habits that emerged from his early life are a bad adaptational fit to the life he wishes to build for himself. Given his intellectual defenses, I will have to be careful not to make this information a substitute for going through the emotional processes required for healing. I will repeatedly reinforce that the goal of therapy is to be able to love and work, and that understanding is the booby prize.

2. Target Problems

My hypothesis is that his core symptoms are generalized anxiety, social anxiety, and complex PTSD from childhood. I suspect they stem from early attachment trauma that have resulted in his symptoms, lack of social skills, and social isolation. Because he presented with his anxiety within the consultation room with his clients, I started by focusing on these issues and moved onto nonprofessional interactions. Beyond that, Michael may benefit from group therapy and involvement in social organizations where he can practice his developing social skills.

3. Biological Issues

No medical conditions, drug abuse, or medication side effects are currently evident or identified. I would hypothesize that his early prolonged stress has impacted his memory processing, executive functioning, and his DMN abilities in ways which are reflected in his symptomatology. Although he is academically successful, I need to be aware of how well he remembers and can build upon prior sessions, especially around emotionally sensitive issues. Chronic high levels of stress can impact hippocampal development and function and result in problems in short-term memory and memory access during stress. I will focus on his autonomic arousal and reactivity early in treatment to lay the groundwork for neural regulation and integration that will allow for success in other aspects of treatment and healing.

4. Psychological Issues

Michael's primary symptoms are anxiety, depression, suspiciousness, and social isolation. His defenses center around isolation, dissociation, and intellectualization. I don't yet know of his sources of meaning and inspiration, but there is no doubt that his survival instincts are strong. His attachment schema is clearly avoidant, which will likely correlate with a lack of recall of events from his life and a dismissing attitude toward the importance of close relationships. This is mostly a defense against rejection and shame, and working toward and through these issues will be a long-term goal of treatment.

What Michael describes as "sleepwalking" suggests a dissociative defense—a shutting down of emotions to decrease fear and anxiety, which leaves him with a distant and surreal experience of life. These experiences can reflect an inhibition of right-hemisphere processing by the left and even a disconnection from signals sent up from the body to the cortex. Clients with these symptoms often report that they feel "one step removed" from life or that they feel like they are watching their lives on a screen. This is something I will have to keep in mind and explore down the line.

5. Social Issues

His social isolation is a central issue. He reports having no friends or real connection to his peers. His training to be a therapist may have been an attempt to find a situation safe enough for him to be able to connect with others. Because we depend on our parents to take care of and protect us, an early awareness of their deficits can be intuitively frightening to a child. Getting his mother to interact with him was always on her schedule. She was largely absent, and he was left to fend for himself. When they did interact, she was a source of as much distress as comfort. His father was a constant source of neglect, misunderstanding, and emotional misattunement. These early attachment experiences led Michael to have little affect regulation, which inhibited his second and third executive systems. This is largely why Michael's mind abandons him when he is triggered and he finds himself without thoughts, words, or memory.

Competent children like Michael often become parentified and, instead of getting their emotional needs met, end up caring for their parents and dissociating from their own emotional world. His mother's unpredictability of mood and behavior terrified him and disqualified her as a safe haven. He reported that she would hug him on occasion but "always too hard and never when I needed it—but I took what I could get." You can imagine that Michael's interactions with his mother did not activate the biochemistry of well-being and safety.

6. Assessment

Michael's avoidant attachment style parallels his lack of recall and the relative absence of autobiographical memory. His ability to modulate arousal is minimal and as therapy progresses, I will institute a program of biofeedback and relaxation training to parallel other modalities of intervention. No formal psychological or neuro-psychological evaluations seem necessary at this time, but the question will be revisited later in treatment.

7. *Collaboration*

Initially, I will collaborate with a pharmacologist on the possibility of prescribing an antidepressant or antianxiety agent. I'll consider referring him to an EMDR therapist when we get to the point of addressing traumatic memories. I'll also discuss with Michael the possibility of becoming involved in group therapy, where he could desensitize to interacting with others, learn some basic social skills, and perhaps develop friendships.

8. *Therapeutic Relationship*

Michael's transference to me mirrored his countertransference to his clients. Sitting across from me initially activated fear, which slowly morphed into suspiciousness. As more trust and a greater sense of safety were established, we were able to talk about these feelings and the sadness beneath them and his longing to feel connected and safe in a relationship. When Michael and I felt more closely connected, he would have thoughts of quitting therapy and killing himself. Sometimes he would miss the next session to reestablish a safe dis-tance. Eventually he was able to "act in" instead of acting out—he could come to session despite these feelings and talk about them as opposed to missing the next appointment.

My countertransference was particularly evident when his child-hood experiences triggered painful memories from my own child-hood. As I sat across from him, I heard the voices in my head yelling, "How could those two people be allowed to have a child?! How could the father not see through his wife's lies? Why didn't the father believe him? He had to know his wife was disturbed!" These are very human reactions, some of which you may have had as well as you read about Michael's experiences. We are naturally protective of children and become angry at those who abuse and neglect them. Many of my clients who feel completely unable to defend themselves will tear into anyone who remotely threatens someone they love. It is a very basic biological instinct. At the same time, we are all trying to protect ourselves against our own pain and can find it difficult to differentiate our experiences from our clients'.

9. Treatment Goals

Michael's central goal is to be able to be in session without anxiety and use what he has learned to build his clinical skills and get on with his career. I associate his goals with a broader goal of him building a social life and being a happier and more fulfilled human being.

10. Strategies and Tactics

I will continue to focus on building trust in the relationship and providing Michael with the experience of having an elder listen to him and hopefully help him feel understood. My tactics will include positive regard, warmth, and understanding. As this is established, I will begin to question some of his negative beliefs and begin psychoeducation to help him understand how his childhood has impacted his brain development and states of mind. I will then introduce the other interventions described above in a sequential manner.

12

TRAUMATIZED

To live is to suffer, to survive is to find some meaning in the suffering.

—FRIEDRICH NIETZSCHE

Brains have evolved to be organs of adaptation in the service of survival. In the process, we have been shaped to stay close to significant others for the safety, resources, and comfort we need to live and work. Autonomic arousal and stress are indicators that we are facing a real or imagined threat to our survival. At low to moderate levels of arousal, what could also be called curiosity, interest, or exploration, stress activates our brains to engage in learning and adaptive behaviors. Hunger pangs, a car drifting into our lane, or an unexpected bill will capture our attention, put us on alert, and signal us to take action. We cope with these challenges by grabbing a sandwich, honking our horn, or calling an accountant.

For most of us and for most of the time, we respond to these challenges with minimum disruption. We get knocked down, get up, dust ourselves off, and carry on. We call this resilience, determination, grit, or getting back on the horse that threw you. But this can be taken too far. The spin-offs of machismo, rugged individualism, and denial can, in the long term, impair our ability to recognize and attend to higher levels of chronic stress and even trauma. For example, veterans are loath to complain or seek psychological help either during or after active duty, choosing to suffer in silence to avoid losing face. Yet they struggle with PTSD and the stressors of civilian life, committing suicide at double the rate of noncombat-exposed civilians.

In the most general sense, humans have evolved to cope with stress for brief periods of time. There is an optimal range of arousal within which neural plasticity, emotional regulation, and executive functioning are maintained and optimized. Below this range (in the absence of stimulation or challenge), our brains and bodies slow down to conserve energy and restore themselves. Some call these times vacation. As stress advances above our optimal range, escalating arousal eventually leads to deficits in brain functioning and psychological well-being. This usually results in the inhibition of brain systems responsible for adaptive and flexible emotional, cognitive, and immunological functioning.

At even higher levels of arousal, neural networks can be functionally inhibited, dissociated from one another, and locked into stable patterns of activation that maintain a traumatized state of mind and body. This we call trauma or PTSD. The old saying "What doesn't kill you makes you stronger" only applies within a moderate range of stress; above it, what doesn't kill you impairs the body's restorative and learning capabilities, and ultimately makes you weaker. At a certain level of intensity (different for all of us), stress shifts from a manageable challenge to a state of arousal that triggers a fight, flee, or freeze reaction. Understanding trauma is not a simple matter because its impact depends on our genetics, life history, temperament, culture, personality, and level of social support. This is why the same situation may be taken in stride by one person and result in PTSD in another.

CORE SYMPTOMS

My childhood did not prepare me for the fact that the world is full of cruel and bitter things.

—ROBERT OPPENHEIMER

PTSD is rare among psychological disorders in that we have a relatively clear idea of its origin and underlying mechanisms. Most everyone seems to agree that the core etiology is sustained amygdala-mediated hyperarousal, resulting in a cascade of biological changes throughout the brain and body. The broad effect is that the threat signals sent out by the amygdala activate the autonomic nervous system, triggering us to fight, flee, or freeze. If this continues long enough, the brain will change in ways that are sustained after the immediate danger has passed. Prolonged arousal signals the brain to remain in a defensive posture and to always be on the lookout for danger. Alternatively, victims can get locked into parasympathetic and dorsal vagal activation that keeps them frozen and withdrawn, and crushes their spirit with feelings of worthlessness and shame.

Beyond the hypervigilance and exaggerated startle caused by amygdala hyperarousal, the most characteristic symptoms of PTSD are nightmares, flashbacks, and memories of traumatic events (intrusions) that are experienced as arising from nowhere. These symptoms result from the dissociation of neural networks dedicated to affect and cognition, explicit and implicit memory, and conscious and unconscious processes. These functional disconnections fragment moment-to-moment experience and generate the symptoms seen in PTSD. Together, hyperarousal, frightening intrusions into consciousness, and the fragmentation of the continuity of conscious experience create a state of brain, body, and mind that amplify the dangerousness of each second. If you have ever had a car accident, you may remember how driving immediately afterward feels extremely dangerous, as if every car is out to hit you. Sustained arousal after traumatic experiences directs our brains and minds to orient toward and exaggerate the potential threats around us. This is the amygdala working to protect us, but no one needs a helicopter amygdala always overhead. Now, imagine if your entire childhood had the effects of a car accident!

As the world comes to be experienced as increasingly dangerous, the third symptom, avoidance of thoughts, actions, and feelings, reflects an attempt to decrease anxiety. Avoidance can include withdrawing from others, keeping a highly routinized schedule and set of activities, and psychological defenses such as denial, dissociation, and even amnesia. Avoidance, therefore, manifests both externally in the form of behaviors and internally through the inhibition of thoughts and feelings. This is why those who have been traumatized, and even those with severe anxiety without trauma, tend to lead very routinized lives and are actually frightened by novelty or change. This is what Michael was likely describing when he talked about sleepwalking through life.

TRAUMA'S NEUROCHEMICAL COCKTAIL

Brain: an apparatus with which we think we think.

—AMBROSE PIERCE

The chemical cocktail resulting from experiences of threat and danger alters our energy level and cognitive processes, and decreases our susceptibility to pain. It also inhibits processes of bodily maintenance and restoration, shifting our energy to survival needs until the danger has passed. Five neurochemicals we know are modified in PTSD include norepinephrine (adrenaline), cortisol, endorphins, dopamine, and serotonin. Increased levels of norepinephrine increase bodily arousal and focused attention in preparation for fighting and fleeing. Cortisol sacrifices long-term maintenance and energy storage by inhibiting protein synthesis and breaking down complex starches to readily available sugars for energy availability. Elevated levels of endorphins serve as an analgesic to diminish physical pain if we become injured so we can stay focused on survival-related behaviors. Higher levels of dopamine drive hypervigilance and cognitive acuity. Unfortunately, the one neurochemical that decreases in PTSD is serotonin, a neurotransmitter which supports a sense of connection to others, safety, and well-being. Lower levels of serotonin are associated with hunger pangs, separation, and danger.

When stress is chronic or when trauma converts to PTSD, these biochemical changes can result in stable alterations of the brain that impact all aspects of life. Chronically high levels of norepinephrine translate into ongoing anxiety, irritability, and a startle response that become resistant to habituation. Higher sustained levels of cortisol are responsible for decreased hippocampal volume, related deficits in learning and memory, and suppressed immunological functioning. Sustained high levels of endorphins can distort reality and result in emotional blunting, depersonalization, and derealization. In the long term, endorphins can have a negative impact on cognition and disrupt our ability to engage in reality-testing and day-to-day life. Chronically low levels of serotonin are correlated with more depression, irritability, violence, and suicide.

DISTURBED NEURODYNAMICS OF EXECUTIVE FUNCTIONING

> *The capacity to self-regulate, to self-heal, and to self-renew may be the most important function of the mind, not only for itself, but also in relation to others.*
>
> —JONAS SALK

Sustained high levels of amygdala and ANS activation, and the subsequent biochemical cascade just described, have profound downstream effects on the activity of many neural networks. Key to understanding PTSD is that the hyperarousal of the amygdala (and the primitive executive system it controls) results in the inhibition of the two other executive systems (and language), all vital to navigating our physical and social worlds: (1) the parietal-frontal executive system, (2) systems of expressive language centered in Broca's area, and (3) the default mode network.

The parietal-frontal network is the cortical system most involved with abstract thinking, problem solving, and intelligence. It consists of the dorsal and lateral portions of the frontal cortex and the parietal lobes. It is within this network that the highest level of processing occurs in the brain's construction of space and time: how we navigate and survive within our physical and social environments. The inhibition of this system is evident in the degree to which stress and anxiety impair our thinking, judgment, and problem-solving abilities. I've seen this in many others and certainly experienced it myself.

Michael demonstrated this phenomenon when he was unable to access his considerable knowledge and intellectual abilities while experiencing his flashback countertransference reactions. His extreme arousal led him to feel that his mind was just unavailable to him. In describing this experience, clients have told me things like, "My brain turned off," "It felt like my skull was full of blackness," and "I thought I must be having a stroke." I experienced this when I took my oral exam to become a psychologist. I looked at the page of writing in front of me, knew it was in English, but was unable to translate the symbols on the page (letters and words) into any meaningful thoughts until I was able to slow my breathing and calm down. There is little doubt that anxiety makes us dumb and extreme anxiety makes us even dumber. Such is the veto power of the amygdala over the parietal-frontal executive network.

A central component of our parietal-frontal executive network is a system for expressive language with its hub, Broca's area, in the left frontal lobe. This area has been shown to become inhibited during high levels of arousal in individuals with PTSD, and there are many indications that fear, terror, and extreme stress result in a kind of transient aphasia often referred to as speechless terror. This is demonstrated when someone tries to scream in terror yet finds that no sound comes out of his mouth. It may also be a part of why individuals who are stressed out, traumatized, or find themselves in front of an audience discover that they are unable to speak. At a less extreme level, this may be why, when we are upset with someone, we find it hard to find the right words, yet are later able to think of all of the things we should have said. The inhibition of language can be especially problematic because we use autobiographical memory in the form of narratives to support neural integration, identify with others, and organize a sense of self.

In conjunction with the temporal lobes and hippocampi, the parietal-frontal system contributes to the construction of a conscious workspace that allows us to focus on problems, consider potential answers, and make conscious choices. When amygdala activation is chronically upregulated, it triggers implicit traumatic memories (such as flashbacks) and other disturbing emotions that break into consciousness and undermine our ability to sustain focus and solve problems. It also actively inhibits the parietal-frontal executive system, vital for navigating space and time, relationships, and the physical world.

The DMN consists of a set of structures within the middle of the brain that become activated when we are not focused on either threat, attraction (amygdala), or external tasks (parietal-frontal). This DMN executive system becomes activated when we are engaged in activities like daydreaming, self-reflection, and empathic thoughts about others. This is likely the system we are attempting to activate when we are teaching our clients to be mindful or psychologically minded, or to engage in metacognition. Extensive experience working with victims of trauma reveals that many suffer not only an estrangement from others, but also seem to live in exile from themselves. They find little comfort in intimacy with others, and don't feel safe in their own skin. These extraordinarily painful and disturbing experiences are likely related to chronic DMN inhibition by the amygdala. I suspect that the high suicide rates seen in traumatized and abandoned individuals are primarily due to these feelings of separation, ostracism, and disconnection from the group mind.

IN EXILE FROM OTHERS

That the world I was in could be soft, lovely, and nourishing was more than I could bear, and so I stood there and wept, for I didn't want to love one more thing that could make my heart break into a million pieces at my feet.

—JAMAICA KINCAID

Until recently, there hasn't been a good way to understand the social consequences of PTSD beyond the physiological, emotional, and cognitive consequences of amygdala hyperarousal. The symptoms of avoidance have been interpreted solely as a protective reaction and the cognitive symptoms a hodgepodge of negative thoughts and cognitive disruptions. The emergence of research on the parietal-frontal and DMN executive systems provides us with a new and more sophisticated way to think about the broader effects of PTSD on cognitive and social functioning. This new look organized around the impact of the inhibition of these executive systems may help us to grasp a broader neural infrastructure to explain a broad range of PTSD symptoms.

A key feature of severely traumatized clients is their loss of social connection. It is often described as an inability to understand the actions and emotions of others. It leads to a feeling of being an observer of the social world instead of engaging as a full participant, followed by a range of reactions from suspiciousness, to social withdrawal, to profound shame. This may be due, in either small or large part, to the loss of TOM abilities secondary to parietal-frontal and mirror neuron inhibition. It is an especially damaging symptom of PTSD because it blocks victims from fully engaging in the healing effects of the positive relationships they may already have in their lives. While the case has always been made that social deficits in PTSD are a consequence of the three core symptoms described in the DSM, the discovery of the DMN suggest that the underlying neuronal causes of social fragmentation may be more complex.

Theory of mind (TOM), seen in primates and other social animals, is an ability to predict the intentions and actions of others via eye gaze, posture, movement, facial expressions, and environmental cues. In other word, humans learn to develop an automatic implicit theory of what others are up to, their intentions, and whether or not we should engage with them. As our brains evolved, an increasing number of cortical networks became dedicated to higher-level social functioning, which allowed for greater attunement, sympathy, empathy, and compassion. The DMN executive, along with other systems of bonding and attachment, has enhanced our ability to link with others and become part of a group mind—a powerful but poorly understood phenomenon that drives mob mentality, emotional contagion, and susceptibility to charismatic leaders and cults.

IN EXILE FROM THE SELF

I yearn to belong to something, to be contained in an all-embracing mind that sees me as a single thing.

—RAINER MARIA RILKE

Given that other primates demonstrate TOM abilities with limited (if any) self-awareness, we can assume that the theory of mind is evolutionarily older than a theory of the self. Given their similar natures, it is likely that both consciousness and self-awareness are evolutionary offshoots of our reflexive TOM for others. In other words, as our abstract abilities increased, we were eventually able to turn our primitive TOM of others inward and began to develop conscious theories and assign motivations to our own behaviors. After all, if others have private thoughts, motivations, and intentions, shouldn't I? And if I have thoughts and intentions, there must be an I, just as there are others.

This evolutionary process parallels what we see in children as they come to realize that they are separate from others, develop their own identities, and begin to recognize and explore their inner worlds. We also see through the history of literature a gradual shift from a focus on external behaviors to an articulation of inner experience. While ancient writings focus on the actions and interactions of humans, motivations, intentions, and free will were reserved for the gods and the forces of nature; God was displeased, brought on the floods, and Noah obeyed and built the ark. Compare that mentality with a 19th-century author like Jane Austen who, in her sophisticated and humorous prose, provides the best proof for both self-awareness and the existence of the social brain.

Given all the data supporting the central involvement of the DMN in our abilities to reflect on minds, it may be that the evolution of this network has contributed greatly to developing the kinds of empathy and self-awareness we have attained as a species. If the DMN is chronically inhibited during early development or after severe trauma during adulthood, the victim's ability to develop a coherent sense of self, regulate affect, be introspective, or have empathy for others become significantly impaired. When stress and trauma occur from early childhood, a sense of having a safe inner world to withdraw to for comfort may never be achieved.

Looking at the many functions of the DMN—from having a sense of self, to reading social cues, to imagining a future—it is certainly possible that chronic inhibition of this important network can drastically change the experience of others and of the self. This theory may be supported by findings that those with PTSD and Borderline Personality Disorder exhibit deficits in empathy, self-referential processing, autobiographical memory, and TOM, all of which appear to involve the DMN. Thus, trauma may disrupt our awareness of both our own and other minds by chronically inhibiting the activation of the DMN. The combination of these deficits would likely result in a surreal and fragmented sense of self and others.

In their book *Healing the Traumatized Self*, Frewen and Lanius (2015) use the term "trauma-related altered states of consciousness" to capture the broad range of experiences reported to them by their research subjects that may support the inhibition of the DMN in PTSD. Here is an abbreviated list of victim reports from their book:

- They often report feeling lost, disoriented, and helpless.
- They often report feeling experientially detached from others, perceiving themselves as distant, far away, and unreachable.
- Within an empty shell, they experience themselves as nameless, faceless, silenced, and forgotten.
- At times, they may feel as if they are inhuman or that they have ceased to exist.
- They frequently feel abandoned, insignificant, alone, and undeserving of normal human contact.
- A disconnection from emotions and bodily feelings soon ensues; they report feeling numb, or in some cases as if already dead.
- A capacity for joy, pleasure, triumph, and all sense of curiosity have ceased to exist.

For many severely traumatized individuals, second and third executive system inhibition may explain many of these painful experiences. Their disconnection from the group mind and their ability to maintain a quiet internal space and a consistent sense of self could be key in perpetuating and worsening their neural, psychological, and social functioning. Just as solitary confinement results in anxiety, depression, self-harm, and suicide, the shutting down of circuitry that allows us to self-reflect and connect with others starves the social brain of what it needs to survive and thrive—connection.

COMPLEX TRAUMA AND SOCIETAL DISSOCIATION

> *Man is only fitfully committed to . . . thinking. . . . Believing is what he is really proud of.*
>
> —MARTIN AMIS

Over the years I have seen many clients suffering from PTSD, yet very few have been a good fit for brief forms of therapy. For a very few, 10 sessions of systematic desensitization involving exposure, response prevention, and relaxation training allowed them to regain full pretrauma functioning. For most, focusing on the current trauma led to a spontaneous uncovering of past trauma, characterological challenges, and lifestyles issues that were all impediments to healing. Adult trauma often opens the door to the reactivation of childhood trauma, abuse, neglect, and insecure attachment, which becomes the focus of treatment.

Although I am unaware of any specific research on the topic, trauma appears to make us vulnerable to subsequent trauma. We seem more likely to find it, and it seems more likely to find us, and each experience can have a stronger impact on us than the one before. The ways in which trauma negatively impacts the development and functioning of our brains is a likely cause of this vulnerability to both more trauma and increasingly negative effects of subsequent experiences. The cumulative effect of traumatized living over years, decades, and a lifetime is what becomes the central work with my clients suffering from PTSD.

The power of the pharmaceutical and insurance industries in pushing for medications and brief therapies for everything that ails us leads psychiatrists to eschew the role of early development in favor of symptoms related to current functioning. In addition, the adult bias toward thinking of childhood as a time of innocence and fun can lead us to underestimate the impact of negative childhood experiences. There certainly appears to be considerable evidence to support the claim reflected in our societal resistance to accepting the incidence, scope, and magnitude of early trauma. Every time a public figure discloses early sexual abuse, for example, a flood of emotion swamps hotlines and fills therapists' offices.

Most people also labor under the false assumption that the longer ago a traumatic experience occurred, the less it should bother them. I've heard countless clients exclaim, "This happened to me so many years ago. How can it still bother me?" Their frustration is based partly on the mistaken assumption that the primitive brain's sense of time is similar to that of the part of the brain which constructs conscious awareness. They are unaware of all of the processing that occurs prior to consciousness in the fast systems of the amygdala and that, unlike cortical memory systems, the amygdala is like the elephant that never forgets. Its strategy is to always err on the side of caution and remember everything that has ever frightened, hurt, or shamed us, and generalize it to all similar types of experiences. What our bodies remember runs deeper than what our minds are capable of recalling.

WAS MICHAEL TRAUMATIZED?

There are no facts, only interpretations.
—FRIEDRICH NIETZSCHE

Despite living his life in a chronic state of frozen alertness, Michael didn't officially qualify for a diagnosis of PTSD. He was never beaten, sexually abused, or abandoned during childhood and didn't suffer from the kinds of nightmares and intrusive thoughts and feelings that you might expect to see in a trauma victim. As an adult, he was never exposed to combat and had never experienced a severe auto accident, been stabbed or shot, or been in a life-threatening situation that he could recall. Despite this lack of "official" trauma, Michael lived in fear, experienced powerful intrusive emotions triggered when seeing clients, exhibited a variety of symptoms associated with parasympathetic/dorsal vagal dominance, and had impressive impairments in his relationships with others and himself.

One could certainly argue, and could collect evidence to support the idea that Michael's challenges are a consequence of the interaction of his genetic inheritance and modeling his parents' behaviors. A combination of being on the autistic spectrum and having some of the cognitive and social difficulties seen in close relatives of schizophrenic individuals could possibly explain his social awkwardness, interpersonal withdrawal, and high level of anxiety. The reason why I didn't pursue this diagnostic line was based on the fact that my experience of Michael was very unlike my experience with individuals in these other diagnostic groups. He was more self-aware and emotionally in tune with others than is commonly seen in these other illness processes. It doesn't sound very scientific, but he didn't "feel" like he was either on the autistic or schizophrenic spectrums. More sophisticated knowledge and testing may, in the future, assist us in having a deeper understanding of these genetic influences on experience and mental health.

Clinical intuition always comes under extreme criticism as the field of psychotherapy struggles for legitimacy. The term "evidence-based" has become the excuse for insurance companies to limit the cost of treatments they are required to provide. Unfortunately, it has also become a term behind which psychotherapists can hide for risk management purposes. After all, if you find the "one true way," why bother thinking any further about how to treat your clients?

Get a manual, give your clients homework, and have them fill out checklists. If they don't get better, label it as treatment resistance to preserve your belief system. It is not a coincidence that this myopic thinking parallels what we see in the practice of medicine and why so many clients seek alternative treatments for both physical and medical illnesses. To the question of whether Michael was traumatized or not, I would have to say yes, in the face of the DSM, the APA, Kaiser, and Blue Cross.

INHERITED TRAUMA

The sad and horrible conclusion is that no one cared that Jews were being murdered. . . . This is the Jewish lesson of the Holocaust.

—ARIEL SHARON

About a century ago, a great debate emerged between Darwinians and Lamarckians. The question was, does evolutionary change occur across many generations through mutation and selective reproduction (Darwin/Mendel), or can a change that occurs in one individual manifest in their children (Lamarck)? In the experiment that put the nail in the coffin of the Lamarckian argument, researchers cut the tails off of female rats and showed that their pups were still born with tails. This settled the argument—or did it? In a study with rats, Dias and Ressler (2014) found that fear conditioning in parents was passed on to their children and grandchildren (Dias and Ressler, 2014). This clearly looks more Lamarckian than Darwinian.

The mechanism of action for this inheritance across generations was found to be changes in the gametes of the first-generation parents, which resulted in epigenetic changes in gene expression that were passed on to the next two generations. In the experiment, an odor that was originally a neutral stimulus to the grandparents (and the species) was converted into a trigger for fear and anxiety in their children and grandchildren. In other words, the grandchildren showed autonomic arousal in response to an odor that, in their experience, they had no reason to be afraid of. Imagine one of these third-generation rats going to psychotherapy for a phobic reaction in response to a smell related to the one to which their grandparents had been conditioned. They could search their memory for years looking for the cause of their phobia and, with enough time and enough possibilities, could probably come up with an acceptable narrative. I suspect you can see where I'm headed—sometimes the traumatic symptoms we experience may not be the result of personal experiences but are inherited from our parents and grandparents—passed down not only genetically, but through the thousands of interactions that can transfer emotions across the generations both consciously and unconsciously.

While I was training as a family systems therapist, my teachers made it clear that in order to understand an individual and a family, we had to know about the family back through at least three generations. We were encouraged to create genograms and collect the oral history of the family for about 100 years. This was based on the belief that the traumas, dramas, missions, and loyalties of each generation are, consciously and unconsciously, carried forward. This almost always proved useful in helping the family understand the broader context for its present struggles and appreciate the continuity of the stories of both parents' families through time. In couples therapy, I was trained to think in terms of both partners attempting to both escape from and re-create their family of origin in their marriage. I also remember being told in substance abuse training that addicts don't form relationships; they take hostages based on their experiences with their families.

Over and over again, I have experienced an adult's struggles that make no sense given their personal history but begin to make complete sense when looked at in the context of their family history. I've had many clients with enough social and financial security that they never have to worry about friends and money for the rest of their lives. Yet they are exquisitely sensitive to the loss of any kind of security. These fears and anxieties don't make any sense in the present, and they may not make any sense in their parents' or grandparents' generations, but they do make sense further back in their family history, tied to economic and social trauma many generations ago.

Could these fears be related to modifications of gene expression a number of generations back, which belong not to their experience but to the experience of their ancestors? And how might experiences like slavery, the Holocaust, the Armenian genocide, and the Russian Revolution be showing up today in the symptoms of our otherwise safe, successful, and healthy clients who find their way to our office? We certainly are not yet at the place where we can know with any certainty, but these recent findings in epigenetics make it incumbent upon us to expand our time frame on the causal processes for current symptomatology.

13

MEMORY WORK

Time moves in one direction, memory in another.

—WILLIAM GIBSON

Psychotherapy is memory work—remembering, unlearning, and relearning. We explore what has come before, how it is remembered in the heart, mind, and body, and how these feelings, thoughts, and behaviors impact our daily lives. Benefiting from therapy requires that we remember what we worked on in sessions and bringing it into our lives through mindfulness and experiments in living. Because therapists aren't privy to a client's everyday world, past or present, we are guided by what is in their memories. Part of the therapist's skill is listening carefully, understanding what is being said, and learning to detect unconscious distortions, half-truths, and misrepresentations.

Memory is so central to our lives because our brains have evolved to automatically apply what we have learned in the present. Unconscious memories are activated faster than conscious awareness and front-loaded to shape our perception٬ awareness, our brains and minds shape our biases ؛ into "objective truths." Because our brains are also our most influential memories are formed in relationships, especially those from early in life. Critical experiences with caretakers are so powerful precisely because they shape the infrastructure of our brains during critical periods of brain development and come to serve as templates for all future learning.

Everyday memory is not stored in locked files, fixed and immutable. While memories need to be stable enough to be remembered, they also have to be flexible enough to be updated. Each time memories are brought into consciousness, they become open to modification for the purposes of ongoing adaptation. Think about the process of studying for an exam as you go over and over the material for clarity, corrections, and reinforcement. This is the way explicit memory works. As we age, it is natural to think back to past experiences and reevaluate the thoughts, perspectives, and decisions we made in light of new experiences and increased perspective. This is how we update our knowledge and our sense of self.

TRAUMATIC MEMORY

> *The critical issue is to allow yourself to know what you know.*
>
> —BESSEL VAN DER KOLK

Traumatic memories differ from nontraumatic memories in a number of significant ways. They are encoded at different levels of biochemical activation, stored within alternative neural systems, and experienced differently than nontraumatic memories. For example, Michael learned early in life not to trust the opinions and judgments of authority figures. This early, unconscious decision, however, also led him to distrust his bosses, his teachers, anyone in government, and any therapist he would work with. When we began working together, he didn't realize he didn't trust me—so reflexive, automatic, and deeply embedded was this way of experiencing the world. His skepticism and self-protective instincts developed so early in his life that he wasn't aware of their existence. It's important to keep in mind that no matter how positive your client's transference appears, a negative transference lies beneath it. This is because we all have been hurt, frightened, and disappointed by those we've depended upon in the past. These experiences leave an impression that we don't forget.

Much of this kind of relearning occurs during psychotherapy, as our own distortions and biases become uncovered. As we reflect upon past experiences, we can reassess our thoughts and conclusions with the advantage of emotional regulation, increased perspective, and the guidance of a therapist. A common example is reflecting on the types of reoccurring problems we may have in personal or professional relationships. Increasing self-awareness allows us to review these conflicts with the addition of new insights about ourselves that lead us to reevaluate the negative interactions. We may find that the inclusion of self-insight leads us to reinterpret events and reevaluate the cause of our difficulties. This is a form of memory updating.

One of the primary characteristics of traumatic memories—and a central challenge of psychotherapy—is their resistance to updating. This is because they are stored within amygdala-centric circuits that are strongly resistant to change that simultaneously inhibit the cortical systems involved in their repressing. This contrast is a clear example of the fact that we have multiple memory systems with different evolutionary histories, developmental processes, and functional roles. Traumatic memories are repetitive and stereotyped because they are organized and stored in primitive systems of procedural memory that evolved to organize bodily memories in time-linked procedural sequences.

This is essentially what posttraumatic states—flashbacks, ˙ ˉht-mares, frozen terror—are like. The programming is more ɾ than the victim's ability to control it because choice anˊ

do not exist below the cortex. When Michael was triggered by his clients and sent back to his childhood, part of him knew better, but it didn't matter. The reptilian fear took over. The amygdala enforced its veto power, inhibiting his other executive systems, and he remained stuck as a helpless victim of his past.

When Freud described traumatic experiences as "surpassing the stimulus barrier," I believe that he was describing the inhibition of our other two executive systems during states of high arousal. When we are terrified, we revert to the dominance of the primitive executive systems we share with our ancient ancestors. These systems do not include language, judgment, perspective, or problem-solving skills—in other words, the executive processes of our cerebral cortex. Reptiles depend on genetically determined behavioral programs that get activated by environmental triggers.

In states of high arousal, the fragmentation of autobiographical memory is common. The cortical executive processes involved with the integration of the multiple tracks of conscious memory can easily become dissociated. This is reflected in how many clients begin therapy with little or no emotion related to memories that should evoke strong emotions. At the beginning of our work, Michael talked about his childhood from the perspective of an objective observer or a documentarian. He described much of it in a play-by-play manner that an anthropologist might use to report the behaviors of a newly discovered tribe. These were his memories, yet his emotions had been edited out or perhaps never fully integrated into his autobiographical memories.

For those who are severely abused, traumatic memories are sometimes remembered as if they were watching from above or from a safe distance, or "looking at the world through binoculars turned the wrong way." This likely occurs when endorphins and dopamine released during high levels of stress distort reality and allow experiences to seem more distant and less threatening. As our work continued and our relationship deepened, we would visit and revisit key events and scenes from Michael's childhood. This reiterative process, leading us to visit and revisit early painful experience, usually resulted in his being able to include, recall, and embody a little more of the emotional and sensory experiences each time.

In a safe state of mind, with lower levels of arousal (and cortical executive systems online) each revisiting of memory has the potential of modifying tracks of memory with new information. In these situations, we take advantage of the fact that memory is fluid and updatable to help our clients heal from trauma. By integrating the various elements of memory and including more and more cortical involvement, they are more easily experienced, modulated, and "updateable." With my encouragement, Michael slowly revisited his memories in different ways. Each time he seemed more involved, the memories became more immediate, the connection to the child within him, a bit more intimate.

THE UBIQUITY OF COUNTERTRANSFERENCE

In each of us there is another whom we don't know.

—CARL JUNG

As therapists, we explore our clients' memories while simultaneously having our own memories and associations. Because we are human animals with social brains, our experience of each client is some mixture of who they are and how we experience them. When our unconscious processing distorts our perceptions of and interactions with our clients, we call this countertransference. Despite the sound of it, countertransference doesn't have to be a reaction to your client's transference, but can be a broader reaction to something that is happening within you that you bring to the session. No matter how many years we do psychotherapy, or how well we are trained, countertransference is always a part of our experience.

When it is broadly defined, every therapist has countertransference with every case. This is because every therapist, like every
client, has a brain and mind that comingles the present with experiences from the past. The question from a professional point of view
is, first, how much work have you done to understand how your
own history has shaped your implicit memory systems and your
experience of others? And second, have you developed a strategy
of self-reflection and consultation that allows you to minimize its
negative impact on your clients? In Michael's case, it interrupted his
work completely, so he was forced to deal with it. But for many, it
is subtler and covertly damaging to the quality of our clinical work.

When Michael walked into sessions with his clients, he found
himself transported back in time to the sweltering afternoons, the
unpredictability of his mother's behavior, and those dumbfounding
family discussions of childhood. He was no longer just an adult in a
professional setting; he was also a frightened child who could only
see his clients as a threat. Worst of all, he didn't understand what
was happening and why he was terrified by someone he knew was
not a threat. Such is the power of implicit memory to trigger the
amygdala to activate a fight-flight-freeze response and to break into
and distort conscious experience. In situations like this, people often
fear that they are going insane because they have no other way of
explaining their terror.

With a lack of accurate information about how the brain's many
memory systems work, those suffering with panic attacks rush
themselves to emergency rooms, convinced that they are having a
heart attack. Again and again, they are told that nothing is wrong
with their heart and that they are perfectly healthy. Eventually, they
are advised to visit a therapist or psychiatrist, which they seldom do,
so convinced are they that their troubles are of a physical nature. If
they eventually give in, I get to meet them. Veterans suffering from
PTSD will anxiously await their return home from combat, only to
find that they can't connect to their spouses and children, or adapt

to civilian life. Their brains have changed. They often begin to use substances, isolate themselves from their families, and think that they may need to go back into combat where "at least things made sense."

At one point, Michael told me that he spent countless nights lying in bed thinking about his parents, his "stuckness," and his "crazy" fears and anxieties. He felt trapped in a life that seemed all too familiar yet simultaneously alien and uncomfortable. It was a struggle for him to hold on to the hope that he would some-day find a way out of his present life and into something almost unimaginable—a sense of peace, safety, and connection to others. After doing well in his classes, running into a wall in his clinical development filled him with a fear of never being able to escape the emotional world of his childhood. Although it had been decades since he had to deal with the terror and complexities of his family situation, his amygdala was still trying to protect him from a reality that had long since passed. But how could he convince this part of his brain that he was no longer in danger?

CONVERTING TRAUMATIC INTO NONTRAUMATIC MEMORIES

> *Time and memory are true artists: they remold reality nearer to the heart's desire.*
>
> —JOHN DEWEY

While countertransference can be subtle and often goes unnoticed, Michael's countertransference was a full-body experience that hit him like a hammer. It was more like a traumatic flashback that couldn't be worked out in the context of supervision. There was no easy answer, mindfulness technique, or cognitive reframing capable of address-ing it because it reflected everything he had battled since childhood. What made it worse was that it also represented a roadblock to cr ating the professional life he had prayed would help to set him f

One of the primary values of a secure, warm, and trusting relationship with the therapist is our ability to serve as an amygdala
whisperer. Put in a less poetic way, the sociostatic processes that we
use to regulate the brains of others can be employed by the therapist
to lower amygdala activation, decrease arousal, and increase cortical involvement and neuroplastic processes. This allows memories
to be experienced at a lower level of arousal, consciously processed
with the cortex online, and gradually integrate dissociated neural
networks. The goal is to subject traumatic experiences to the same
updating processes and cortical modulation that occur with nontraumatic memories.

A LITTLE PSYCHOEDUCATION

Knowledge is power. Information is power.

—ROBIN MORGAN

With many clients, especially those with intellectualizing defenses
like Michael, psychoeducation concerning anxiety and panic can be
a very helpful adjunct to treatment. It is especially useful because
the narrative it provides creates cortical activation that can be paired
with the frightening input. When a therapist is sitting across from a
client, he can both experience his activation and think about what he
has been taught. Because the amygdala is responsive to descending
inhibition from the cortex, the cortical activation stimulated by the
psychoeducational narrative provides added top-down modulation
and inhibition. Describing to a client what is happening inside her
and predicting the consequences can serve as a bit of stress inocu-
lation via cortical activation and involvement. This is one piece of
become his or her own amygdala whisperer.
hael already had a general sense of how the amyg-
vagal system worked from his clinical training, I
tables below to expand his thinking and boost his

cortical activation. The first chart is a list of nine amygdala targets in the brain stem that cause some symptoms of anxiety and panic (with their fancy Latin names to enhance their legitimacy). My goal was to have Michael shift from associating his startle reaction with his parents and clients to thinking of the stimulation of the central gray or his lateral hypothalamus. In other words, this is a conditioned biological process and not something metaphysical, supernatural, or life threatening. It's just your amygdala trying to protect you. Here is the list of amygdala targets I shared with Michael.

Amygdala Targets in the Brain Stem and How They Make You Feel

Lateral hypothalamus	> Sympathetic activation	> Tachycardia > blood pressure
Dorsal vagal	> Parasympathetic activation	> Stomach discomfort
Parabrachial nucleus	> Respiration	Panting, problems breathing
Ventral tegmental area	> Dopamine	Agitation
Locus coeruleus	> Norepinephrine	Enhanced vigilance
Dorsal tegmental nucleus	> Acetylcholine	Stress memories
Nucleus R P caudalis	> Reflexes	Startle response
Central gray	< Behavior	Freezing, withdrawal
Trigeminal, facial nerve	Mouth open, jaw movements	Fearful facial expressions
Paraventricular nucleus	ACTH release	Overall stress response

To reinforce his understanding of the physiological processes, I also shared with him a list of the symptoms of a panic attack. I wanted him to shift from being a fearful victim to an expert about fear so that his mind (cortex) could maintain maximum activation as his arousal increased. The repetition across these two charts is intentional—the more overlearned knowledge becomes, the more resistant it is to the inhibitory actions of the amygdala. This parallels the repetitions you engage in learning to play a sport or an instrument—the more overlearned it becomes, the more reflexive the moves.

Panic Symptoms Triggered by Amygdala Arousal

Palpitations, pounding heart, or accelerated heart rate

Sensations of shortness of breath or smothering

Sweating

Trembling or shaking

Feeling of choking

Chest pain or discomfort

Nausea or abdominal distress

Feeling dizzy, unsteady, lightheaded, or faint

Derealization (feelings of unreality)

Depersonalization (being detached from oneself)

Numbness or tingling sensations

Chills or hot flushes

Fear of losing control, going crazy, or dying

When a client describes a symptom he is experiencing, you can find it on the list of panic symptoms and then see if might be on the brain stem target chart. Cross-reference the emotions, thoughts, and bodily reactions to the aids in stimulating cortical circuits to connect and inhibit fear circuitry.

SYSTEMATIC DESENSITIZATION

You're braver than you believe, stronger than you seem, and smarter than you think.

—A. A. MILNE

Systematic desensitization is a tried and true way of working with trauma and traumatic memories. It is essentially a process of pairing exposure to traumatic memories with relaxation training with a warm, caring, and competent therapist. In other words, it pairs repetition and reinforcement, increased affect regulation, and cortical activation during recall. Many newer forms of trauma therapy are essentially repackaged systematic desensitization.

The nature of Michael's recall changed as his brain slowly began to reprocess and store his memories utilizing more cortical circuitry. The addition of the safety of our relationship allowed him to be better able to integrate his current experience with recall. Reality matters, and one of the things that trauma therapy must do is allow current realities to be woven into memories of a frightening and vulnerable past. In other words, turning the past into the past.

When Michael and I got down to the nuts and bolts of working on his panic reaction when sitting face-to-face with a client, we began by making a list of all the things that made him anxious about being with a client. He told me that his anticipatory anxiety began the moment he made the appointment. He reported instantly feeling a tightness in his chest and shallow breathing as he entered the appointment into his schedule. He said that this was the lowest level of anxiety he would feel about seeing a client, so we started creating a hierarchy of arousal with this at number 10. He then told me that the highest level of arousal occurred when he was sitting across from a client who had become silent, and it felt like he should say something. In this situation, he was in a panic state, resisting the urge to jump up and run out of the room. Thus we had our two anchor points:

1. Sitting across from a silent client (most arousing)
10. Entering the appointment into my schedule book (least arousing)

As we discussed his experiences in depth, Michael said that even if he wasn't paying attention to the calendar, he noticed that his anxiety would get worse with each passing day. He described how he suffered the night before, lying in bed, feeling frightened, and unable to sleep. Michael described his racing heart as he drove to the clinic on the day of the session, and how his heart sank when the receptionist told him that his client had arrived. We discussed these and other experiences, rated each association with a level of distress, and then came up with the following stress hierarchy:

1. Sitting across from a silent client
2. Walking into the waiting room to get the client
3. Being told his client had arrived
4. Driving to the clinic
5. Waking up on the morning of the session
6. Lying in bed thinking about it the night before
7. Realizing that the session was one day away
8. Realizing the session was two days away
9. Realizing over the weekend that the session was during the upcoming week
10. Entering the appointment into my schedule book

The next step was to figure out the best ways to help Michael regulate his arousal, anxiety, and fear as we activated these challenging associations. We tried various breathing techniques, visualizations, and biofeedback to explore how he could be more aware of the subtleties of his anxiety and learn to gain some control over it. Biofeedback helped him to better detect muscle tension and learn how slowing and speeding up his breathing impacted his arousal. Later, coupling this with a mental image he found relaxing, sitting at the top of a mountain trail he would sometimes hike, he slowly found that he could use his mind to regulate his arousal—in my terms, causing enough cortical activity to employ downward modulation of the amygdala, ANS, and other regulatory processes. During the five learning sessions, I encouraged him to practice using them in his day-to-day life across as many stressful and nonstressful situations as possible.

Armed with a deepening awareness of his arousal, we began to pair relaxation with each situation in his hierarchy, starting with number 10. We would begin with a breathing exercise that would lead into a visualization and description of the stressful situation. I would have him describe the situation in as much detail as possible to make it as real for him as possible. I would ask him about the sights, sounds, colors, and even the smells associated with, for example, entering the appointment into his book. I would interrupt his visualization from time to time and ask him what he was feeling, what his level of distress was (on a scale of 0–10), and remind him to employ his relaxation skills. When his level of distress reached 0 for a particular stressor, we would move up the hierarchy to the next stressful event and repeat the same process. I was careful to do this as slowly as possible and to move forward only when Michael appeared to grow impatient with our pace. This helped me to be confident that I wouldn't go too quickly for him and risk triggering feelings of anxiety and loss of control.

This process moved along, evoking many memories and feelings which we took time to explore and process. These detours served the general process of therapy while allowing Michael to better control the pace. In my experience, systematic desensitization is more of a circular and reiterative process that can be woven into therapy in a flexible manner. In the ongoing process of exposing the client to arousing memories and then switching over to relaxation, we can optimize neural integration and memory reprocessing. By helping a client to relax via relationships and specific skills, his cortex stays online and new learning happens, which includes the building and activation of descending fibers from the cortex to the amygdala. It is these new connections that allow us to not have a fight-flight-freeze response in the face of something the amygdala has tagged as dangerous: in Michael's case, sitting across from someone who might become emotional.

EYE MOVEMENT DESENSITIZATION AND REPROCESSING

Nothing fixes a thing so intensely in memory as the wish to forget it.

—MICHEL DE MONTAIGNE

A few decades ago, a somewhat different approach to working with traumatic memories emerged, eye movement desensitization and reprocessing (EMDR). It is the brainchild of Francine Shapiro, who discovered that she was able to decrease the emotional arousal associated with her own negative memories subsequent to repeated visual scanning from left to right. Over time, she worked this into a structured intervention that paired exposure to painful memories with the eye movements she found helpful. There was a great deal of pushback against EMDR, but it eventually gained traction and is now accepted as helpful treatment for trauma and PTSD. Like any other treatment, it doesn't work for everyone, but it helps enough people to add it to the list of possible interventions when working with traumatized individuals.

Some believe that the active component of EMDR is not the eye movements (or alternating sensory stimuli) at all, but the gradual exposure to traumatic experiences in the context of an attentive other who is employing standard cognitive-behavioral techniques. (In other words, just another form of systematic desensitization.) I suspect this is true for some subset of clients who benefit from EMDR, and there is no arguing with success. I know of more than a few clients who are dismissive of the process and unwilling to engage in it because of the sensory stimulation. In my experience, alternating sensory stimulation with the recall of conflictual, painful, or traumatic experiences does make a difference. Dr. Shapiro did not claim to know the mechanisms of action for EMDR, but the most commonly voiced belief is that it is related to integrating both cortical hemispheres in memory processing.

If a client finds EMDR helpful and that the sensory component is part of its success, why would this be? Is hemispheric integration really the best explanation? In other words, how could looking back and forth or being tapped alternately on your right and left knee make your brain process information in a different way that could help you to heal? My guess is that the secret to the success of EMDR, for those with whom it works, has to do with the orienting reflex. When we compare the brains of individuals with and without PTSD in memory tasks, we find that trauma often results in a significant change in the neurodynamics of memory consolidation and retrieval.

When nontraumatized individuals are confronted with new information, what is called a saliency circuit is activated in the cingulate and insular cortices along with regions of the temporal lobe and hippocampus. This puts systems of memory on alert to prepare us to learn something new and perhaps update old memories b' on new information. Another way to think of the saliency circuit is as a lookout for important or novel information that sounds the alarm in memory circuits when it sees something that fits the bill. It seems that for individuals with PTSD, the saliency system is inhibited and instead, the system for autobiographical memory is activated.

This change in neurodynamics results in novel experiences triggering anxiety and traumatic memories instead of orienting toward and learning from new experiences. This is likely why traumatized and highly anxious individuals tend to live limited and routinized lives. By structuring your life to avoid novelty, you protect yourself from being triggered—a very logical means of self-protection. The symptom of neophobia, or fear of anything new or unexpected, has been recognized in trauma victims for decades. This basic change in the neurodynamics of memory may be a key to what keeps many victims locked into endless rounds of recall, retraumatization, and avoidance of potentially curative experiences. The question then becomes how the sensory stimulation components of EMDR might disrupt this closed system. A possible answer to this question may rest in bypassing the saliency network of the cingulate and insular cortices by utilizing a more primitive saliency system called the orienting reflex.

Neural systems organizing sensory, motor, and memory abilities have been involved in collaborative coevolution since we were fish. One piece of evidence for this is that when we use the large muscles of our legs to walk or run, they secrete neural growth factors that cross the blood-brain barrier and stimulate neuroplasticity and learning. This suggests that our muscles evolved to tell our brains ͻy attention when we are moving because something important happening. In the same way, our animal ancestors without ͻtices likely used primitive orienting responses to trigger ͻory systems to pay attention and learn.

Although humans have evolved a more complex cortical saliency system, the more ancient orienting system has been conserved. My suspicion is that EMDR leverages our orienting response to bypass the inhibition of the cortical saliency circuit disrupted and bypassed by severe trauma. The eye movements and other sensory stimuli used in EMDR trigger the orienting response and activate temporal-hippocampal circuits of explicit memory. This allows for an integration and reprocessing of traumatic memories into the now activated cortical systems of nontraumatic memory.

Support for this theory may be found in the processes of memory updating that occur during the rapid eye movement (REM) stage of sleep. On the face of it, we certainly don't need to move our eyes to see what is going on in our imaginations. These rapid eye movements during sleep likely reflect that our systems of memory updating and consolidation coevolved along with our orienting reflex. While the window to this process may have been via side-to-side eye movements, the orienting reflex is also activated via touch, sound, and other sensory modalities.

14

TAKE-AWAYS

Doubt is not a pleasant condition, but certainty is an absurd one.

—VOLTAIRE

In my opinion, the most important single idea contained in this book is that humans are complex beings that have been shaped by evolution across the eons to adapt to an ever-changing world. Nothing about us is simple, and no simple solution fits all people. Every one of us is an experiment in nature, as is every group, and each and every therapeutic relationship. Therefore, any one-size-fits-all solution is, in my opinion, destined to fail most clients. I also believe that a successful therapist needs to be part performance artist, part improviser, but most importantly a knowledgeable and well-trained psychotherapist with access to as much knowledge and information as possible. Beyond these core principles, I decided to conclude this small volume with what I feel to be the main take-away messages of this book and my work.

   1. The Social Brain: If we are to progress in our understanding of the human brain, we need to understand and study it in the context of relationships. Excellent research has been done in mapping the architecture and function of neural systems, yet very little of the social sciences have been considered by those who study functional neuroanatomy. Our brains have evolved to interact, cooperate, and regulate one another. To truly understand them, they must be studied in their natural habitat—relationships. It is much better to think of the brain as part of a family or a tribe.

2. **The Social Synapse:** The synapse between neurons is a biochemical ecosystem that evolved to communicate complex messages at lightning speed from one neuron to the next and back again. Nature has replicated this same strategy in the space between individuals we can call the social synapse. Biochemical communication across the social synapse continues in the form of odors and pheromones, along with a range of other channels of communication including eye gaze, facial expressions, touch, language, metaphors, and ideas. This broad bandwidth of conscious and unconscious communication across the social synapse allows us to imitate, attune, and synchronize our thoughts, feelings, and behaviors, allowing us to create superorganisms called couples, families, tribes, and nations.

3. **Sociostasis:** Because our brains have evolved to be such exquisitely social organs, we now have the ability to affect each other's neurochemistry, metabolism, and neuroplastic processes. We leverage these abilities in nurturing relationships to raise our children, help our students to learn in the classroom, and assist our clients to heal in psychotherapy. This is why regulated parents raise securely attached children, why loving teachers are able to teach children deemed unteachable by educational institutions, and why clients consistently report that their positive feelings for their therapist appear to be a central mechanism of emotional healing.

4. **The Potential Therapeutic Value of Countertransference:** We are linked across the social synapse through many conscious and unconscious levels of communication. Because of this, we sometimes discover that we project into others and sometimes they project into us. These projections might come into our consciousness in the form of emotions, bodily sensations, visual images, or memories from our past. When we become aware of them, it is

our responsibility to determine their origins as best we can. Sometimes they may have more to do with our clients than ourselves. When this is the case, they can serve as valuable bridges to communication, attunement, and empathy. This is why we need to spend considerable time in therapy to be insightful about our inner worlds. To use them successfully in therapy, it is important to present them as hypotheses and take responsibility for the fact that you may well be wrong. If these two skills are in place, you will be able to use your inner experience with your clients to their advantage.

5. The Centrality of Arousal to Psychotherapy: New learning requires a state of mind and brain that allow for cortical participation and integration, both of which are inhibited during high states of arousal. Therefore, mental health, learning, and positive outcomes in psychotherapy depend on the successful modulation of arousal. This allows the cortex to stay online, learn, and help to heal a brain that has been dysregulated, wounded, or traumatized. Therefore, identifying and treating stress is not only a special focus of psychotherapy, it should be included in all forms of treatment for nearly every presenting problem.

6. The Invisible Half Second: We don't live in the now, but about a half second behind the now. During this half second, the ways in which our personal, cultural, and species memories influence emotion, perception, and cognition come to shape our conscious experience. Within this half second exists the workings of the Freudian unconscious, the mechanisms of implicit processing of cognitive neuroscience, the biases of social psychology, and the perceptual principles of Gestalt psychology. This idea seems to be a unifying principle of all areas of study that attempt to understand the deep narrative of human experience.

7. Executive Functioning: Contrary to the prevalent dogma, executive functioning is not a straightforward cognitive process emerging from one region of the brain. It is a full mind-brain-body process that relies on at least three complex executive systems with different evolutionary histories, developmental courses, and skill sets. To understand executive functioning, you have to grasp all three systems and how they work together to guide our emotional, intellectual, and social abilities. In addition to the intellectual intelligence we have traditionally been told to pursue through education, we have to develop our emotional and affective intelligence to regulate our primitive executive. In addition, we need to develop the self-awareness and empathic capacities of the third executive system to be able to integrate with others and develop a reliable relationship with ourselves. Optimal executive functioning at work or in our personal lives requires the participation of all three areas of learning and understanding. Wisdom is something that has to be nurtured throughout life—otherwise, old age will show up all by itself.

8. Neurodynamics: As a parallel to psychodynamics, neural systems within the brain and nervous system need to communicate, integrate, and successfully cooperate with one another for normal adaptive functioning. Dissociation and disconnection occur at both the psychological and neurological levels and cause psychological distress and disruptions of cognitive functioning. While neurologists have studied disconnection syndromes that result in disruptions of perception and cognition, therapists have explored the disconnections that occur after trauma which disrupt behavior, emotion, identity, and emotional regulation. We are at a point where we can begin to integrate neurodynamics and psychodynamics into a functional whole. This is at the core of the project for a scientific psychology.

9. Integration: The concept of integration is central to both psychological and neurological functioning. Both the mind and the brain consist of many component parts that together give rise to consciousness. In the realm of the mind, we work toward expanded awareness of thoughts and feelings that have been defensively excluded from conscious awareness. The purpose is to expand clients' understanding and appreciation of as many parts of themselves as they are able to tolerate. Similarly, optimal neurological functioning depends upon the development and integration of the many neural systems required for everyday activities. Both psychological and neurological function can be described as optimal when all systems have developed properly and are in cooperative communication with other functions and networks, respectively.

10. **Epigenetics:** After a century of exploring the correlations between childhood experiences and challenges in adulthood, we finally have a convincing causal model for the underlying mechanism of action, epigenetics. Through epigenetics, early experiences, both good and bad, are translated into the biochemistry, neuroanatomy, and functional relationships within our brains. The structures of our nervous systems become, in a manner of speaking, a physical record of our past experiences and learning histories. They develop in the environment in which we have to survive as children, which thus is the environment for which we are most adapted. The challenges that bring people to psychotherapy are often the result of the mismatch of their neural programming and the environment they are now trying to navigate. Because epigenetics is an ongoing process, early biological programs can potentially be reorganized in the context of successful therapy.

11. **The Biopsychosocial Triad:** The growing recognition of the fact that we are social animals with minds led to the notion of a biopsychosocial orientation to treatment. It means that to understand and treat our clients, we need to appreciate the multiple ways in which both their mental health and mental challenges exist in a matrix of interactive biological, psychological, and social influences. These three factors have been woven together during evolution and are rewoven in unique ways during development.

12. **Memory Work:** Because our brains have evolved to remember the past and to anticipate the future, our minds are in a constant state of reflection and anticipation. The psychological wisdom of Buddhism points to this automatic process as the source of much of human suffering, an idea largely corroborated by all forms of Western psychotherapy. Early memory, in its many forms, influences and guides us throughout our entire lives. The transference and countertransference manifest during psychotherapy are treasure troves of memory if we learn how to see and understand them. Psychotherapy can't be isolated from the rest of a client's life. The client needs to remember what has happened in psychotherapy and not just become an excellent client in session yet continue to suffer all the other hours of the week.

13. **The Significance of Narrative Coherence:** The coherence of a client's narrative contains a great deal of information about what is unconscious and inaccessible to autobiographical memory. It provides a window into the level of stress during childhood, the quality and nature of the available caretaking relationships, and the development and integration of many neural networks dedicated to cognitive, emotional, and social functions. The many neural systems that need to be online and active when communicating narratives to others means that we can develop ideas about what systems are not functioning by examining the missing components that render a narrative incoherent. This is something we can do in session with a little training and lots of experience.

14. **Psychoeducation:** For many clients, coming to understand how the brain and mind work helps them to see beyond the reflexive fear that they are broken or crazy. If you can help them to see the logic of how their brains and minds have been shaped, they can come to understand the past adaptive value of their thoughts, emotions, beliefs, and behaviors. Further, they can come to realize that they had no choice and that what was done to them was not their fault, despite the egocentric attribution style and distorted notions

of causality that we all have early in life. Perhaps just as important is that they can learn that all of humanity struggles with navigating life with an imperfect and Paleolithic brain that is a poor match for our current existence.

15. Experiments in Living: In line with translating clinical work into a client's life, most forms of psychotherapy should include structured experiments in living. This is where the insights derived from therapy are applied in the workshop of life where fears are confronted, limitations are tested, and new ways of being are tried out. These experiments should be carefully crafted in a graduated manner to ensure success by not overwhelming the client with stress and shutting down the brain's ability to learn. The opposite of trauma is the ability to remain cortical when confronted with a challenge—a principle at the heart of parenting, teaching, and psychotherapy. In psychotherapy, understanding is the booby prize, so we need to do all we can to help clients take the learning out of therapy and into their lives.

16. Build a Solid Case Conceptualization: Most new and many experienced therapists never spend the time to formulate a case conceptualization. Despite the fact that therapy is an art form and requires flexibility and improvisation, I'm always surprised that when pressed, many therapists admit that they are just winging it. Being with a client in session is an emotional and interpersonal experience. It is often difficult to even remember what happened during a session because we get so involved with active listening and interacting with our clients. Yet there are many defenses, road-blocks, and pitfalls in treatment that can't be seen from the ground. When you put the time into building, updating, and refining a case conceptualization, you have the ability to go up to 10,000 feet to get a look at what is happening in treatment from a helpful vantage point. Often, revisiting your case conceptualization will remind you of theories, strategies, and techniques that will allow you to go back in with fresh eyes and new and valuable ideas.

These ideas or core principles are nowhere carved in stone. They are all working hypotheses I encourage you to experiment with, modify, and even discard if something better comes along. There is still so much to learn about these ideas, and about all of the ideas presented in this book as we try to optimize and leverage them in ways that will prove helpful to our clients.

A FINAL STORY

Political ideology can corrupt the mind, and science.

—E. O. WILSON

As doctoral students, my peers and I were heavily steeped in CBT. We were discouraged, shamed actually, for showing interest in other schools of psychotherapy, all of which were considered to be psychobabble. After many years in the rich intellectual environment of Harvard's psychology department, where both debate and collaboration were encouraged, I was well prepared to resist the prevailing dogma of my new academic home. As I learned the theories and methods of CBT (which I often found useful), I continued my readings in psychoanalysis, family systems, neuroscience, and behavioral medicine. Early on, I was fortunate enough to meet and work with a number of professors in psychiatry and neurology who were a far better match to my eclectic approach to mental health. These brilliant and dedicated thinkers helped me stay sane in the challenging political environment of my own rigid department.

In the later part of my first year, I was reading a book by Wilhelm Reich called *Character Analysis*, the first half of which had been the inspiration for many forms of somatic therapy and the deep exploration of transference. To avoid being ridiculed, I carried Reich's book around in a small wrinkled paper bag. Unbeknownst to me, the paper bag had raised suspicion and stirred gossip that I had a drinking problem. What other explanation could there be for a bag about the size of a pint of whisky that was always mixed in with my CBT texts and stat books? It was around this time that I was called into my advisor's office for what was described as an important meeting.

As I lowered myself into the seat beside his desk, I could tell by his expression that this was serious. Although I couldn't think of anything I had done wrong in either my academic or clinical work, I assumed I was in significant trouble for something. I had already been witness to the mistakes of my colleagues being dealt with quickly and severely. My mind flashed back to the speech during orientation when we were told that only two-thirds of us would make it to graduation. It felt like a hammer was about to fall, and all of my feelings of inadequacy and shame began to glow white hot within me. I must have looked like the proverbial deer in the headlights when, with obvious discomfort, he began to speak: I braced myself for the worst.

He began by telling me that he was aware of my problem, and that he was concerned for my welfare. He continued to say that there were resources available to help me and that one of the other faculty, a long-time member of Alcoholics Anonymous, had volunteered to connect me with a sponsor. Although I understood his words, it took me awhile to process what he was saying. I don't know if it was because I was so anxious or because I hardly ever drank. The program had left no time for any kind of social life, and I spent most of my time trying to figure out statistics and research methodology. I stared at him in confused silence.

When I was finally able to wrap my mind around what he was saying, I said, "But I don't have a drinking problem." He shot me a patronizing expression, sat silently for a few moments, and pointed at the books on the table next to me. He said, "Let me see the bag." As I handed him the bag containing the Reich book, I could tell he was surprised by the feel and weight—it wasn't what he was expecting. I can still see his face as he pulled the book out of the bag;

his expression of surprise gave way to one of mild horror when he finally realized what it was. He eventually whispered, "This is even worse."

Apparently, a drinking problem was understandable, but how do you help someone who has gone over to the dark side? This was a wake-up call to the politics of academia and the intellectual limitations of the professors I had admired. As in politics, this kind of academic partisanship has stultifying consequences for both thinking and intellectual progress. After graduation, I went on to study family systems therapy, neurology, and neuroscience and have continued to explore multiple fields ever since. I tell this story to emphasize the dangers of replacing curiosity and exploration with dogma and groupthink.

APPENDIX 1

EVOLUTION

Evolution is a problem-solving and problem-creating process.

—JONAS SALK

The word "evolution" is widely used but seldom understood. In everyday language, it has become synonymous with all aspects of change, metamorphosis, and growth. People are described as having personalities, skills, and emotions that are in the process of evolving. Ideas that are modified, theories that are expanded, or beliefs that change are also described as evolving. While we all understand that change and evolution are somehow connected, the changes we witness within individuals are not what was described by Charles Darwin in *On the Origin of Species*.

Darwin's evolution is a process of modification within a biological community of plants or animals across multiple generations via changing patterns of genetic inheritance. The three core concepts of evolutionary change are biodiversity, mutations, and natural selection: Biodiversity is reflected in the variability of inherited traits that arise within individuals; mutations, which result from the modification of genes or their organization within our DNA; and natural selection, which describes the process by which individuals whose traits are the best fit for the current environment are those who tend to survive, reproduce, and thus spread their traits within the community. A commonly used example of biodiversity and natural selection is a species of peppered moth that inhabited London during the time of Darwin.

Before the Industrial Revolution, buildings made of a lighter stone favored lighter-colored moths while darker ones were easy prey against the lighter sandstone backgrounds. As industry expanded, soot from the factories darkened the buildings, favoring the survival of the darker colored individuals of that species. Light moths didn't turn into darker moths, but the darker ones became a better fit within the changing ecosystem, reproduced at greater rates, and resulted in overall change in coloration of the peppered moth population. This is natural selection in action. The lighter-color moths, which were once a good fit for the environment, slowly became less fit while their darker children increased in fitness because the darkening buildings provided them with better camouflage. Sometimes an entire species will disappear, which is called extinction. Scientists estimate that since the beginning of life on earth about 4 billion years ago, more than 99% of species have gone extinct. Yet over a trillion species remain. Now that's biodiversity!

In contrast to natural selection, artificial selection is directed towards a desired outcome rather than flexibility in the face of changing environmental demands. A good example of artificial selection is seen in dog breeding. Certain traits deemed desirable by breeders are found in individual dogs who are bred with other dogs with similar traits. This leads to the intensification of these traits in some of their children, who are then selectively bred to further concentrate those traits, and so on. This is how we get dogs with marked herding abilities, flat faces, or large or small size. Of course, this inbreeding also results in a higher concentration of genetic defects which occur less with random breeding. Artificial selection parallels natural selection, but survival and fitness are based on the intentions of the breeders rather than the survival demands of an environment. Eugenics, such as were practiced in Nazi Germany and the United States in the 20th century, is a term for artificial selection applied to desired traits in humans; in these cases, so-called Aryan physical traits and the eradication of imbecility, respectively.

Few ideas have caused as much controversy as the theory of evolution via natural selection. We are all familiar with the debate between evolutionists and those with a theocentric view of the universe who believe in intelligent design. Although the evidence for evolution is overwhelming, many believe that everything we see was created by the hand of god according to scripture. Even scientists who have spent their life studying evolution and have no doubt about its truth have extremely heated debates among themselves about how evolution works. The positive outcome of these debates has been the gradual expansion of evolutionary biology via new theories and discoveries. What has yet to be successfully integrated into evolutionary theory is the relative impact of being highly social creatures who depend on groups to survive. We have yet to understand how our membership in social groups influences natural selection.

THE EVOLUTION OF THE BRAIN

> *Brains exist because the distribution of resources necessary for survival and the hazards that threaten survival vary in space and time.*
>
> —JOHN ALLMAN

When things are difficult to comprehend, we tend to use simple metaphors to try to understand them. The brain has been likened to everything from an air conditioner, to a calculator, to an enchanted loom, depending on the prevailing images of the day. Today, the most common metaphor for the brain is a computer that stores information and launches applications like our laptops and smartphones. Metaphors, while helpful, need to be used with caution. While they can help us get started in the process of understanding, we have to be able to let them go when they reach the end of their usefulness.

Of the ways in which brains do parallel computers, the most compelling are (1) the use of vast processing and storage capacity, and (2) the strategy of converting all types of information into a binary code—patterns of 0s and 1s for computers and patterns of excitation and inhibition for the brain. The brain's patterns of excitation and inhibition can represent everything from motions, to emotions, to abstract thoughts, to a sense of purpose. Just like a computer, the most complex processes usually boil down to a basic binary code. But the more deeply you dig into the brain, the more you find that the metaphor of brain as computer begins to break down.

For example, years ago, I learned that if you press your index fingers against the palms of an infant's hands, she will grasp your fingers with so much strength that you will be able to pick her up. Of course, I couldn't resist trying it when my son was a few days old. Sure enough, this little being who didn't yet have the strength or coordination to hold a bottle was able to hold his own weight while suspended above his crib. Impressive! I did this periodically for entertainment and to demonstrate his strength to friends and relatives. After a few months, and to my dismay, he stopped holding on. I wondered whether he had grown bored of the trick or had simply become too heavy to hold his own weight. I soon came to learn that he had lost that ability to grip. But why?

This reflex, called the Palmer grasp, is one of a number of reflexes that was organized by the brain stem way back in our evolutionary history. Theory has it that this grasping reflex originated with our primate ancestors so small children could hold onto their mothers' fur as they moved from tree to tree, hunted for food, or drove off predators. And even though parents no longer swing from trees and can buy all sorts of devices to hold their infants as they go about their day, the grasping reflex is conserved within our genetic blueprint. Its current value, if it still has one, might be to enhance the experience of bonding as parents become captured or captivated by their baby's grasp.

The reason why my son was able to do this in the first place was the activation and excitation of the primitive reflex. The reason it stopped is because of the inhibition of these neural circuits. The activation of the Palmer grasp reflex had become inhibited by the cortex through descending neural networks that went all the way from the top of his brain down to its most primitive lower regions. Put in a slightly different way, the early excitation required to grasp from our ancient past was later inhibited by the more recently evolved need for the cortex to gain control over the hands and fingers. Thus, in the first few months of life, we get to see a little bit of evolutionary history in action—the primitive arising first, followed by more recent stages of evolution. For in order for us to learn to use our hands in dexterous ways that are under cortical control, we first have to free the hands from the "grip" of the brain stem.

Here is something even a bit more interesting. If, later in life, a person begins to have neural loss in the frontal and temporal lobes related to Alzheimer's or some other disease process, the Palmer reflex will return. What this means is that for most of our lives, the cortex is exerting an inhibitory influence on some portion of our brain stem to quell this reflex. The return of primitive reflexes—called cortical release signs—indicates that the neurons dedicated to inhibiting this reflex during the early months of life are no longer able to fulfill this function. That is why the return of primitive reflexes is considered to be an indication of cortical damage and neuronal loss.

Returning for a moment to our comparison of brains and computers, this example highlights a major difference between the two. Computers are built and programmed in the present with specific tasks in mind and are organized in a logical, linear, and coherent fashion. Computers don't need to be programmed in ways that interrupt or impede other aspects of their programming; their programming is simply modified. Alternatively, the brain has been organized and reorganized, piece by piece, over millions of years in response to the process of natural selection resulting from changing environmental and social demands. Sometimes, the adaptation to particular challenges in one era becomes a problem for later generations.

SPLINTER SKILLS

> *If you got rid of all the autism genetics, you wouldn't have science or art.*
>
>   —TEMPLE GRANDIN

When we think of the brain as a computer and forget that it is a complex adaptive system, we miss the fact that a great deal of the way it works seems illogical. While a computer is programmed to store information and make it readily available, our brains are designed to remember and forget, to develop abilities but not too much, to comprehend reality but not too accurately. You have probably seen or heard stories of individuals considered to be autistic with extraordinary skills and abilities. One example is a person who can listen to an hour-long piano concerto for the first time and immediately sit down and play the piece, note for note. Another might draw scenes they saw briefly in amazing detail, or be able to tell you on which day of the week any date in the past or the future will fall. These types of abilities are considered splinter skills because they exist in stark contrast to the individual's general level of functioning.

Why would someone with the type of atypical neurological development seen in autism have such phenomenal abilities while being impaired in everyday abilities like language, emotional regulation, or social skills? The answer, I believe, can be found in one of the ways in which inhibition and excitation work in our brains. Because we are social animals shaped by the needs of both individual and group survival, we have to take care of ourselves and contribute to our groups in ways that support group survival. If we as individuals or our groups don't survive, then our genes don't get passed on either. The importance of the balance of individual and group needs is reflected in our morals, laws, and codes of conduct.

The somewhat unnerving truth may be that tribes survive best when most people are about average, with just a few outliers. In other words, greatness (reflected in splinter skills) is sacrificed in the service of what's best for the group. The tribe can only tolerate so many savants because they don't contribute to the day-to-day survival of the group. Most everyone needs to contribute to basic survival. Although shooting for the lowest common denominator sounds maladaptive when applied to education, it may have been selected for the needs of group survival. Here inhibition acts to average out abilities across members of the tribe in a way similar to biochemistry dictating the morphology of the members of an ant colony to serve the group. Cortical areas inhibit each other in order to attain and maintain an average-functioning brain. This makes the best case for the popular notion that we only use 10% of our brains—just as the cortex expends some of its activity to inhibit the Palmer grasp, the cortex appears to expend considerable energy inhibiting itself so that most of us turn out average—the group needs lots of soldiers but only one general.

Further support for transcortical inhibition comes from patients without autism but who experience brain damage later in life. In a phenomenon referred to as acquired savant syndrome, a number of patients with brain damage have developed splinter skills later in life. The ability to play an instrument, engage in complex mathematical calculations, or draw impossibly complex images of fractals have emerged after concussions, brutal beatings, or being struck by lightning. In a fashion similar to the reappearance of a Palmer reflex in Alzheimer's disease when damage to one area of the brain releases another portion of the cortex, a region that may specialize in music, mathematics, or drawing will start to explode with previously inaccessible capabilities. The variabilities seen in autistic individuals reflect the kind of diversity that can occur when developmental brain processes relating to the averaging of abilities are disrupted. The emergence of splinter skills shows that brains have amazing capacities despite the fact that most of us don't display them.

Left-handedness, which reflects another experiment in brain development, correlates with a higher incidence of learning disabilities and mental disorders. On the other hand, it also correlates with creativity and artistic accomplishments. Left-handedness may be consistently limited to 10% of the human population because natural selection has "estimated" that this is an optimal percentage of this phenotype in the population to ensure group survival. Alternative neurodevelopmental patterns may result in a process that parallels mutation at the level of brain and mind that contributes to cultural innovation and the adaptive flexibility of the group. To label lower-frequency occurrences like autism and left-handedness pathological, may be to miss the real purpose of these individuals for group survival.

THE EVOLUTION OF THE SOCIAL BRAIN

The brain is embodied and the body is embedded.

—GERALD EDELMAN

When we compare ourselves to our closest primate cousins, chimpanzees and apes, we notice things like an increased contrast between the dark and light parts of our eyes and having hairless faces full of fine capillaries and muscles. These changes, which make little difference to our survival in the physical environment, have had a huge impact on our ability to communicate with one another and coordinate group behavior. Social animals certainly survive as individuals but more so as members of groups that are competitively fit. The selection pressures experienced by social animals come from the necessities of both individual and group survival. For this reason, the brain has evolved into both an organ of adaptation to the physical environment and a social organ of adaptation.

An understanding of evolutionary theory is extremely important to all of biology, especially neuroscience. Contemporary brain functioning doesn't always make sense when looked at from a current perspective. An intelligent neural designer who took on the challenge of engineering a brain would focus on developing an efficient biological mechanism adapted to the present environment. The brains in our heads have been shaped over millions of years via countless adaptational challenges, just like the peppered moths of London. Changes in food supply, followed by shifts in climate, followed by the arrival of a new predator or the appearance of a rival tribe all resulted in successive adaptational changes over thousands of generations.

Each adaptational challenge was faced by the neural diversity within individuals and tribes in the endless experimentation of natural selection. All of these compounded adaptations have resulted in countless neural reorganizations, much repurposing, and the birthing of new systems preserved within the brains of those members of the fittest human tribes. The contemporary human brain is a byzantine labyrinth of neural systems that only begrudgingly yields its secrets. Its structures reflect not only biological solutions to adaptational dilemmas but, to some degree, the sequential evolutionary history of our species. These are some of the reasons why we are often stumped by the logic of neural processing and surprised when we finally discover how the brain accomplishes a specific task. The solution never reflects the straightforward and logical strategy of a single intelligent engineer.

Another example of the evolutionary process is the existence of vestigial organs, which were useful to us in the past but have faded from a lack of survival value. A prime example may be our wisdom teeth, which have been conserved in most humans despite the fact that our jaws have become smaller with changes in our diet. As fetuses, humans start developing tails like their primate ancestors, which begin to fade by about eight weeks of gestation. Some babies are born with remnants of a tail when this process isn't successfully terminated. The only significance of the appearance of a tail during gestation is as a reminder of our evolutionary history. In a sense, the genetic memory of our tails is conserved during early development but later discontinued.

We also appear to have some behaviors and reflexes that serve no current purpose but are believed to have had survival value in our evolutionary past. The toe curling of a human infant (along with the Palmer grasp described above) is believed to have helped us grasp onto the mother's long hair and on branches when our ancestors lived in trees. The goose bumps we experience when cold or under stress once had the effect of raising body fur so it could trap more heat, and also made us appear larger in threatening situations. Some have postulated that the human hiccup is a descendant of a reptilian reflex used in respiration, where air is gulped in a similar manner. They support this claim with the fact that premature infants will hiccup more frequently until their lungs have matured. We stand to gain a great deal of understanding of ourselves by contextualizing our behaviors and experience within our evolutionary history.

On the surface, evolution is about adaptational change. Just below the surface, evolution is a dynamic interaction between innovation via processes like mutation and natural selection, and conserving traditional strategies and structures, some of which go back to the beginnings of life on earth. This is why an appreciation of our evolutionary history is vital to understanding how our brains and bodies function. In everyday language, the word "conservation" refers to concepts such as environmental sustainability, recycling, and the protection of natural habitats. In the realm of evolution, we use the term in a somewhat different way. For our present purposes, it can be used to mean both (1) the process of maintaining basic strategies across different levels of complexity, and (2) the continuation of primitive structures alongside later-evolving structures and functions.

The first category, conservation of strategies, includes processes such as using patterns of excitation and inhibition and systems integration across levels of increasing complexity. For example, we witness the balance of excitation and inhibition within cells, among individual cells, and between neural systems. In the complex government of systems within our brains, the visual and motor systems need to integrate in order for us to have hand-eye coordination. The homeostasis of sodium and potassium inside and outside of neurons allows them to fire and reload while the balance between the cortex and brain stem regions allows us to both sustain attention and orient to novel and potentially important stimuli.

Decades ago, the neuroscientist Paul MacLean (1985) presented a theory of the brain that focused on the conservation and juxtaposition of neural structures from multiple stages of evolution. His triune brain theory describes it as a three-part layered system—the modern human brain atop a primitive mammalian brain, atop a reptilian brain—with each ascending layer devoted to increasingly complex functions and abilities. At the base, the *reptilian brain*, relatively unchanged through evolutionary history, is responsible for activation, arousal, homeostasis, and basic drives. The *paleomammalian brain* (what some call the limbic system), central to learning, memory, and emotion, wraps around the reptilian brain. The highest layer, the *neomammalian brain* (cerebral cortex), is responsible for sensorimotor behavior, problem solving, conscious thought, and self-awareness.

Central to MacLean's theory and something especially important for clinical and social psychologists is the idea that our three brains don't necessarily communicate or work well together because of their differing functions and ways of processing information. In addition, only a small portion of the neomammalian brain is capable of verbal expression and self-awareness. Some of what therapists call dissociation is the result of inadequate communication and integration among these different brains. Further, MacLean's description of the reptilian and paleomammalian brains unconsciously influencing the conscious processing of the neomammalian brain roughly parallels the interaction of conscious and unconscious processes we focus on in therapy.

A superficial reading of MacLean's work might lead us to the idea that each layer of the triune brain evolved sequentially and independently from one another, but that is clearly not the case. In reality, the reptilian and paleomammalian brains have continued to evolve along with the neomammalian brain. Earlier structures are not simply conserved (unchanged) from past generations, but also undergo a process called *exaptation*—the modification of earlier-evolving brain structures for new applications. Thus, all three layers continue to evolve along with the emergence of ever more complex vertical and horizontal neural networks that connect them. This simultaneous conservation and modification of neural networks has led to an amazingly complex brain capable of a vast array of functions, from monitoring respiration to performing mathematical computations.

The amygdala and hippocampus work together and regulate one another in the realms of memory and reality testing. They are also components of different executive systems that can work together or inhibit one another under certain conditions. Deep in our brains lies the vermis, which evolved from fish to help them stay upright as they swim. It now sits at the core of a structure called the cerebellum that helps us not only to stay upright, but also to maintain our cognitive and emotional balance. The reason why so much of our language is grounded in physical metaphors is that much of our cognitive and emotional processing is based in somatic experience and the history of our physical evolution.

A prime example of conservation of structures that are most often of concern to us in our everyday lives is the primitive executive system of the amygdala. The amygdala is an organ of appraisal, responsible for associating internal and external stimuli with positive and negative reactions. It decides what we should approach and avoid; what is life threatening and life sustaining, attractive and beneficial or disgusting and repugnant. The amygdala is best known and most studied for its role in an animal's reaction to dangerous stimuli in the external environment and its activation of our fight-flight-freeze response to threat. We have learned a great deal about this system in humans from the study of rodents because so many essential components have been conserved from our earliest mammalian ancestors.

During the evolution from the rodent to the human brain, there was obviously a great deal of neural expansion and increased processing sophistication. The primitive amygdala executive system, which was once a large proportion of the mammalian brain, has been overshadowed by later-evolving cortical processors. But don't let its size fool you! It still exerts an oversized influence on our experience and behavior. In fact, this primitive executive still holds veto power over our other executive systems.

The amygdala executive and the fight-flight-freeze system it oversees were shaped by natural selection early in evolution and remain relatively unchanged to this day. It was specifically designed for coping with direct threats to our physical survival that would resolve relatively quickly for better or worse. All of our biochemical responses of adrenaline and cortisol halt the maintenance functions of the body, like our immune system, neuroplasticity, and new learning, in an all-out struggle for immediate survival. But here is the rub—it now resides in a far more complex brain that exists within a more complex culture. To make things worse, the primitive amygdala executive has difficulty distinguishing between those things which are truly life threatening and those that are simply negative. So now we become fearful, agitated, or have panic attacks at the thought of getting less than an A on an exam, speaking in public, or driving on the freeway. Our Paleolithic amygdala executive is out of its element in modern technological society, making anxiety disorders and the impact of sustained stress a ubiquitous physiological and psychological challenge.

THE PRICE OF EVOLUTIONARY CONSERVATION

> *With modern parts atop old ones, the brain is like an iPod built around an eight-track cassette player.*
>
> —SHARON BEGLEY

When we begin to examine the brain in the context of evolution, a pattern of sequential adaptations through conservation and innovation emerges into focus. Put in a slightly different way, successful adaptation seems to have leveraged a combination of old structures put to new purposes along with newly evolved structures to navigate survival challenges. Evidence of this is reflected in how the brain processes social rejection. As humans grew increasingly social, survival fitness came to be equated with our ability to stay connected and stick together. The social brain networks that arose to support connectedness (e.g., attachment, theory of mind, social engagement) recruited existing networks transmitting physical pain to motivate us to cooperate and stay connected. In addition to feeling good when we are with our friends and family, we also feel pain when we are separated, rejected, or shamed. So now when we are rejected, our primitive pain circuitry creates pain in our chest that we call heartbreak. This is why the pain of social rejection has been shown to be decreased by taking two Tylenol.

The problem with conservation is that what may deal well with a current adaptational challenge could become a problem later in evolution. Now that we have so many systems dedicated to positive attachment, is it still the best survival strategy to feel so much pain related to loss? Given that loss is such a normal part of life, might we be better off if it didn't result in so much depression, grief, and even suicide? In another example of conservation, observing a predator triggers specific brain networks that make us fall silent in order to avoid detection. This automatic reflex works fine for mammals and other primates and has been strongly conserved in humans. Humans, however, have evolved to be highly dependent on the use of language for essential processes involving memory, social connectivity, and self-awareness. Narrative also came to play a significant role in the integration of neural systems among the two hemispheres and between cortical and subcortical processing. In other words, the use of language in narratives enhances neural, psychological, and social integration.

When people are traumatized, these primitive fear circuits are activated, and the impulse to startle, freeze, and fall silent are activated as well. The speechless terror seen in trauma and the subsequent inhibition of language results in deficits in all of the functions that it has evolved to serve. Thus, what may have enhanced the survival of our nonverbal ancestors has now become a significant liability for neural integration, psychological well-being, and social connectedness—in other words, key components upon which our brains depend for our ongoing adaptation and survival. For our primitive ancestors, environmental and social conditions remained relatively constant throughout life, meaning that early learning served them well. With the rapid changes of modern society—increased mobility, new technologies, and extended life spans—being locked into old ways of thinking, feeling, and acting is a much greater liability for well-being and survival.

APPENDIX 2

GENETICS AND EPIGENETICS

I am a trained psychologist and I think of all human issues in terms of psychology, neuroscience, genetics, and evolutionary history.

—HOWARD GARDNER

A central topic of discussion during most of my training as a psychotherapist was determining whether a client's illness was organic or functional, a result of nature or nurture. Organic illnesses were those with agreed-upon biological causes such as Alzheimer's and Korsakoff syndrome. Functional illnesses, such as depression and anxiety, were believed to be the result of stress, trauma, and emotional conflicts. If an illness was deemed organic, clients were referred to physicians, while those with functional illnesses were referred to psychotherapists. Sorting disorders into dichotomous categories made us feel a bit more confident that we understood something about the human condition. When clients didn't fit exactly into either category, which happened regularly, we would consider them to be exceptions to our rules. We became so attached to these categories that they became difficult to question. It was a rare health professional who crossed over the line to suggest that those with organic illnesses might benefit from psychotherapy, or that a person's anxiety or depression might be the result of an underlying physical illness.

Some illnesses, like schizophrenia, became theoretical battle-grounds. Some were convinced that it was a genetically transmitted brain disease, while others believed that it was a consequence of conflictual family dynamics. For me, the study of schizophrenia was my gateway beyond the organic-functional distinction. It was clear from both the research and my clinical experience that genetics, brain functioning, and family dynamics played a meaningful role. Yet each theoretical camp refused to give the other camp any credit. Eventually, the research proved that all three were at play, and my experiences taught me that scientific objectivity was more aspiration than actual.

We now know that nature and nurture (genetics and experience) work together to shape our brains, abilities, and disabilities. We also know that the mind arises from the interaction between our developing brain and social interactions, and that all psychiatric illnesses involve both organic and mental processes. Nature and nurture become one during development, and the line between organic and functional illnesses, and the separation of body and mind, dissolves into an interactive process now referred to as experience-dependent plasticity. Experience-dependent plasticity means that our brains are structured and restructured by our interactions with the social and natural environments during development.

Although we are born with the genes given to us by our parents, which of those genes are expressed in the building of our brains and bodies is guided by experience. Neurons and genes are different forms of coded information that remain flexible for the purpose of adaptation. Together, they build our brains, minds, and bodies while modifying them in ways that help us cope with the environmental and social challenges we face during development. This last sentence would have blown my mind 30 years ago—now it just puts a smile on my face.

GENETICS

The truth, it is said, is rarely pure or simple, yet genetics can, at
times, seem seductively transparent.

—IAIN MCGILCHRIST

I still remember the lecture in my high school biology class about
the monk Gregor Mendel. Growing pea plants in the garden of the
abbey where he lived, Mendel discovered many of the basic principles of genetic inheritance. Because of the conservation of basic
genetic mechanisms during evolution, his discoveries with plants
turned out to apply to all animals, including humans. It turned out
that he uncovered the underlying mechanisms of genetic inheritance that apply to all complex life forms on earth. His findings
included the discovery of *dominant* and *recessive genes* and the principles of *segregation* and *independent assortment*. Centuries later, with
Crick and Watson's discovery of the double helix, Mendel's observations were understood to be the effects of template genetics, or
the way in which genes and chromosomes combine to pass along
traits from one generation to the next.

We now know that the genetic information we inherit from our
parents is coded in four amino acid bases (adenine, thymine, gua-
nine, and cytosine) wound together within our DNA—a kind of
twisted spiral ladder. The approximately 23,000 pairs of these amino
acids, spun tightly together within the double helix, are embedded
within the nucleus of each of our cells. The genetic code within our
DNA contains the formula for all of the components of our brain
and body. When egg and sperm come together during conception,
genetic information from both parents comes together in a similar
way to Gregor Mendel's fertilized pea plants, and traits from both
parents are expressed or repressed (dominant or recessive) based on
similar principles.

What has been called the central dogma of molecular genetics is the process by which the genetic code contained within our DNA is converted into the building blocks of our brains and bodies. Depending on what structures we need to build, the double helix will "unzip" in certain regions that contain the appropriate code for what is required. When the proper code becomes available, molecules called messenger RNA (mRNA) match the sequences within the DNA and build the protein structures we need. These structures are then transported out of the nucleus to where they are used to construct needed structures. The central dogma is this flow from DNA, to messenger RNA (mRNA), to protein, a process called transcription. The initial assumption about the transcription of our genetic code into biological structures was that the structure was predetermined by the genes we inherit. The experiences of an animal were not thought to impact the expression of the genetic code unless something like radiation resulted in genetic mutations.

Although articulating the process of transcription was a huge leap forward in our understanding of genetics, it left many unanswered questions. A central one concerned why individuals who share the same genetic material (genotype) would come to express different traits (phenotype). I worked with a family of 10 children, all from the same parents, where 5 of the 10 developed schizophrenia. I spent countless hours (as did the family) trying to account for who became ill and who did not. What was obvious in this family was that inheriting identical genetic material and even growing up in the same household did not result in identical outcomes, but how?

It has been learned more recently that the portion of the genetic information that participates in transcription appears to be relatively small. The majority of what was initially called junk was thought to perhaps serve as placeholders or simply be the accumulated debris of natural selection. It turned out that some of this junk participated in guiding molecules called introns and exons involved in the selection of portions of the genetic code to transcribe. It is this selection process that begins to tell the story of how individuals with the same genetic material can have different developmental outcomes (phenotypes). If you think of the genetic code as a keyboard with 23,000 keys and each song selects the use of certain keys, we have a more sophisticated way of thinking about our genetic information. The genes we are born with, the expression of which the good abbot studied so long ago, is only half the genetic story. The other half of the story is the selection of which genes are expressed and which are suppressed. It is when we turn to this question of expression that epigenetics comes into focus.

EPIGENETICS

Genetics is not your destiny.

—GEORGE CHURCH

The biologist C. H. Waddington coined the term *epigenetics* by placing the prefix *epi* (Greek for over or above) in front of *genetics*. The clear message here is that there are forces that control genetic expression, many of which are yet to be discovered. The field of epigenetics is the study of the forces that guide the choice of which genes are chosen for expression and why. Going back to the piano analogy, epigenetics would be the selection of which keys to use for each song. More directly, what sections of our DNA are selected for transcription and what principles guide their selection?

Much of the foundational work in epigenetics has been carried out by Michael Meaney and his colleagues. The research they began publishing during the 1990s has explored the effects of a rat's maternal behavior on the developing brains of her young pups. The central question was whether the amount of grooming, retrieving, and nursing received by the pups would have an impact on genetic expression. The strategy was to compare the brains of rat pups who received the most attention with those who received the least. Some studies even examined the effects of being deprived of a mother's attention altogether. The implications of this research for human development and well-being are mind-blowing.

The research in epigenetics is central to connecting the field of neuroscience with the broad study of human development, education, and psychotherapy. After a century of research demonstrating positive correlations between childhood experience and adult outcome, we now have a biological mechanism that may provide us with causal relationships that can guide future research. Meaney's work also provides us with an animal model for Bowlby's theories about the influence of caretaker availability and contact on the developing brain. It also provides us with a very specific mechanism of action that explains how early experience is translated into the wetware of the brain. With these two foundational pieces in place, we can better understand the connection between early experience and adaptation later in life. This is especially important in exploring the challenges to resiliency of adults who were stressed and traumatized as children and adolescents.

Overall, the results of this research have shown that more attention received by rat pups is correlated with biochemical changes in their brains that support (1) neural health, plasticity, and learning; (2) the regulation of stress and arousal; and (3) future maternal behavior. In each category, there are measurable changes in the neuroanatomy and biochemistry in specific regions of the rats' brains that support these functions. For example, pups that receive more attention have more synapses, dendrites, and neurochemicals supportive of plasticity and learning. These pups tend to have more cortisol receptors in their hippocampi and endorphin receptors in their amygdalas. Just these two differences, among the many that were discovered, protect their brains from high levels of stress and help them to benefit from regulating biochemicals present in their brains. When they grow up to have pups of their own, the daughters who received more attention demonstrate enhanced metabolic activity in social brain network areas as well as more oxytocin and estrogen receptors in those areas that organize maternal behavior. See the box below for a summary of these findings.

More maternal attention correlates with:
- More synapses, longer dendrites, increased survival, increased neuronal and growth hormone activity
- Increased expression of glucocorticoid receptor gene promoter in the hippocampus and lower cortisol secretion in response to stress
- Increased levels of benzodiazepine and adrenalin receptors
- Decreased fear reactivity, startle response, and helplessness behavior
- Enhanced metabolic activation in the medial cortex and anterior cingulate cortex
- Increased levels of oxytocin and estrogen receptors in the medial preoptic areas (a maternal center in rats)
- Less sexual behavior and less likely to become pregnant shortly after birth

Less maternal attention correlates with:
- Decreased synaptic density in medial prefrontal cortex
- Increased neuronal and glial death; decreases in growth hormone levels and glial density
- In the amygdala, reduced benzodiazepine receptors and increased mRNA expression
- Increased startle response and greater cortisol secretion in response to mild stress
- Decreased exploratory behavior, avoidance of novelty, and greater vulnerability to addiction
- Increased anxiety, fearfulness, and response to stress
- Decreased cell survival in the medial preoptic areas (a maternal center in rats)

In epigenetics, we see nature's recipe for a balance between flexibility and stability via information conserved from the past and its alteration to new challenges in adapting. When genetic inheritance (template genetics) is combined with epigenetic processes (transcription genetics), we have dual mechanisms that allow for the mixing of mostly successful genes from the previous generation and the ability to adapt to changes in survival demands of the present. In the final analysis, survival depends upon information, whether it is in the form of genetic codes, the organization of neurons, or the social hierarchies of our tribes. At each level, a delicate balance must be established between consistency and change.

STRESS AND EPIGENETICS OF CHILDHOOD TRAUMA

We are never so defenseless against suffering as when we love.

—SIGMUND FREUD

The relationship between childhood stress and problems of adaptation later in life have been a central focus of study since the beginnings of psychology and for writers and philosophers for millennia. What we haven't had before is a mechanism of action; in other words, how these early experiences are preserved to shape our lives decades later. Before the discovery of epigenetics, we used theories of internal psychological processes and literary metaphors to try to understand the hypothetical causal relationships that guided these processes. With epigenetics, we not only have a theory that can be tested, we also have a model of development that unites social, psychological, and biological factors in a developmental framework. The brain changes related to variations in maternal behaviors are measured by chemical assays of the rat pups' brains after they are sacrificed. Because we can't do research with humans in the same way, the epigenetic research was done with rats. A variety of other methods need to be used to examine these processes.

The modern research that has galvanized the idea of a direct causal relationship between childhood stress and adult adaptation is referred to as the ACE (Adverse Childhood Experience) Study. While the results only demonstrate a correlational relationship between early stress and health later in life, the fact that it was a long-term study with 17,421 subjects from diverse populations added substantially to its value as a likely reflection of epigenetic processes found in the rat research. It makes a powerful case for the cost to society of childhood stress and its widespread impact on our patients. Adults in this study were asked about ranged from parental separation and divorce to being exposed to drug abuse in the home and domestic violence. The study found that the prevalence of each of the eight stressors within this particular population varied from 5% to 28%. See Table 1 for the percentages of subjects reporting each adverse experience.

Table 1
Percentage of Subjects
Reporting Each Adverse Experience

Physical abuse by parents	28
Household alcohol or drug abuse	27
Parental separation or divorce	23
Sexual abuse by anyone	21
Mental illness in household	17
Battered mother	13
Emotional abuse by parents	11
Incarcerated household member	5

These stressors were not evaluated individually but were all considered to contribute to the overall level of stress in the subjects' childhood environments. It is a safe assumption that these factors would significantly influence parents' caretaking abilities, the availability of resources, and the level of safety and stability in the home. The medical and psychological illnesses encountered by these adult subjects later in life were correlated with the number of ACEs reported, from 0 to 8.

The number of ACEs correlated positively with negative lifestyle factors such as smoking, drug abuse, promiscuity, and obesity. These behaviors were associated with higher levels of lung disease, COPD, and unintended pregnancy, as well as heart and liver disease. Greater exposure to ACEs also correlated with a history of depression, suicide attempts, hallucinations, alcoholism, homelessness, problems getting and keeping work, and domestic violence. Logical connections between the ACE studies and the epigenetic research lead us to hypotheses about potential mechanisms of action.

The early social stress of these human subjects would result in adaptations of brain development that would make them more likely to experience higher resting levels of cortisol and lower levels of serotonin. Just these two biological changes alone could directly result in increases in anxiety and depression and a less robust immune system, making them more vulnerable to a range of physical illness. Of course, the psychological and social impacts of these kinds of negative childhood experiences can never be underestimated. What the epigenetic research helps us to understand is the deep synergy among biological, psychological, and social factors in development.

EFFECTS OF CHILDHOOD TRAUMA ON THE DEVELOPING HUMAN BRAIN

Without health life is not life; it is only a state of languor and suffering—an image of death.

—BUDDHA

I've spent a long time thinking about the impact of early experience on the developing brain. In line with the results I just described, my assumption has always been that the effects of trauma are mediated by a general stress response and that the effects will be equally distributed across the brain and will be nonspecific to the type of trauma endured. For many years, the changes found in the adult brains of those traumatized as children seemed to support this point of view. For example, when the brains of abused and nonabused adult suicide victims were compared, those with histories of abuse in childhood had lower levels of cortisol receptors in their hippocampi. Research demonstrated decreases in the size and development of the cortex and corpus callosum, decreases in activation in the cerebellum, and electrical instability in the limbic system. All these findings seem to reflect more general challenges to optimal brain development and functioning.

To my amazement, newer research suggests that the epigenetic encoding of early trauma may be more specific than expected. In other words, in addition to a general stress response, there may also be particular imprints on brain development that reflect the specific type of trauma endured. There may be an adaptational response to specific types of trauma that is reflected not only in a victim's symptoms but also in the wetware of the brain. For example, one study found that young adults exposed to parental verbal abuse had abnormalities in the white matter tracts within left-hemisphere circuits involved in language and social memory. Could the epigenetic pro-

cesses that build these networks have impeded the development of
these systems as an adaptation to the verbal abuse? Might symptoms
related to language processing and social interaction that we see in
some victims of complex PTSD actually be protective epigenetic
adaptations to early negative experiences? Could this be the biological substrate for later receptive and expressive language problems
that so many of these children experience in school?

In the same year, it was found that young women who experienced sexual abuse as children demonstrated gray matter reduction
in many regions of their visual systems, which were directly related
to the duration of abuse before age 12. Again, is this a general
impact of stress or the physiological infrastructure of what we might
call denial, motivated forgetting, dissociation, or sensory neglect? A
year later, another study found that adults exposed to regular childhood emotional maltreatment had a "profound" reduction in medial
prefrontal cortical volume, which was especially significant in the
left dorsal medial prefrontal cortex, a region centrally involved with
attachment, attunement, and social interactions. Involving the same
neural circuitry, abused adolescents have reduced functional connectivity within top-down networks involved in the inhibition of
nondesirable actions.

Perhaps most striking of all the studies to date, it was discovered
decreased representation of cortical somatosensory areas dedicated
to the genitals after childhood sexual abuse in adult females. They
also found that emotional abuse was associated with cortical thin-
ning in the anterior cingulate, a central structure of bonding, maternal behavior, and attachment. These more recent studies have forced
me to rethink my prior assumptions about the general and specific
impacts of early stress and abuse. The structures and functioning of
the brain are looking more and more like biological recordings of
our learning and adaptational histories.

Evolution is not in the least bit sentimental or romantic—it is
all about survival of the fittest. A child's job is to adapt to what-

ever social and physical environment he finds himself in, including abusive and stressful environments. It would be maladaptive for children born into abusive relationships to have secure attachment schemata and develop sensory processes that take in all of the information around them, especially the input that is most painful to them. The difficulty for those children who adapt well to abuse and then move into a nonabusive world is that they have brains, minds, and bodies that have been built for a defensive stance toward the world and need help to adapt to positive, warm, and loving relationships.

20 KEY FIGURES IN NEUROSCIENCE

Antonie van Leeuwenhoek (1632–1723)

A Dutch businessman, his interest in making lenses led him to invent the microscope and discover the world of microorganisms, which led to the establishment of microbiology as a scientific discipline. Among his discoveries are bacteria, spermatozoa, single-celled organisms, and the banded pattern of muscle fibers. Although he never published a paper or a book, his numerous letters to the Dutch Academy of Science led his work to be known throughout Europe.

Paul Broca (1824–1880)

The son of a French physician, Broca followed in his father's footsteps, eventually becoming a professor of surgery at the University of Paris. He studied a wide range of areas including the histology of bone, aneurysms, and infant mortality. His interest in evolution and comparative anatomy led him to make valuable contributions to knowledge of the limbic system. Broca is best known for his studies of the brain and speech. His discovery associating damage to left frontal cortex areas with loss of expressive speech led to the naming of both Broca's area and Broca's aphasia. The localization of language to Broca's area became a key support of the localization school of neurology, which posited that specific areas of the brain are solely responsible for specific behaviors.

John Hughlings Jackson (1835–1911)

Jackson was an English neurologist who had a long career as a clinician and theoretician. Although best known for his work with epilepsy, his application of evolution to the brain, his theory of a three-layered brain, the role of the cortex in inhibition, and his related ideas of positive and negative symptoms had continued influence on neuroscientific theory for over a century. His clinical observations, especially applied to epilepsy, are considered to be unmatched.

Camillo Golgi (1843–1926)

An Italian anatomist, Golgi is best known for a staining technique that allowed the study of individual neurons. Golgi's "black reaction," now called the Golgi method, involved applying silver nitrate and potassium dichromate to neurons, which caused silver chromate to fix to all the structures of a particular neuron and turn them black. For reasons still unknown, this staining occurs in random cells, making them stand out against the yellow background of their neighboring neurons. The Golgi method supported Cajal's anatomical studies and drawings.

Carl Wernicke (1848–1905)

A neurologist and psychiatrist from what is now Poland, Wernicke spent his career as a clinician and professor at a number of hospitals and universities. His central discovery was that damage to a portion of the left temporal lobe resulted in deficits in language comprehension. This region was later named Wernicke's area, and the diagnosis of receptive aphasia was called Wernicke's aphasia. Wernicke's life was cut short as a result of injuries sustained in a bicycle accident, a reminder to us to always wear our helmets.

Santiago Ramón y Cajal (1852–1934)

A Spanish anatomy professor, Cajal is considered to be the father of modern neuroscience. It was Cajal who first demonstrated that neurons were separate contiguous structures as opposed to the nervous system being one continuous structure (the neuron doctrine). In addition to discovering interstitial cells (involved in peristalsis), he was also an advocate of the existence of dendritic spines. His detailed drawings of neural structures remain valuable teaching tools to this day. Along with Camillo Golgi, Cajal won the Nobel Prize in physiology and medicine in 1906—a wonderful achievement for a boy who was sent to prison at age 11 for blowing up a neighbor's gate with a homemade cannon.

Sigmund Freud (1856–1939)

Although everyone has heard of Sigmund Freud, most are unaware of the fact that he started his career as a neurologist and was a fellow under Charcot at the Salpêtrière Hospital in Paris. His early book, *The Project for a Scientific Psychology*, was an attempt to relate mental processes to neural functioning. In this book, Freud stated his belief that mental processes would eventually be understood via biological processes. He blocked its publication while he was alive, and it was only made available to the public years after his death.

Charles Scott Sherrington (1859–1952)

Perhaps best remembered for his poetic description of the brain as an "enchanted loom," Sherrington was a key figure in the early stages of the exploration of the nervous system. His work solidified the belief that the nervous system consisted of individual neurons. He coined the word *synapse* to describe the space between them through which they communicate and believed that they can be excitatory or inhibitory in function. His most influential book, *The Integrative Action of the Nervous System* (1906), established the idea of a nervous system as a coordinated and interactive government of systems. Sherrington won the Nobel Prize for his work on the integrative action of excitation and inhibition within the reflex arc, which demonstrated his general system principles.

Wilder Penfield (1891–1976)

An American neurosurgeon, Penfield pioneered the mapping of relationships between brain regions and behavior. He developed a method of treating epilepsy by destroying the cells in the area of origin of the seizures. As part of his preparation for this surgery, he would electrically stimulate areas of the patient's brain around the site of the seizure while the patient was under local anesthesia. This allowed him to record the patient's experience and learn what function each region participated in. While the original goal of this stimulation was to decrease the negative side effects of the surgery, it allowed him to map various areas of the cortex to see which regions of the brain represented physical and sensory experiences. Penfield also discovered that stimulation of the temporal lobes would result in vivid memories, hallucinations, déjà vu, and out-of-body experiences.

Alexander Luria (1902–1977)

A Soviet developmental and neuropsychologist, Luria's work during his long career as a clinician and theoretician pushed the envelope of studies in neurodevelopment, traumatic brain injury, aphasia, and executive functioning. Along with Alexei Leontiev and Lev Vygotsky, Luria developed cultural historical psychology, which combined the influences of evolution, personal history, and culture—especially language—on cognition and the development of higher mental functions—a synthesis we are attempting to create to this day. Two of his books, *Higher Cortical Functions in Man* and *The Working Brain*, are standard texts in neuropsychology, along with two of his case studies, *The Mind of a Mnemonist* and *The Man with a Shattered World*. The Luria-Nebraska Neuropsychological Test is a standardized test based on his theories.

John Eccles (1903–1997)

Eccles was an Australian neurophysiologist and a student of Charles Sherrington at Oxford University during the 1920s. His early work focused on understanding the nature of neural communication and the summation effect of neural firing, for which he won the Nobel Prize in 1963. Although he initially believed that neural communication was strictly electrical, the research he and his colleagues performed led to the discovery that neural transmission is electrical along a neuron and chemical across the synapse, hence the electro-chemical neural transmission we know today.

Donald Olding Hebb (1904–1985)

Hebb was a Canadian psychologist best known for his studies of the relationship between neuronal connections and learning. In his most influential book, *The Organization of Behavior* (1949), he explored the neuronal mechanisms of action that underlie memory. In what came to be called Hebbian learning, he described what we now mean when we say "neurons that fire together, wire together," sometimes called Hebb's Law. He described a process of metabolic changes in two firing cells that make it easier for them to fire together. A major contribution of Hebb's work was to connect what was then considered psychology to the biological sciences.

Roger Sperry (1913–1994)

Sperry was an American neurobiologist and psychologist who won the Nobel Prize for his work on laterality with split-brain patients.

His research on neural connectivity with cats led to the discovery that severing the corpus callosum could be a treatment for epilepsy in humans. Along with his students Joseph Bogen and Michael Gazzaniga, Sperry performed experiments that led to many discoveries about the different contributions of the right and left hemispheres. It was learned from his work that each hemisphere has its own way of processing information and possesses its own system of consciousness.

Arvid Carlsson (1923–2018)

Soon after the discovery by Kathleen Montagu that dopamine was present in the human brain, Arvid Carlsson, a Swedish neuropharmacologist, demonstrated that it served as a neurotransmitter. He created a way to measure the amount of dopamine in different brain regions and found it in high concentrations in the basal ganglia, centrally important in movement. He also showed that drugs which block dopamine result in movement symptoms similar to Parkinson's disease. His research led to the use of a synthetic form of dopamine, levodopa, for the treatment of Parkinson's disease. For this work he won the Nobel Prize.

Marian Diamond (1926–2017)

Diamond was an American neuroanatomist whose primary research focus was the exploration of the impact of environmental stimulation on the development of the brain. Her work in neuroplasticity demonstrated that enriching environments can have a positive and even healing impact on neural structures. This had a profound effect on neuroscience theory and laid the conceptual groundwork for the influence of experience and epigenetic processes in brain development. Her analysis of Einstein's brain also led to a greater understanding of the role of glial cells in neural processing.

Eric Kandel (1929–)

For many the public face of neuroscience, Kandel is an Austrian researcher and professor at Columbia University. Trained as a psychoanalyst, his interests led him to study memory. Through a series of collaborations over his long career, Kandel and his associates have discovered multiple biological changes within neurons involved in short- and long-term memory, supporting the theory of Hebbian learning. His work has also supported his theory that these biological mechanisms of learning have been conserved during evolution in both invertebrates and vertebrates. Kandel won the Nobel Prize for his work on the biology of memory.

Edward O. Wilson (1929–)

E. O. Wilson is an American biologist and the world's leading authority on ants. Just as significant is his founding of the field of sociobiology, which examines the relationships between natural selection and social behavior. He will perhaps be best remembered for his work on consilience, the integration of the different scientific disciplines into a unified theory of nature. He is one of those rare individuals who has demonstrated expertise in both the most specific details of science and its broadest theoretical implications.

Oliver Sacks (1933–2015)

Oliver Sacks was a British born neurologist who spent his career as a clinician and author in the United States. He is best known for his many books and articles, which made him the premier spokesman and most visible member of his profession for decades. His keen observations, coupled with his interest in and compassion for his patients, made his case studies highly relatable and educational for professionals and laypeople alike. His studies included in-depth explorations of topics such as migraines, hallucinations, color blindness, and the impact of a wide range of traumatic brain injuries.

John O'Keefe (1939–)

O'Keefe is an American neuroscientist who has spent his career exploring the functioning of the hippocampus as a cognitive map. His discoveries include place cells, boundary cells, and the coding of location via temporal coding of brain wave activity. For his work in understanding how the brain orients us in space, he won the Nobel Prize in 2014. He has been at the University College of London since 1967.

Antonio Damasio (1944–)

Antonio Damasio is a Portuguese neuroscientist who has explored how the brain processes information and gives rise to self-awareness. His most well-known theory is the somatic marker hypothesis, which describes the role of bodily states, motivation, and emotion in decision making. His influential book, *Descartes' Error* (1994), describes the fundamental error of separating mind from brain and body, which he supports with an array of neurobiological and behavioral studies.

Michael Meaney (1951–)

Michael Meaney is a neuroscientist primarily known for his ground-breaking work on the impact of maternal care on gene expression. His most important work sheds light on the impact of the amount of maternal attention on the growth of various biological and neuroanatomical aspects of brain development in rat pups. He demonstrated the mechanism of action that shapes the actual wetware of a pup's brain and its ability to learn, cope with stress, and attend to its own offspring.

1OO KEY TERMS FOR NEUROFLUENCY

NEURONS

action potential: The electrical firing of a neuron once it is adequately stimulated by neurotransmitters.

axon: The extension from the soma across which electrical impulses are sent to the dendrites at its tip.

dendrite: Ending point of the axon that connects with other neurons via chemical messengers called neurotransmitters.

glia: A variety of nonneuronal support cells interwoven with neurons throughout the nervous system.

myelin: Insulation around axons that increases the speed and fidelity of electrical conduction.

neuron: A nerve cell that transmits information via electrical and chemical impulses.

neurotransmitter: The chemical messenger that passes from one neuron to another.

nucleus: The part of the neuron with the soma that contains DNA, mitochondria, and other structures central to neuronal functioning.

soma: The cell body of a neuron that contains the nucleus.

synapse: The space between neurons across which chemical messaging takes place.

vesicle: Packet of neurotransmitters that is released from the dendrite into the synapse.

NEURAL SYSTEMS

autonomic nervous system (ANS): The network of the nervous system that controls basic functions of metabolism and survival.

central nervous system: The brain and spinal cord.

enteric nervous system: A branch of the ANS that controls the gastrointestinal tract via peristalsis and enzyme secretion.

ganglion: A cluster of neurons organized into functional units (plural, ganglia).

neural network: An ensemble of neurons that can extend throughout the brain, working together to perform one or more functions.

neurodynamics: The interaction, integration, and homeostatic balance of neural networks. It is a conceptual parallel to psychodynamics, which was originally conceived as the dynamic tension between the ego, id, and superego, but can be applied to any model of the psyche that includes multiple interactive components in dynamic tension to one another. The fact that our brains consist of a complex network of interacting systems means that the nature of their integration and balance is directly related to mental health and mental distress.

parasympathetic nervous system: A branch of the ANS that down-modulates arousal and supports bodily maintenance.

peripheral nervous system: The nervous system beyond the brain and spinal cord that extends throughout the body.

reticular activating system: A set of nuclei throughout the brain stem that regulates consciousness and arousal.

sympathetic nervous system: A branch of the ANS that regulates processes of activation and the fight-flight-freeze response.

THE LIFE AND GROWTH OF NEURONS

apoptosis: Programmed neural death as a part of normal brain development.

arborization: The growth of dendrites to establish communication with other neurons.

critical and sensitive period: Genetically timed period of exuberant neural growth within different neural systems.

necrosis: Cell loss due to trauma, metabolic problems, or illnesses such as Alzheimer's disease.

neurogenesis: The birth of new neurons.

CORTICAL STRUCTURES

allocortex: The more primitive three-layer structure of the cingulate and insular cortices.

Broca's area: An area in the left frontal lobe responsible for expressive speech.

cingulate cortex: At the center of the cortex, running from front to back, the cingulate is involved with sensory and affective integration.

corpus callosum: The major bundle of nerve fibers connecting the left and right cerebral hemispheres.

cortex: The outer layer of the brain above the midbrain; cortex means bark.

cortical blindness: A situation in which cortical visual systems are offline, so the victim is not consciously seeing but does avoid objects because of visual information that is processed subcortically in networks of the thalamus.

cortical release sign: The return of primitive reflexes that were successfully inhibited by the cortex until cortical damage occurred.

frontal lobe: The area of the cortex with the primary role of sensory and motor integration.

fusiform face area: An area of the occipital lobes that specializes in face recognition.

hemineglect: A condition in which a patient with right-hemisphere damage becomes unaware of the left side of the body and visual field.

insular cortex: Organized as a topographical map of the body, the insular cortex organizes and processes bodily information.

laterality: A term describing the relative specializations of the left and right sides of the brain.

localization: The theory that specific areas of the brain are responsible for specific functions.

neocortex: The six-layer structure of the frontal, temporal, parietal, and occipital lobes.

occipital lobe: The central cortical area involved in the construction of vision.

parietal lobe: Located above our ears, this cortical area evolved from the hippocampus and is involved with spatial organization, orientation, and executive functioning.

prefrontal lobe: The front-most portion of the cortex, involved in emotional regulation, abstract thinking, and executive functioning.

temporal lobe: Beneath our temples, this region is involved in memory and emotional activation.

ventricle: One of four fluid-filled cavities within the brain where cerebrospinal fluid is produced and connected to the spinal cord, through which the fluid circulates. The ventricles also serve to cushion the brain from the effects of impacts and changes in vascular pressure.

Wernicke's area: An area in the left temporal region responsible for the encoding of receptive language.

SUBCORTICAL STRUCTURES

amygdala: Located beneath the temporal lobes and behind the prefrontal cortex, the amygdala is an organ of appraisal of positive and negative stimuli and plays a major role in bodily activation in response to threat and pleasure.

basal ganglia: A complex nuclei at the base of the cortex with diverse functions and connections to many areas of the brain. It is commonly thought of as being involved with action selection in association with the prefrontal cortex.

brain stem: The base of the mammalian brain linking the brain with the spinal cord. Major components of the brain stem are the medulla, pons, and midbrain.

cerebellum: Sometimes called the "little brain," the cerebellum sits below the rest of the brain at the very rear, where it has a complex connectivity with most of the cerebral cortex. It is involved with such functions as emotional regulation, language production, timing and sequencing, and executive functioning.

hippocampus: Located at the bottom of the temporal lobe on both sides of the brain, the hippocampus originally evolved as a spatial map of the physical environment and has expanded to play a central role in the consolidation of short-term to long-term memory.

hypothalamus: Lying just below the thalamus, the hypothalamus coordinates the autonomic nervous system, mechanisms of arousal, and multiple areas of homeostatic regulation.

thalamus: A structure that serves as both a sensory relay station and a center for pain perception.

NEUROTRANSMITTERS AND NEUROHORMONES

acetylcholine: An excitatory neurotransmitter whose many functions include arousal, muscle activation, memory, and attention.

cortisol: A steroidal hormone (and glucocorticoid) released in response to stress to enhance flight-flight processes. Cortisol inhibits protein synthesis, increases blood sugar, and suppresses immunological functioning in the service of immediate survival needs.

dopamine: A neurotransmitter that primarily serves neural networks involved in reward motivation and motor control.

endorphin: Endogenous opioid that takes multiple forms involved in the inhibition of pain signals and can induce a state of euphoria.

GABA: The major inhibitory neurotransmitter in the central nervous system of mammals, also involved in muscle tone.

glutamate: The most common excitatory neurotransmitter, it is known to play a key role in learning and long-term memory.

neurotrophin: Growth factor that serves to enhance the development, functioning, and survival of neurons.

norepinephrine (adrenaline): A hormone with the primary function of activating and mobilizing the body for the fight-flight response.

oxytocin: A hormone that plays a key role in bonding, attachment, reproduction, and childbirth—called the love hormone.

serotonin: A neurotransmitter involved in cognition, learning, memory, and feelings of well-being.

testosterone: A hormone that supports the development of male reproductive structures, hair, bone mass, and muscle.

GENETICS AND EPIGENETICS

central dogma: The flow of information from DNA to messenger RNA to protein structures that build the brain and body.

epigenetics: Involves the ways in which organisms are shaped and modified based on experience via the processes of the central dogma.

genetics: The study of genes, genetic variation, and inheritance in living organisms.

genotype and phenotype: The genotype of an organism describes the genetic makeup of an individual while the phenotype describes observable characteristics. For example, an individual may have genes for both blue and brown eyes (genotype) but may express brown eyes (phenotype).

transcription: The first step in the process of gene expression, where a segment of DNA is made available to be copied by messenger RNA.

EVOLUTION

biodiversity: The range of the organization of genes and the organisms they result in.

conservation: The maintenance of earlier genetic sequences, structures, and functions from more primitive to more complex organisms.

fitness: The adaptive match between the way an organism functions and current environmental conditions.

natural selection: The process in which those organisms better adapted to the environment survive and reproduce.

neural Darwinism: Gerald Edelman's theory of neural survival and organization based on functionally driven selection.

NEUROSCIENCE AND RELATED FIELDS

neurology: A clinical field that studies and treats brain-related illnesses which very often have psychiatric consequences.

neuropsychiatry: A clinical field that focuses on the interface between neurological compromises and their behavioral consequences.

neuropsychology: A clinical field that focuses primarily on the assessment and rehabilitation of brain-related disabilities.

neuroscience: The vast area of study of the anatomy and functioning of the brain and nervous system.

psychoneuroimmunology: The scientific study of the relationships between the mind, brain, and body and their impact on health.

psychopharmacology: The field focused on the development and use of medications to treat psychological illnesses.

LEARNING AND MEMORY

childhood amnesia: The absence of autobiographical memory for the first few years of life. It is believed to occur because the cortical-hippocampal systems upon which autobiographical memory depends do not mature until later in childhood.

cranial nerves: The 14 central nerves that connect the brain with the rest of the body.

explicit memory: Refers to all forms of memory that involve conscious awareness, such as autobiographical, verbal, and visual recognition.

Hebbian synapse: The coordination of two neurons that leads them to tend to fire together, which assists learning.

implicit memory: Describes all of the ways the many memory systems within the nervous system have learned to respond and adapt to the environment that operate outside conscious awareness and control.

long-term potentiation: The strengthening of connectivity among neurons built on past activity. The opposite process, long-term depression, results in a decrease of synaptic strength.

neuroplasticity: The many ways in which neurons change in order to hold information to support new learning.

procedural memory: Implicit and unconscious learning that usually involves motor learning such as walking, sewing, or playing tennis.

ACTIVATION AND EXECUTIVE SYSTEMS

amygdala executive system: The first executive system, which appraises situations, triggers arousal, and directs approach or avoidance behavior.

default mode network: An executive network that becomes activated when the amygdala and parietal frontal executives are not engaged, allowing for self-reflection and empathy.

parietal-frontal network: A network that organizes the experience of space and time and allows us to navigate our physical and imaginal environments.

reticular activating system: A hierarchical and widespread network that modulates arousal, directed action, and sleep.

saliency network: A network centered in insula-cingulate connectivity that guides and focuses our attention on novel and important stimuli.

SOCIAL REFLEXES AND NEURAL NETWORKS

attachment system: The interaction between regions of the orbital and medial prefrontal cortex and the amygdala that helps us learn to use the proximity of caretakers to modulate and inhibit anxiety and arousal to form an attachment schema and, later, the ability to autoregulate.

grasp reflex: A primitive brain stem reflex that makes the hand grasp when the palm is stimulated, which is responsible for allowing our primitive relatives to hold onto their mother as she navigated through the environment and which now jump-starts the attachment and bonding process.

mirror neuron system: Specific neurons in the frontal and parietal lobes that map information about others onto our own neural networks involved in sensory, motor, and emotional processing. It is believed that mirror neurons provide the foundation of imitation, learning, attunement, and empathy.

orienting reflex: A reflex that leads us to orient to the sound of a caretaker's voice and to circles and complex images such as eyes, nipples, and faces. This reflex aids bonding as well as stimulating cortical areas to become expert in facial recognition so that we can distinguish familiar people from strangers.

reflex arc: A reaction of the nervous system that takes place at the level of the spinal cord and does not involve the brain. An example is pulling your hand away from a hot stove or reflexively braking a car in an emergency.

social engagement system (aka the polyvagal theory): The cluster of functions of the vagal nerve network (physiological and affect regulation, emotional communication through facial expressions, constriction of the inner ear, and dilation of the pupil) that aid emotional attunement and sustained bonding and attachment.

theory of mind: The ability to automatically attribute mental states—intentions, desires, knowledge—to others.

REFERENCES AND RECOMMENDED READINGS

Carlson, E. A. (2018). *How scientific progress occurs: Incrementalism and the life sciences.* Cold Springs Harbor, NY: Cold Springs Harbor Laboratory Press.

Changeux, J.-P. (2002). *The physiology of truth: Neuroscience and human knowledge.* London: Belknap.

Cozolino, L. J. (2014). *The neuroscience of human relationships* (2nd ed.). New York: W.W. Norton.

Cozolino, L. J. (2017). *The neuroscience of psychotherapy* (3rd ed.). New York: W.W. Norton.

Damasio, A. (1996). *Descartes' error.* New York: Putnam.

Dana, D. (2018). *The polyvagal theory in therapy.* New York: W.W. Norton.

Dias, B. & Ressler, K. (2014). Parental olfactory experience influences behavior and neural structure in subsequent generations. Nature Neuroscience, 17(1), 89-98.

Edelman, G. (1987). *Neural Darwinism.* New York: Basic Books.

Frewen, P. & Lanius, R. (2015). *Healing the traumatized self.* New York: W.W. Norton.

Graziano, M. S. (2013). *Consciousness and the social brain.* New York: Oxford University Press.

MacLean, P. (1985). Brain evolution related to family, play, and the separation call. Archives of General Psychiatry, 42, 405-417.

Minuchin, S., & Nichols, M. (1993). *Family healing: Strategies for hope and understanding.* New York: Simon and Schuster.

Panksepp, J., & Biven, L. (2012). *The archaeology of mind.* New York: W. W. Norton.

Porges, S. (2011). *The polyvagal theory: Neurophysiological foundations of emotions, attachment, communication, self-regulation.* New York: W. W. Norton.

Stolorow, R., Atwood, G., & Brandschaft, B. (1994). *The intersubjective perspective.* Northdale, NJ: Aronson.

Wilson, E. O. (2012). *The social conquest of the earth.* New York: Liveright.

INDEX

Note: Tables are noted with a *t* following page number.

Gramsci, A., 63
Grandin, T., 260
grandparents and grandchildren, plasticity of
    attachment circuits and, 14
grasping reflex, 258–59, 301–2
Grice's maxims, coherence analysis and, 164
grit, 7
group mind, 217, 219
groupthink, 8, 254
GSR. *see* galvanic skin response (GSR)

Hamilton, E., 16
Hampton, L., 89
Healing the Traumatized Self (Frewen &
    Lanius), 219
Hebb, D. O., 289
Hebbian synapse, 300
Hebb's Law, 289
hemineglect, 296
Higher Cortical Functions in Man (Luria), 289
hippocampus, 10, 27, 45, 53, 109, 113, 266,
    297
Hippocrates, 31
Holocaust, the, 225
human connectome project, 101
humans, as biopsychosocial organisms, xii
hyperarousal, addressing, 157–58
hypothalamic-pituitary-adrenal (HPA) axis,
    44, 47
hypothalamus, 12, 109, 297

illness, organic-functional distinction in,
    271–72
imitation, via mirror neurons, 90
imitative learning, 119
immunological system, 43
implicit memory, 17, 18, 26, 41, 46, 67, 77,
    144, 145, 150, 189, 197, 232, 300
implicit processing, architecture of, 42–44
independent assortment, 273
inherited trauma, 223–25
insecure attachment, 26, 67, 70, 74, 75,
    97, 98
inside-out integration, 107–8
insight-oriented therapy, 89
insular cortex, 16, 107, 296
integration, 248–49
    brain health and, 25–26
    failure of, 106, 111–13

integration patterns, 103–11
    front-back, 109–11
    inside-out, 107–8
    left-right, 104–7
    top-down, 108–9
Integrative Action of the Nervous System, The
    (Sherrington), 288
intelligence
    top-down, prefrontal cortex view of, 81–82
    wisdom *vs.*, 94
interconnectivity, truth of, 115
internal mother, biochemistry behind
    invoking of, 74
introns, 274
intuition, 50–51
invisible half second, 40–41, 43, 44, 247
IQ, 15, 81, 85

Jackson, J. H., 286
James, W., 12, 91
Jesus, 115
Jung, C., 14, 231

Kahneman, D., 178
Kandel, E., 135, 189, 291
Keller, H., 194
Kincaid, J., 216
Kording, K., 155

Langs, R., 118
language
    early abuse and impairment of, 167–68
    hyperaroused amygdala and inhibition of,
        182, 214, 215
    lateral specialization and, 105–6
Lanius, R., 219
laterality, 104–7, 296
learning, 107, 242, 268
    Hebbian, 289, 291
    imitative, 119
    memory and, 144, 300–301
    neuroplasticity and, 113–14
left-handedness, 262
left hemisphere of brain, 104–5, 107
left-right integration, 104–7
Leontiev, A., 288
Levine, P., 185
Li, F. F., 25
limbic system, 12

ABOUT THE AUTHOR

Louis Cozolino has been a writer, professor, and practicing psychologist in Los Angeles since 1986. In addition to holding degrees in philosophy, theology, and clinical psychology, he has studied, worked, and written in the areas of neuroscience, neuropsychiatry, and education. As a professor at Pepperdine University, he has, and continues to be, involved in the training of hundreds of Masters and Doctoral students.

His research interests have included working with clients with schizophrenia and their families, the long term effects of childhood stress and abuse, and the application of evolutionary theory, social and cognitive neuroscience, and attachment theory to the practice of psychotherapy.

In addition to his clinical and consulting practices, Lou lectures around the world to professional and lay audiences on attachment, child development, evolution, and the synthesis of neuroscience and psychotherapy. In addition to *The Pocket Guide to Neuroscience for Clinicians,* he is the author of seven books including *Why Therapy Works, The Neuroscience of Psychotherapy, The Making of a Therapist, The Neuroscience of Human Relationships, Timeless, The Social Neuroscience of Education,* and *Attachment-Based Teaching.* In addition, Lou has also authored and co-authored articles and book chapters on child abuse, schizophrenia, language, and cognition. Lou is the editor for the Norton Series on Interpersonal Neurobiology.

Also available from

THE NORTON SERIES ON INTERPERSONAL NEUROBIOLOGY

*The Birth of Intersubjectivity:
Psychodynamics, Neurobiology, and
the Self*
MASSIMO AMMANITI, VITTORIO
GALLESE

*Neurobiology for Clinical Social
Work: Theory and Practice*
JEFFREY S. APPLEGATE, JANET R.
SHAPIRO

*Being a Brain-Wise Therapist:
A Practical Guide to Interpersonal
Neurobiology*
BONNIE BADENOCH

The Brain-Savvy Therapist's Workbook
BONNIE BADENOCH

*The Neurobiology of Attachment-
Focused Therapy*
JONATHAN BAYLIN, DANIEL A.
HUGHES

*Coping with Trauma-Related
Dissociation: Skills Training for
Patients and Therapists*
SUZETTE BOON, KATHY STEELE,
AND ONNO VAN DER HART

*Neurobiologically Informed
Trauma Therapy with Children*

*and Adolescents: Understanding
Mechanisms of Change*
LINDA CHAPMAN

*Intensive Psychotherapy for Persistent
Dissociative Processes: The Fear of
Feeling Real*
RICHARD A. CHEFETZ

*The Healthy Aging Brain: Sustaining
Attachment, Attaining Wisdom*
LOUIS COZOLINO

*The Neuroscience of Human
Relationships: Attachment and the
Developing Social Brain* (Second
Edition)
LOUIS COZOLINO

*The Neuroscience of Psychotherapy:
Healing the Social Brain* (Second
Edition)
LOUIS COZOLINO

*Why Therapy Works: Using Our
Minds to Change Our Brains*
LOUIS COZOLINO

*From Axons to Identity: Neurological
Explorations of the Nature of the Self*
TODD E. FEINBERG

For complete book details, and to order online, please visit the Series webpage at wwnorton.com/Psych/IPNBseries